Lifestyle

Conversations
with Members
of the Unification Church

Edited by Richard Quebedeaux

Lifestyle

Conversations with Members of the Unification Church

Edited by Richard Quebedeaux

Distributed by the Rose of Sharon Press, Incorporated

Conference series no. 13
First Edition
© 1982
Unification Theological Seminary
Barrytown, New York 12507

Design by DCBruner and Lynn Musgrave

Distributed by
The Rose of Sharon Press, Inc.
GPO Box 2432
New York, New York 10116

Library of Congress Catalog Number 82-50799
ISBN 0-932894-13-5
Printed in the United States of America

Contents

Introduction   vii

Engagement, Marriage and Children   1
Discussion   27

Piety and Spirituality   51
Discussion   56

Social Action and Politics   73
Discussion   84

Evangelism and Witnessing   93
Discussion   102

Women's Caucus   113

Fundraising   125
Discussion   133

Life in the Northern California Church   141
Discussion   152

History of the Unification Church in America   163
Discussion   178

Results of Research on American Unificationists   185
Discussion   196

Participants   215

Introduction

As a result of interest generated at the first introductory summer conference which presented and critiqued Unification theology (held in the Virgin Islands in 1979),* two smaller, advanced seminars were convened early in 1980 in the Bahamas to address the concerns that emerged. One focused on Unification hermeneutics,** and the other on Unification lifestyle, namely, the concrete ways theological beliefs in the Unification movement impact the day-to-day lives and behavior of its members. This latter gathering of Unification seminarians, doctoral students, and church leaders with scholars of other religious traditions to discuss lifestyle issues *per se* was the first of its kind, and it spawned others in the years following.***

The seminar centered on informal presentations by especially articulate Unificationists on certain important (and sometimes novel) aspects of their lifestyle—including their highly controversial methods of fundraising and membership recruitment (i.e., evangelism)—and on group

*See *Proceedings of the Virgin Islands' Seminar on Unification Theology*, ed. Darrol Bryant (Barrytown, N.Y.: Unification Theological Seminary, distr. Rose of Sharon Press, 1980).

**The proceedings of this conference have been published under the title *Hermeneutics and Horizons: The Shape of the Future*, ed. Frank K. Flinn (Barrytown, N.Y.: Unification Theological Seminary, distr. Rose of Sharon Press, 1982).

***Another volume on Unification lifestyle is being prepared by Gene James using material presented at subsequent conferences and other sources.

discussions following those presentations. It concluded with a more formal paper by a noted non-Unification comparative religionist on his assessment of the Unification movement, based on the results of an in-depth survey among the "Moonies" in the U.S. in 1976. Although the positions taken here do represent a variety of common feelings shared by numerous Unificationists, they should in no wise be taken as normative. Indeed, the dialogue itself demonstrates the presence of considerably more heterogeneity in lifestyle within the Unification movement than is generally supposed by the public.

The seminar begins with presentations on engagement, marriage, and children in the Unification movement by Hugh and Nora Spurgin, who were one of the 777 couples married by Rev. and Mrs. Moon in a single ceremony in Korea in 1970. They talk about the stringent spiritual disciplines Moonies undertake prior to marriage ("the Blessing"), the "matching" process itself (i.e., engagement) in which couples are often brought together for the first time by Rev. Moon, and the distinctive features of married life and families within the larger Unification community. Here the Blessing is viewed as the prime "sacrament" for believers, and children born of blessed parents are thought to be free of "original sin." The Spurgins stress that "our marriages are for the benefit of mankind, not merely for ourselves," and they go into a discussion describing the manner in which self-sacrifice is an integral part of life in the Unification movement, both before *and* after the Blessing. Arthur Eves, who had been married and divorced prior to joining the movement, then speaks about male-female relationships from the perspective of the unmarried Moonie. He focuses on the Unification practice of premarital celibacy in the midst of a permissive society, and how it serves as a discipline that helps persons to develop their love for others.

At this point, Patricia Zulkosky offers a presentation on Unification piety and spirituality—the rituals, prayer, and worship of the movement. She talks about the workshops in which *Divine Principle* (Rev. Moon's "new revelation") is taught, the spiritual "conditions" set by members (sacrificial offerings to God like extended periods of fasting and prayer), and the spirituality of communal living (practiced by most Moonies in the U.S. at the present time). She also explains the meaning of the weekly "pledge service" at 5 AM on Sunday and the distinctive church holidays celebrated by members. In Zulkosky's words, Unification spirituality as a whole is built on the "goal of relieving the suffering of God by fulfilling the ideal of creation—namely the building of the Kingdom on earth."

From there, Kurt Johnson, a research biologist and the innovator of a number of "social action" projects for the Unification movement, presents his views on *Divine Principle*'s perspective on social concern and politics. For him, the theology offered by the Principle is centered on "doing" (*praxis*) rather than on metaphysical speculation. He talks about the Unification doctrines of restoration and eschatology as they bear on politics, then compares the Marxist vision of a new economic and political order with the "counterproposal to Marxism" suggested in *Divine Principle*. In so doing, Johnson presents a picture of Unification political and economic ideals far different from the stereotyped "reactionary anticommunism" Rev. Moon is sometimes accused of promoting.

The practices of witnessing and evangelism as an integral part of life in the Unification movement, and the new institution of "home church" as a specific method of evangelism and witnessing, are discussed by Jaime Sheeran and Diana Muxworthy, who had both been state directors for the movement. They elaborate on the difficulties of living "principled" (or what traditional Christianity has termed "sanctified") lives in a secular environment, and relate this issue to the development of the home church ideal. The presentations of these two women are then followed by an unplanned, but very interesting, ad hoc discussion on the role of women as a whole in the Unification movement and on feminism more generally. This particular discussion was attended by members of the concurrent seminar on Unification hermeneutics as well as this seminar's participants.

From here, the agenda moves on to a lively (if not heated) discussion of the controversial and innovative methods of raising money for church activities within the Unification movement, *and* the spirituality and theology of material goods behind these practices. The presentations were made by Stephen Post, who had spent a year and a half fundraising and was a "champion" in this task, and by Esteban Galvan, who came from a Chicano family of migrant workers and spent four years on the Unification movement's Mobile Fundraising Teams (MFT) in the U.S. Post concentrated on the theology of fundraising, while Galvan gave a passionate account of the day-to-day life of a typical MFT member and the spiritual and social benefits he or she derives from the experience.

The conversation then proceeds to a quite heated dialogue, this one concerning daily life in the movement's Northern California (Oakland) church—the specific target of accusations by the mass media and distraught parents concerning allegedly deceptive methods of membership recruitment.

The presenter here is Dr. Mose Durst himself, then the director of the movement in Northern California and now president of the Unification Church in America. Durst emphasized the theology of self-sacrifice that lies behind the hard work and singlemindedness of the Northern Calfornia church, the centrality of fasting and prayer and aggressive evangelism in the daily lives of members, and the character of the "notorious" weekend teaching seminars at "Camp K" (where anti-cult proponents charge that potential recruits are methodically "brainwashed"). He was quick to admit mistakes made by the movement in its evangelistic efforts in the past, but stressed also the sincerity and good intentions of the recruitment process in Northern California as a whole. *

The final two presentations in the seminar are made by Neil Salonen and Stillson Judah. Salonen, then completing a long term as president of the Unification Church in America, gave a fascinating lecture on the history of the movement in the United States and its Korean origins. Here he focuses on the Unification notion of "providential history" and its working out in the present era. He talks about the first Korean missionaries to the U.S. who arrived in the early 1960s and how the various "strands" of a then tiny organization came together into one movement when Rev. Moon took up residence in New York in 1972. From there, Salonen discusses Moon's national speaking tours and large public rallies in the mid-70s, and the movement's growth and development since then. Stillson Judah, professor emeritus of the history of religions at the Graduate Theological Union in Berkeley, concluded the formal part of the seminar with a presentation on the contemporary social significance of new religious movements and the Unification movement in particular in a time of rapid cultural change in America.

The group discussions after each presentation were simply not long enough to deal adequately with *all* the questions raised, but they were very stimulating, to say the least, and always integrally related to the issues at hand. If the text of this book is not the definitive statement on Unification lifestyle—and it surely isn't—it does represent a significant first attempt to bring something about the reality of what it means to be a Moonie today to the reading public.

Richard Quebedeaux
Berkeley, California

*More testimony by Dr. Durst on this matter can be found in *Hermeneutics and Unification Theology*, ed. Darrol Bryant and Durwood Foster (Barrytown, N.Y.: Unification Theological Seminary, distr. Rose of Sharon Press, 1980).

Engagement, Marriage and Children

Hugh and Nora Spurgin
Arthur Eves

Hugh Spurgin: I would like to begin by mentioning briefly Nora's and my experience. Nora and I were married in Korea in 1970 in one of the mass weddings performed by Rev. and Mrs. Moon, the "777" wedding. Seven hundred and seventy-seven couples were married simultaneously, including seven from America. Our situation is somewhat different from that of couples in more recent weddings, because we were engaged and married before Rev. Moon came to America to live. Our engagement was based on consultation with Dr. Young Oon Kim* who was at that time one of the missionary leaders of the Unification Church in America, rather than directly with Rev. Moon. After Dr. Kim returned from a trip to Korea, she spoke with a few older Unification Church members in America and asked who among them wanted to go to Korea to be married and with whom. She had individual interviews with several people, including Nora and me. Based upon those interviews she selected seven American couples to go to Korea and recommended them to Rev. Moon. Then when we arrived in Korea we each had personal interviews with Rev. Moon at which time he said we were accepted into the marriage ceremony.

I don't have time to tell our entire story, but let me just mention that we had been attracted to one another but didn't reveal that, either to

---

*Dr. Young Oon Kim presently teaches at the Unification Theological Seminary. She is the author of *Unification Theology*, a series entitled *World Religions*, and others.

1

one another or to anyone else, until Dr. Kim spoke individually with each of us. It was through Dr. Kim that we found out that our attraction was mutual. Moreover, both before and after speaking with Dr. Kim, Nora and I had several spiritual experiences in which God let us know clearly that we would be right for each other. My philosophy had been that if I concentrated upon doing the work of God, primarily evangelical work, He would find an ideal wife for me. That felt more secure than relying only upon myself. Nora and I feel that our marriage was chosen in heaven. It was decided by God, not by us—although we participated in that decision through our consent. That's our belief and that's the attitude that Unification people in general have when they are matched. Nora and I had that attitude at the time of our engagement.

Today's matchings are different because Rev. Moon is in the United States and is directly involved in the matching process—that is, he is directly involved in the selection of mates for people. The process is somewhat similar to an arranged marriage, but different because there is opportunity for the expression of personal preferences.

Some of you may know about the engagement of 705 couples in New York in May of 1979. Unification members gathered with Rev. and Mrs. Moon in a large ballroom in the World Mission Center (the former New Yorker Hotel). More than fifteen hundred people assembled on that occasion to be matched. In short, the procedure was as follows. Based upon both divine inspiration and consultation with the members, Rev. Moon selected potential mates. Then each couple selected left the ballroom to speak privately in order to decide whether to accept or reject the match. If either of them rejected, they returned to the ballroom to await another match. If they accepted, they returned briefly to bow before Rev. and Mrs. Moon and the entire congregation, signifying their acceptance.

In my experience, there are generally two types of engagements. In one case a person is matched to someone who is obviously suited for him. Coming from similar backgrounds, these couples usually have minimal difficulty getting along. In the other case a person is engaged to someone who normally would be incompatible with him if they were not both members of the Unification Church, because of cultural or personality differences. One cannot assume, however, that such couples are unhappy. For instance, in 1970 when Nora and I were married, there were several international couples. There was one couple in which the woman was German (and unable to speak English) and the man was British (and unable to speak German). Initially, without a common language, they had some difficulty communicating, but now—ten years later—they have a successful marriage.

There are many miraculous stories of what happens during the engagement. For the period of the matching, I believe, Rev. Moon is especially inspired; his spiritual senses are open, and he is able to communicate directly with God and with the highest realms of the spiritual world. There is no other way for me to understand what happens.

Several times I have witnessed what I consider supernatural occurrences, but I have time to give you only one example. At the matching last May, there was one young man whom Rev. Moon talked with several times during the course of the day about a mate. Let's call him Tom. But each time Rev. Moon talked with Tom, Rev. Moon asked him to sit down without resolving anything. In the meantime while Tom waited, other people were engaged. Then, rather late in the day, suddenly Rev. Moon made a beeline toward a girl who was sitting in the back of the room. I do not think Rev. Moon could physically see her (because she was far in the back of the room and seated behind other people) but he hurried toward her without regard for aisles; people scurried to get out of the way. When he reached her (let's call her Jane), he asked Jane to stand and come to the front of the room. Once having reached the front, Rev. Moon asked Tom to stand and he proceeded to match them. It's a nice match; I know the couple. There are countless situations that are similar. People often have psychic experiences during, before or after the engagement process. As I indicated, Nora and I did.

I'd also like to give you an example of what the Unification attitude toward marriage ideally should be, and often is. Assume that you are a Unification person sitting in the engagement room with fifteen hundred other people. However, after having sat there all day, suddenly you realize there is only one other eligible person left, everyone else having been engaged. What would your attitude be? If you were not a committed Moonie, you might start to worry and to think about other people you'd like to marry or about all the characteristics you'd detest in a spouse. However, as a Unificationist you would most likely look at the situation from another perspective—that God saved this one person for you. That is to say, you would take the view that *from the beginning* of the matching God knew who was best for you.

Certainly God is always looking out for our best interests based upon His superior knowledge about our situations, preferences and interests. Hence Rev. Moon's desire is, of course, that we as Unificationists experience the best marriages possible. When Rev. Moon matches a couple, he thinks not only of that couple's immediate situation; he is also concerned with broader, providential concerns. He is thinking about their ancestors, their descendents, their futures, and God's will for their lives. Because he is in constant contact with God, he knows more than we do about what is best for us.

The doctrine of marriage and the family in the Unification Church is the central concept of Unification thought and lifestyle. It is interrelated with most other aspects of the Principle—Rev. Moon's teaching—with the doctrine of creation, the doctrine of the fall, the doctrine of redemption, and eschatology.

According to *Divine Principle** God gave man three blessings: to be fruitful (or attain individual perfection), to multiply (to have a family), and to have dominion over creation. Adam and Eve were not intended by God to marry until they had perfected their individuality to the point where they could stand in relationship to their children as perfect parents, just as God can be trusted as our Parent. Adam and Eve were to participate in the creation of their own character by keeping God's commandment not to eat of the fruit (which we take to mean *not* to have a sexual relationship without God's blessing in marriage). By keeping the commandment, man would become a co-creator with God of his own character, enabling him to embody God's nature and become His true child. Also, this would entitle man to dominion over the natural world, since the things of creation take no responsibility for perfection of their nature but grow automatically to maturity through the operation of natural laws.

Unfortunately Adam and Eve had sex before God blessed them in marriage, and it is only on the foundation of thousands of years of God's dispensational work that we are now living at a time when marriages can be without reservation blessed by God. This is why we call a Unification marriage, including the wedding ceremony, "the Blessing."

*Divine Principle is one of the names given to Rev. Moon's teaching as a whole. Another, more simple name is the Principle. *Divine Principle* is also the name of the primary English text in which Rev. Moon's teaching is presented. See *Divine Principle* (New York: Holy Spirit Association for the Unification of World Christianity, 1977). This text was not written by Rev. Moon himself. Often *Divine Principle* is used to simultaneously refer to the teaching and to the text in which it presented.

When a Unification Church member is single and new to the church, he does many things—fundraising, witnessing, working in church businesses, studying theology. From a Unification perspective, however, these are secondary to what's happening within him internally. Moonies are trying to become true people—true sons and daughters of God in order to become ideal as husbands and wives and parents. This effort is fundamental to the Unification way of life.

What is special about marriage in the Unification Church? For Unificationists, the Blessing is a passport to heaven. Marriage has that purpose and significance. It is conceived in relationship to God. The Blessing ceremony has sacramental qualities. It has elements of the traditional Christian sacraments, as well as much that is new or different. For example, during the wedding ceremony, holy water is used in a baptismal fashion and holy wine in an eucharistic manner. During the time of the Blessing ceremony, according to Unification theology, one's sins are forgiven and new life is given.

In the world today, Rev. Moon is God's primary spiritual instrument. Unification marriage is lived in accord with the tradition that Rev. and Mrs. Moon have established through the example of their sacrificial, loving lives. Rev. and Mrs. Moon have reached a level of spiritual maturity that makes them ideal or true as people, as husband and wife, and most importantly, as parents. That is to say, they are parents capable of giving unconditional love to their children and to others without expecting anything in return. For me Rev. Moon is not only a leader, nor just a brother in Christ or a friend. He is all those things, but he's more. He's a spiritual father, Mrs. Moon is a spiritual mother, in the sense that I can inherit a spiritual tradition from them that can lead me to God.

For Unification marriages there is a deep sense of mission and of a sharing of God's love. Our marriages are for the benefit of mankind, not merely for ourselves. Moonies are taught to sacrifice their comforts and desires (and even to leave their families if necessary) in order to serve others first and best. Rev. Moon inspires a willingness to sacrifice one's own good life for a higher purpose.

There is an aspect of romantic love in the Unification marriage ideal; I don't want to de-emphasize that. However, the ideal highlighted by Rev. Moon is that we should be willing to marry and care for anyone. What is important is the attitude with which one approaches marriage. Rev. Moon stresses that no marriage ever begins perfect and no mate is ideal in the beginning. Rather we should enter the relationship with the attitude that we will do whatever is necessary to make the marriage work for our mate, treating him or her as a son or daughter of God. We are taught to give to that person the best possible marriage, the marriage that God would want for him or her. Regardless of the difficulties involved, Unificationists are taught to make the marital relationship a success, not to give up.

According to Unification theology, we are at the beginning of an era when we all can have truly God-centered families. Moonies see themselves as helping to usher in a new age in which all men and women (including all the people who have ever lived) will reach spiritual perfection. Restored families, communities, and nations—indeed an ideal world is ultimately possible.

George Exoo: Could you specify questions in the interview process? I gather these are not private interviews. What kind of questions are nonetheless asked?

Hugh Spurgin: OK, Nora's and my situation was unusual because in 1970 the church was small and Rev. Moon was able to spend some time personally with each candidate. Obviously that is not the current situation. We are now part of a larger movement. There is an informal group called the Blessing Committee which is composed of older Blessed wives. They gather information for Rev. Moon on members eligible for the Blessing. In this presentation I have not discussed all the details of either the matching or the public wedding—some of you have seen the film of the wedding of eighteen hundred couples—but in order to be eligible for the engagement and marriage activities a single person is asked to fill out an application. He usually has to meet certain external guidelines. For instance, as it now stands, he is expected to be a member of the church for at least three years. He should also be a certain age. My wife would know more, but recently, I believe, the guideline was that men be over twenty-six years of age and women over twenty-four. Is that correct, Nora?

Nora Spurgin: Actually it is twenty-four and four years in the church or twenty-six and three years in the church. Those are just the external boundaries to work with.

Hugh Spurgin: Those may change, as they have changed in the past. There are also other guidelines for previously married couples. Spiritually the most important qualification is recruitment of spiritual children. Moonies are evangelists, trying to take their message of hope to the world, recruiting people for the church and helping them grow in their relationship with God and with other people. If I interest someone in the church that person becomes my spiritual child and I am responsible to help him grow in his understanding of and relationship with God.

I myself can learn by raising spiritual children, just as I can by raising my own natural children. The theory is that if I raise spiritual children before getting married, then later on I will be a better parent to my own children. In the process of learning and growing in my relationship with my spiritual children, hopefully I will become emotionally more mature and better able to raise natural children in the future.

George Exoo: Now you mean—I'm being a little facetious—you get S & H green stamps for winning converts, and at the time you've filled five books, you get married, no?

Hugh Spurgin: No. But at this time there are external guidelines for being married by Rev. Moon. But I will leave that question to my wife. She has served on the Blessing Committee and can discuss candidacy.

Prior to the matching, Rev. Moon looks at the pictures of eligible members and sometimes at the applications. Once he enters the meeting room, however, Rev. Moon doesn't use any notes and rarely consults with anyone other than the participants; he relies primarily on divine inspiration.

Let me conclude by saying that there are both internal and external aspects to the wedding. The internal part is called the holy wine ceremony. It has deep providential significance, particularly soteriological importance. During that part of the ceremony often the feeling of forgiveness of sins comes. Nora and I felt that; during that simple, private ceremony we felt reborn. The external aspect is the public wedding. Often, but not always, those are mass weddings.

There are other things to say, but I'll stop and introduce you to my complement, my wife Nora. Nora, can you talk about the Blessing Committee and requirements?

Nora Spurgin: It's not legalistic in terms of having a certain number of spiritual children, but it is the desired ideal that we have the experience of having guided and raised people through their growth in the church. So of course not everyone has brought three spiritual children. Some people have brought many more. I just want you to know that it's not legalistic.

George Exoo: But there is a minimum.

Hugh Spurgin: At this point in time I don't think there is. There are certain guidelines for being married in the church, but Rev. Moon can waive those kinds of qualifications and sometimes he does. And those qualifications vary from wedding to wedding. Actually, I was only two years in the church when I was married. Nora was older in the church than I, but in my case Rev. Moon waived the three-year membership requirement. So it's not legalistic.

Nora Spurgin: I'd like to talk about goals, patterns and traditions in family life in the church. Let me preface this by saying that we consider the present time a period of transition, a period when a great deal of restorative work is taking place. So, although we talk about ideals, in reality, at this point we do not live in a time when those ideals can be fully realized. Many of the things we do are geared toward restoring the world. We are also restoring our own personal lives; so the patterns are not set and you will find couples in many different situations. You can't look at any one couple and say, "This is the pattern of a Unificationist marriage—a Blessed couple." Rather, you see what that particular couple is going through, their situation and particular contribution to the providence at this time.

For example, you may see one couple working side by side in the same mission. Hugh and I have had this experience, working together with a team of people. It's a growing experience for the marriage. Being together forces you to constantly work everything out. Therefore, it's been one of the most growing and one of the most fulfilling experiences for us. At other times, you see people working in individual missions, as Hugh and I are doing right now. He's going to graduate school, a mission which I share only internally.

Next, what are some of our goals as Blessed families? We as Unificationists do not expect to *find* a perfect mate or a perfect marriage but rather we expect to *make* a perfect marriage. So we enter our marital relationship with an attitude of making it a good marriage. We have been trained by Rev. Moon not to fear struggle. We know that through struggle we become better people; I become the right person for my spouse and he becomes the right person for me. Single life in the church is considered a time of preparation for marriage and for development of an unselfish heart. We enter our marriages with an attitude of considering not just ourselves and our own personal happiness, but hopefully we have developed some ability to extend ourselves to others. My own father used to always say marriage is a "sixty-sixty" proposition, not a fifty-fifty one. To make it work each partner has to give sixty percent. I think he was right. Because of our training as single people in the Unification Church, we are educated not to think only of our own needs. We may approach marriage with a willingness to give more than fifty percent, rather than to think, "I will give only fifty percent and no more."

As Unification couples, we feel that it is God's blessing for us to have families, and we believe that our position as Blessed couples is different before God. We are part of a new, heavenly lineage—free from the hold (but not from the influence) of evil.

We feel responsible always to seek what is God's will for our lives and to respond to that to the best of our ability. Recently couples, like all Unification members, have been asked to develop "home churches." If we are living as a couple in a community, for instance, then our mission is to extend ourselves and to become a vital part of that community, relating as friends to our neighbors and inviting them into our homes and hearts. We will thus learn to know the community and become solid families within it. This is the offering of the nuclear family as a unit.

You may wonder whether there are any regulations on the married life of Unification couples. Ideologically, we want to make ideal marriages—fulfilling our fullest potential as couples as well as individuals. In an ideal state of oneness with God and of spiritual maturity, we are completely united with the Lawmaker (God) and are absolutely free. This is Rev. Moon's basic attitude. There is an ultimate state of absolute freedom. Realistically, of course, we are merely in the process of getting there. Therefore, we must exercise discipline in order to reach a point where we can experience absolute freedom. Hence, we need to discipline ourselves to live righteously by following some basic principles. Most people are surprised by the fact that Rev. Moon has given Unification couples very few specific guidelines, however. Fidelity to one's partner is an absolute. Other than that he expects us to find the best way for us, experimenting through trial and error and finding out what's workable within the structure of *Divine Principle*, but without specific marital directives.

One of the questions often asked is: "Do we have rules regarding birth control and abortion?" A lot is left up to the individual. Rev. Moon encourages us to have large families, but he doesn't talk of birth control as sinful. We certainly have to take personal responsibility for raising our families. When Rev. Moon discourages using birth control, he talks about it in terms of not limiting our families for the sake of our missions. He exhorts us to go ahead and have many children. Our children are the only thing we can attain in this world that is eternal. Therefore, because it has eternal consideration we may regret having limited our family too much at a time when it seems that there is so much else to do. Children are our future. Blessed children are a contribution to the world.

What are our goals for our children? Basically the goals are internal; we want to help our children have a sense of respect and reverence for God, for other people, and for creation. Therefore, Rev. Moon suggests that we have a special place in our homes, no matter how small our homes are, for prayer—a spot that is a sanctuary. We have such a place in our house which is set aside for prayer. He also teaches that we should pray in front of our children, not just have our devotional life separate from them. Rather let them feel and learn the pattern of reverence and attendance to God by observing our example. We also try to instill in the children a sense of dignity, self-worth and confidence. Because they are Blessed children (children born after the Blessing) we consider them special. Of course we don't want to raise them to be self-centered or arrogant by considering them too special. They, too, will develop character by learning to be selfless and sacrificial. But definitely we try to instill in them a sense of being God's children, which in itself gives them dignity and self-worth. They need to be respected as individuals; Rev. Moon says, "Give your children respect." Over the years Rev. Moon has given some instruction on how to raise children, but it is still surprisingly little.

We are also concerned to develop our children's potential, because we want them to make a contribution to mankind. We, thus, try to be in a position to develop whatever potential they express, and expose them to as many opportunities and different experiences as possible. Here, too, Rev. Moon has advised us not to place too many limitations on our children, to let them live a full and stimulating life.

In terms of religious training, we try to give them an understanding of the Christian foundation which they inherit. We have Sunday school for them, taking them all the way through the Bible in a format very similar to any other Christian Sunday school; and in addition we teach them *Divine Principle* and hence the *Divine Principle* interpretation of biblical stories and passages.

We are concerned about the environment in which they are growing up. Our own children go to public school—in other areas where the public school is not so good, the children go to Catholic school or some other kind of private school. Our public school is a good one and so far they have not had bad experiences. However, as they become older there may be problems, especially in the area of sexual morality. We're very concerned because, of all the things we want to teach our children, a strong sense of sexual ethics is very important, but this is something that is hard to control in the contemporary environment. Through television and school, the corrupt attitudes of our society creep into our everyday lives. Recently our eight year old daughter came home from school and said that a little girl in her class said she was "too sexy." She is only in the second grade but children are thinking about these things and we have to deal with them. I asked her if she knew what "sexy" meant and she didn't. We, like all parents, have to deal with influences we don't initiate, and it's not easy. We have no guarantee that our children are going to grow up to be Unification Church members, even though that is our ideal—our desire.

What, then, are our goals as a Blessed family? Probably the highest goal would be to pass on the values of unselfishness in service to God and humanity—to help our children experience the various kinds of love (a child's love, mutual love, and ultimately parental love). We attempt to instill these values first through example and, second, by family traditions. We don't have many rules or strict traditions, but we do have several ceremonies. When the child is eight days old, we have a dedication ceremony in which the father and mother offer the child to God. This is similar in attitude to a baptism or christening ceremony in other churches. The parents dress in white robes and offer prayers for the child.

We also try to have devotions in our homes, prayer and grace before meals, good music, and a peaceful and happy home atmosphere. There are always many people around so the children are exposed to many different social relationships—intercultural, international, and interracial. We're religious, but involved in the world around us; our kids are Brownies and Cub Scouts and go to camps and take lessons.

As one of the patterns or traditions of our church, I'd like to comment briefly upon our attitude toward sacrifice. We feel that marriage is important and should be enjoyed and all want to experience joy and happiness. We also believe that willingness to offer ourselves to the larger mission's needs will ultimately bring us the greatest amount of joy and satisfaction in our marriage.

Some couples' sacrifice is very different from the sacrifices others make. I'd like to give an example. Rev. Moon may call for couples to go out and work in individual missions—foreign mission fields, for instance— so they may live separately for a while. Yet, at the same time another couple—let's say an interracial couple, Black and white—is living together in Harlem. The interracial couple's whole mission is different; their sacrifice is different. They may be struggling and suffering and working just as much as the couple that is working on separate missions. I hope you can understand that we're looking for the meaning behind these sacrifices.

Why are couples separated? What is the purpose of it? Actually, in terms of separation, many of you know that our Unification couples are sometimes separated for the sake of a larger concern. Is this a basic pattern for everyone? Not necessarily, even though we all think in terms of living sacrificially. The couples who were married in 1969 and those who were married in 1970 waited forty days before they began their married life. That is an absolute condition in the Unification Church. This forty-day period of abstinence before beginning one's married life is a time to offer to God one's marriage, first making a spiritual foundation for a God-centered marriage. We liken it to Jesus fasting in the wilderness for forty days prior to beginning his public ministry.

Then in 1975, the couples who were Blessed were asked to wait three years. It came as a surprise to everyone that there could be a longer separation period. However, these couples were given a special providential mission. Their marriages were to be the foundation for the worldwide spiritual work, whereas previous couples had laid national foundations. So many of them (either one or both) went to foreign nations as missionaries. They were asked to give three years as a spiritual foundation for the worldwide work; after that they would begin their marriages. Since then many are continuing their mission work together as couples.

While some were beginning the missions in other countries, the other couples who were back home in America were also asked to make sacrifices by helping to solidify the American mission. I specifically remember three occasions when Rev. Moon called upon American Blessed women to leave their families and go out and work on a mission. The first time he called for American women to do this was in 1971. I was pregnant, Hugh was working at an outside job, and we were leading the local center in Philadelphia. Because I was pregnant, I did not go out. Five of the women went to work as itinerary workers for one year. They were representative of all the married couples; their mission was to travel throughout America serving as spiritual counselors to the young leaders in each state, helping to guide them, and helping them to understand the problems of the members. This was an important role, a valuable mission. I remember having mixed feelings about staying behind while others went out. A part of me wanted to be out there doing spiritual work—being on the front line. But because I was soon going to have a baby I stayed at the center in Philadelphia with my husband. However, in addition to doing what I could regarding the spiritual work, I cared for the eighteen-month-old son of one of the women who went out, having to separate temporarily from her family. Her husband as well as her son lived with us and the center members.

Taking care of two families wasn't easy either. Sometimes I wondered which was the greater sacrifice! Mine at that particular time wasn't so glorious, yet it demanded a great deal of sacrifice and internal fortitude. Three days after our second child was born, Hugh left Philadelphia to go out to the Midwest to lead an evangelical bus team, traveling from state to state publicizing our movement and trying to recruit members. So that meant that I was left home with three children (including my friend's son) while Hugh was called to another mission hundreds of miles away.

After a few more months, however, the first group of I.W.s (itinerary workers) came back, and the mother of the little boy for whom I had been caring rejoined her family, and I went to Minnesota to join Hugh. Hugh and I worked together for several months until Rev. Moon asked again for some wives to go out as itinerary workers, traveling from state to state visiting local centers, giving counseling to leaders and members and providing an overall perspective to the work of the local church. I was asked to go and I did. The women who went out the first time were not asked to go this time.

There are two purposes in this type of sacrifice and work. One, it serves a very pragmatic purpose in our church because the wives have a great deal to offer. We are generally older members and because of our experience of marriage and motherhood, we have a different perspective from single members who have just recently joined the church. Ideally we've learned a lot in marriage and grown a great deal so that emotionally we are in a different space. We have a different perspective on the church, on people's individual problems, and hopefully a more mature attitude toward life in general. Our role was concerned with helping young state leaders to develop and mature as leaders.

Although in many ways it was more exciting to be out in the field than to be at home, it wasn't an easy life. I would like to share with you some of the mixture of feelings that many of us experienced in separating from our families. I think of the times when I cried myself to sleep just thinking about my children and husband and wishing I could be with them, yet wanting to make this sacrifice at the same time for providential reasons. I think that you'll find that most of the couples want to contribute to the dispensation on the most sacrificial level they can. If they are in a situation, practically or emotionally, where they cannot do what is asked, then they generally make whatever offering they can. I don't know if that makes sense to you; what I mean is that a couple may feel they cannot both work and do a church mission at a given time, but they will try to do the best they can within their circumstances to contribute to the movement. Even though we feel a certain joy in being able to offer ourselves to God and our church in this way, it is always with a deep sense of internal suffering and pain. It is this very experience of suffering that makes us more qualified to appreciate and understand the suffering of other people. Rev. Moon specifically teaches that we need to experience and thus understand this kind of struggle and suffering.

Each of the times Rev. Moon has called for the wives to go work "on the front line," as we call it, that sacrifice has been really needed. For example, when the couples in 1975 went to the foreign mission field, their sacrifice was needed to make a spiritual foundation for the worldwide mission. Here in the United States, the older couples were making a spiritual foundation for this nation. We view the time that we are living in as a time of spiritual warfare, as if our nation were at war. If an enemy stood at our borders ready to invade, we might have to leave our families to protect our country. The same is true spiritually; we in the Unification Church feel we are leaving our families now for the sake of protecting our nation and ultimately ourselves from the lack of God-centered values. We believe that there is an ultimate purpose for such sacrifice; but people won't always be living such extremely sacrificial lives.

I'd like to mention something about my personal experience with regard to my children, as an example. During the Yankee Stadium and Washington Monument rallies in 1976, we worked as an entire movement to give something of ourselves for the sake of this country. We believed this nation needed a spiritual revival and we sought to bring it about.

At that time I was pregnant with my third child (we now have four children). I could have chosen not to work in those campaigns. But I felt that this would be such a tremendous spiritual condition for my child as well as for the nation for me to participate. Some day she can say, "My mother worked in those rallies even though she was pregnant. She helped sweep the streets of New York City and handed out leaflets while carrying me." So I deliberately chose to work during both campaigns. In fact, during the Washington Monument campaign, Mr. Salonen, the president of our church in America, said, "You don't have to go. Are you sure you want to?" I wanted to go and make a contribution.

Thus, even though responses to these kinds of missions and interruptions to family life differ and the capacity to handle the subsequent separations are not the same, the attitude of most couples is similar. We all try to work with whatever capabilities we have. It is important that we evaluate our limitations honestly and communicate them to our church leaders.

During the time that mothers are working on front line missions, the church has provided care for the children. I'd like to talk about that. There was a nursery established for full-time care for children of mothers with church missions. I personally felt that the children were happy and well cared for when they were living in the nursery. I feel that many children can handle this type of social and nurturing experience if they have absolute confidence that their parents really love them, care about them, and care for each other. There is no fear that their parents may get a divorce, that kind of fear among the children generally does not exist in our Unification family units since the value of the nuclear family is strong for us.

Personally, I used to keep a journal for each of my children, a continuous letter written to each child while I was out traveling. I would write my deepest feelings and desires for them in that journal when we were separated because of my mission. Now my two oldest children are seven and eight years old, and they love to have me read from those journals, their personal book written by mommy. I would write, for instance, "I really wanted to be with you, but I felt I should do God's work. Someday you will understand, but now maybe you don't. I went out, separating from you and Daddy, because I want to make a better world for you and for others." I feel that even now they have some deep feeling—a small sense of appreciation—for what I did, and in the future they will have even more appreciation.

Recently Rev. Moon has been expressing a great deal of concern about our children and their education. He's been concerned all along, but now there are many more children and they are growing older, so he wants to establish an educational system for them. When parents have three children, it is a mission in itself to educate them; therefore mothers with three or more children are generally being freed from other church missions to do this. Occasionally there are exceptions to this, but in general after having three children a woman is freed to take just the mission of raising and educating the children. By that time usually the oldest child is ready to go to school.

I'd like to mention something about the future. That's really where it's at for our movement. What we're doing right now is only preparation for the future. Rev. Moon often talks about creating more trinities among the couples; a trinity is three couples or families that are especially responsible for helping one another. It's like an extended family and they would be financially concerned for each other. Right now we live in a communal system, but that will not always be the case, especially not for families; already the transition has begun. So then the three couples will make up a small community. To what extent such a system will work we don't know, but that is an ideal; the plan is to possibly even live together in the same apartment house.

For me this would be a beautiful system, although I know from the reality of living with other couples over the last few years, that there is much to work out. It's just like a marriage (where you have to work out all the little personal problems and idiosyncrasies)—the same is true when you live with other couples. You have to come to love one another, almost like you come to love your marriage partner. You have to come to accept the other people and be willing to think of them and their needs and concerns as well as your own and your own family's. When you live with another family with children and you see their children doing things that you don't particularly like—and your children doing things that they don't like—it requires some stretching to reach a point of workability. Again we see this as part of our road to maturity or perfection. If we are raised within the church to be loving, then it makes it much easier.

In terms of education, we're concerned about setting up our own schools in the future. Even now we are developing a nursery, and as the children grow, it will develop into an educational system. Hugh's and my children are a little older than most of the children in the American church, although not older than the Blessed children in Japan or Korea. As the number of Unification children in America increases we will provide an educational system for them. Rev. Moon wants to have the best education for them—in every way the best. We are a paradox—we often live sacrificially, but our goal is to ultimately have the very best. Heaven is to be on earth. In the nurseries now, three-year-old children speak two or three languages quite fluently. It's really amazing. In a way I'm sorry that my children aren't currently there, because they are not getting such an education.

Next, I'd like to speak about home churches as part of the future plan. This is a new providential era and the Unification Church is developing a pattern or system of helping other families spiritually—of helping not only individuals but entire homes to become God-centered. An elder couple in our church would serve as a central hub for a neighborhood, helping the people around them. Externally, they would be as responsible as pastors, but centered upon their homes in the community, not necessarily upon a church building. This system is just developing, but I feel it is a pattern for the future.

We Unification members feel that through our philosophy of life we have a world view that can break down barriers from which society suffers. We are preparing our children for intercultural, international, interracial marriages and societies. We foresee a breakdown in cultural and international barriers in the future—we see that happening more in the next generation than in ours.

I want to say more about the Blessing Committee: The concern is basically that members are prepared and able to handle marriage and families, in addition to meeting certain external qualifications. There are some situations where people are counseled extensively to help them determine whether they feel they are ready to handle a family. For example, if someone has some deep-seated personal problems that he or she might do better to work out before marriage, then they may choose not to attend a particular matching. Or, there may be other reasons, personal reasons, why they may decide not to go.

Also, as we have said, the church has specific requirements, including three years membership, an age requirement, and also celibacy (which Hugh did not mention, but which is very important prior to marriage). Our assumption is that if you have been dedicated to the church's values and work for three years, you also have remained celibate for three years. However, of course, we are all fallible and things happen and some people have difficulties maintaining such standards. Those things are often discussed with the Blessing Committee.

Richard Quebedeaux: Thank you very much. Do you have any more comments?

Hugh Spurgin: Could I make one more comment? I want to discuss a paradox. On the one hand, Unification theology stresses the importance of family life, yet the reality is that often we as Unification couples are separated. Several times, Nora and I have been separated; most other Unification couples have been separated. It is the same paradox that Jesus mentioned when he declared, "He who seeks to gain his life will lose it, and he who loses his life will gain it." In other words, if you do God's work it will be better for you and your family because ultimately you and your children will gain. Rev. Moon, in accord with Jesus, teaches that such a paradox is a basic law of the universe. For example, Rev. Moon told Nora and several other women who were working as I.W.s while they were pregnant that the reason he asked them to work so long separated from their families was that, in addition to helping other people, they personally would gain by sacrificially doing God's work. He said that because of their faithfulness, both they and their children would gain spiritually. I believe that. That is to say, I believe that God will help our children to prosper spiritually if we do His work. Problems arise, however, when doubts and confusion enter one's mind and one becomes halfhearted in doing God's work. It seems to be the worst of all possible worlds when one is neither fully committed to a mission, nor fully with one's children. Then you are in a gray area of confusion. If one is *really* dedicated and committed to doing God's will and believes what Jesus said when he told us that in the process of sacrificing we'll gain, then I believe, paradoxically, we do benefit.

Richard Quebedeaux: Thank you very much. Now I'd like to do something evangelical. I'd like to read a portion of Scripture. This is the twelfth Chapter of Romans in the Phillips translation:

18

With eyes wide open to the mercies of God, I beg you, my brothers, as an act of intelligent worship, to give him your bodies, as a living sacrifice, consecrated to him and acceptable by him. Don't let the world around you squeeze you into its own mold, but let God remold your minds from within, so that you may prove in practice that the plan of God for you is good, meets all his demands and moves toward the goal of true maturity.

As your spiritual teacher I give this piece of advice to each one of you. Don't cherish exaggerated ideas of yourself or your importance, but try to have a sane estimate of your capabilities by the light of the faith that God has given to you all. For just as you have many members in one physical body and those members differ in their functions, so we, though many in number, compose one body in Christ and all are members of one another. Through the grace of God we have different gifts. If our gift is preaching, let us preach to the limit of our vision. If it is serving others let us concentrate on our service; if it is teaching let us give all we have to our teaching; and if our gift be the stimulating of the faith of others, let us set ourselves to it. Let the man who is called to give, give freely; let the man who wields authority think of his responsibility; and let the man who feels sympathy for his fellows act cheerfully.

Let us have no imitation Christian love. Let us have a genuine break with evil and a real devotion to good. Let us have real warm affection for one another as between brothers, and a willingness to let the other man have the credit. Let us not allow slackness to spoil our work and let us keep the fires of the spirit burning, as we do our work for the Lord. Base your happiness on your hope in Christ. When trials come endure them patiently; steadfastly maintain the habit of prayer. Give freely to fellow Christians in want, never grudging a meal or a bed to those who need them. And as for those who try to make your life a misery, bless them. Don't curse, bless. Share the happiness of those who are happy, and the sorrow of those who are sad. Live in harmony with one another. Don't become snobbish but take a real interest in ordinary people. Don't become set in your own opinions. Don't pay back a bad turn by a bad turn, to *anyone*. See that your public behavior is above criticism. As far as your responsibility goes, live at peace with everyone. Never take vengeance into your own hands, my dear friends: stand back and let God punish if he will. For it is written:

Vengeance belongeth unto me: I will recompense.

And these are God's words:

If thine enemy hunger, feed him.

If he thirst, give him to drink:

For in so doing, thou shalt heap coals of fire upon his head. Don't allow yourself to be overpowered by evil. Take the offensive—overpower evil with good!

I will turn over the next half hour to Arthur who will talk about life as a single person in Unification Church. After that we'll open it up to discussion, conversation and interaction. Even though we'll be moving from topic to topic, that doesn't mean that a question that isn't answered can't be asked again later. I hope that every person will be able to ask his or her burning questions and feel that those questions get satisfactory answers. Feel free, of course, in your free time to ask people questions and to interact with each other. If two or three of you are bothered about something, don't hesitate to bring that up at a later point. With that I'll introduce Arthur Eves.

Arthur Eves: You're going to see the principle of unity within diversity. We come from different experiences, different backgrounds, different perspectives within the church.

In this framework, there is an important issue that runs through *Divine Principle* and generally in society: the creative tension between novelty or creativity and order. On the one hand, *Divine Principle* affirms traditional values, yet, on the other hand, it's something radically new and different. These facts lead to the questions about whether it is fundamentally a reactionary stance or something radically new.

An important point here is what is the purpose of morality as we see it in the Unification Church? The purpose of creating orderly relationships is growing, and developing the greatest possible love. Thus, the reason we emphasize the family is that we see it as developing a child's capacity to love as a child, then developing his or her capacity to love within a conjugal relationship, and next developing his or her ability to love children as a parent.

Don Jones: Could I ask a clarifying question? I'd like to go back to what Nora said. You've both used the term *morality.* When Nora used it the term seemed to pertain to sexual morality. I wonder if you could tell us how that term functions for you.

Arthur Eves: Right. In terms of particular behaviors?

Don Jones: I don't know, you used the term. Does morality mean being generous to others, or does it mean not being unfaithful to your spouse or not having sexual intercourse before marriage and that sort of thing?

Arthur Eves: I'd say all of the above and for different reasons. Being generous to others is definitely an expression of love, an affirmation of the other. With premarital intercourse, although love is involved, it's a premature demonstration of affection. Consequently, it hinders further development. We usually express it in different terms but . . .

Nora Spurgin: From my point of view I would put sexual morality first, but that doesn't exclude other forms of morality.

Arthur Eves: In terms of order, we see purpose as absolute and the purpose to us is the development of the ability to love, and the means are relative. Guides and values are considered as means to fulfill the purpose.

We really emphasize family ethics. Some will say that this is because of the Oriental origin of Unification thought and the influence of Confucianism, but it is more fundamental than that.

Now Richard asked me to address several questions on attitudes toward celibacy, homosexuality and other areas. These things I have to deal with from a personal perspective; I can't make generalizations for the movement.

For me celibacy is part of a process. During the period of celibacy I'm developing my ability to love in individual relationships and perfecting that level of relationship.

At the beginning, after conversion, we're full of abstract feelings of love, and there is a feeling of love toward everyone. But over time, you learn how to act on those feelings concretely and practically; that is much more real, much more important. This is a common experience among all religious groups, the tendency to love everybody, but finding that when it comes down to the nitty-gritty of daily life it is very difficult to express that. Our communal lifestyle helps love to develop.

We talk about religion and family and these things are touchy for many people. They're very powerful symbols and most people have strong but ambivalent feelings about them. I think people, especially in recent years, have blamed a lot of problems on religion and the family, so when we use those words it creates an emotional response, especially if we talk about an ideal family. Some aspects of the ideal family, such as the parental relationship, need to be more clearly defined. We're talking about a radical shift. Given what we are coming out of, we have many distorted perceptions, distorted experiences, and a very wide range of understandings of what family is.

Among people I have talked to, there is a fear that we are creating dependencies, but the role of a true parent is to raise people beyond the dependencies that they project on a parent figure, to independence. I think that's what Rev. Moon has been trying to do. All of us, in our search for authority and for something we can count on, put responsibility on others, and in our religious life we are gradually taking that responsibility back. The purpose of the moral teachings on how you treat other people in general is to guide one from a state of dependence and not knowing how to deal with the world to a state of freedom and of being able to live in love, united with God and God's ideal.

There is considerable accusation of the Unification Church regarding the use of peer pressure. But peer pressure within any kind of community is very strong because of the intimacy, because of the concern about other people within the community and how they feel about you and respond to you. I think this side of our life is very real. But in our situation there is also an emphasis on developing a person's relationship with God, with an absolute ideal outside of the social environment, so that one is connected to the transcendent ideal and working within the immanent situation.

The points that Hugh and Nora made about spiritual children and home church were also, of course, about developing one's ability to love. When I first joined the church I was in Oakland, mostly witnessing. My experience of concern for individuals and their spiritual growth and other needs was very important in developing my ability to love. Also in the home church experience we had in London several years ago, there was a feeling that each of us was responsible for everyone in the area. There we knew a very deep love, one in which we had the satisfaction of really giving, really being concerned, without requiring anything in return.

My feelings about marriage within the Unification Church are sometimes mixed, because there is a fear of the unknown. You don't know what's going to happen. I was married for four and a half years before the church. It was about three years after that that I met the church. After my marriage I felt betrayed by love. I decided that I didn't owe anybody anything in terms of my relationship to them, that I didn't have any responsibilities to them. This led me into an amoral ethic for a period of several years. But at a certain point there was a need to separate from this new-found ethic, and an internal conflict needed to be resolved. So with that kind of situation I began to lead a more spiritual life. Also in developing deeper levels of communication and communion with others, I found a value greater than I had known in my marriage. Communion and communication are fundamental to the development of sexual relationships and I became voluntarily celibate previous to joining the church, not as a rejection of sexuality, but because I felt that I was missing something fundamental to the full appreciation of sexuality. This is something that I feel is taught by *Divine Principle*—that there is a fundamental discovery of another person as an individual prior to entering into a marriage relationship with them. There has to be a deep appreciation of them as a complete person before that. Also I became convinced that sexual activity was not necessary for knowing somebody fully, and that sometimes it could cut someone off because it was a substitute for real communication. I think that *Divine Principle* teaches a way to get around that, to know people and really communicate.

The church lifestyle offers a great deal in terms of brother-sister relationships; there is often a group intimacy, trust, and openness which leads to fuller self-expression and confidence in other people. This leads to an ability to overcome social pressure and mores. It's paradoxical, because the group intimacy leads to feeling more social pressure; and on the other hand it leads to freedom from the social pressure, because there's enough trust within the group that you can do what you want, express yourself in any way as long as you don't hurt anyone. You know that you are accepted for who you are and not for what you do or what you think. I've definitely found an ability to enter into deeper levels of intimacy and deeper levels of communication with other people than were available to me before.

Now there are some difficult questions. I don't think the Unification Church has an official policy on homosexual celibate members. There have been problems in the past with local center leaders who couldn't deal with a gay person as a full person. There is a real feeling within *Divine Principle* that every person is a child of God, but that we're also all sinners. But a difficulty arises, one which has been brought up by Richard and others: What happens to a person who is gay and has become a Moonie, likes the lifestyle, likes the people, likes the theology, likes everything except for the part about marriage? It's a difficult question because marriage is central in the theology. Definitely within *Divine Principle* there is room for acceptance of an individual as a person, but we believe in the importance of fulfilling the three blessings. So, according to our theology, for the homosexual there is only the possibility of fulfilling the first blessing: individual fulfillment, ability to love on an individual level, ability to relate to God on an individual level.

In terms of the marital relationship, on the one hand, it would be denying of a person's nature to ask him or her to enter into a relationship which he/she thought went against his/her inclinations or tendencies. On the other hand, it seems that the logical part of the theology requires marriage for the fullest expression of love. We leave that up to the individual in terms of decision, because there are many reasons why a person might not want to get Blessed, although there is peer pressure—people wanting to know why you don't want what they feel is the greatest thing in the world.

There is a desire to keep things as open as possible for the individual within the framework of the Principle; we want people to express themselves to the limit they can within its framework. This is based on our belief that the Principle helps people to become the most that they can be. If a person doesn't feel that it does that, he must find some kind of internal resolution, either with his position in regard to the movement—in terms of what he does or doesn't like about it, what he does or doesn't accept—or in regard to himself and change. We are very supportive of the person who wants to change and who wants counseling. If a person is gay and wants to remain single and to remain celibate, and wants to remain in the movement, we can go with that. There isn't any clear policy in the church.

Of course, if we're actually accomplishing the restoration of family relationships and it turns out that homosexuality arises due to problems within the family then it's only a temporary problem. If, however, homosexuality arises from the androgynous nature of humanity, then we'll have to understand that. We can't really afford to close ourselves off from any possibilities until all the information is in.

Also, as far as child-care is concerned, whatever the situation is now, I know that within the movement there is much interest in what's to be done. Right now there are nurseries, but it's wide open and there's much concern for finding the best possible means and methods of education and child rearing. It's experimental and pragmatic at the present time, along with being spiritual.

A big thing at the present time, not just in the church but in society as a whole, is male-female roles and male-female relationships. This is being worked out and developed in church practice. There is a strong Oriental influence, but I think that women are gaining a more diversified role within the Unification Church. In fact, they have played a prominent role throughout, but there's a definite awareness that there are differences between men and women and a desire to utilize those differences in working out what a person does. For example, many of the I.W.s are women, because of the belief that women tend to be more compassionate, more supportive, and more understanding than men. But these are generalities. There are both male and female fundraising captains. I want to make it clear that the androgynous nature of humankind is also recognized. Certain traits are considered more masculine, some more feminine and all persons have a mixture of both. As a metaphor the yin-yang, masculine-feminine polarity principle is powerful and very useful.

William Shive: That is related to Richard's question about the cultural context from which you come.

Arthur Eves: Right. Much Unification thought comes from the very traditional, male dominated society in Korea. But not too long ago, Rev. Moon himself was in Korea and was received officially. He was invited to review a parade and insisted that Mrs. Moon sit on the reviewing stand with him. He said he would not participate unless she sat beside him. He is very radical for a Korean. A woman doesn't normally assume such a public role there.

Hugh Spurgin: When I joined the movement in Washington, D.C. in 1968, the leaders were predominantly women. It was a female-run movement. In fact, as far as I know, everywhere in the Unification Church in the early stages, including America and Korea, women were the major leaders. It was quite obvious that in America the men were not impressive at that time, and women held the major leadership positions. That changed around 1973-74 (when Rev. Moon came to America), but I think there is a providential reason for that change. At that time we were getting more men into the movement and consequently they were given leadership opportunities. More importantly the stress was placed upon having a man and a woman jointly lead various church activities.

Arthur Eves: In terms of the question of celibacy, I find from experience that it's not so difficult to live a celibate lifestyle if there is some sort of transcendent vision for which one is living, rather than for self-gratification. If one is living for something higher, whether it be another person or the vision that one has of the future, or whatever it might be, then as long as one maintains that transcendent vision, the problem is not so great. I think it only becomes a problem when people begin to lose that vision. I think people leave the movement because they lose the vision or they lose hope of accomplishing the vision. After that they think, well, what's the point of it all, why sacrifice anything? Then they leave the movement.

One problem that arises in terms of relationships between brothers and sisters, men and women, is that because we have a very strong ideal, we also have a very strong realization that mutual attraction can overpower that ideal. Because of that, many times there is a fear of developing relationships, a fear of risking the ideal. As the movement develops, as people mature, and as their hold on the ideal becomes more real there is a willingness to risk that, to develop brother-sister relationships, to overcome romantic aspirations, or whatever, and to emerge finally on a plane of really feeling as though another person is truly your brother or your sister. It's a completely different level of relationship. From my experience it involves having even romantic kinds of feelings toward somebody but recognizing that those feelings are not the only important part of life. There always exists a temptation to stop a relationship before it can develop into a deep appreciation of the person and to focus on horizontal or external aspects. It is essential to discover who that person really is instead of who he externally seems to be.

These are my reflections on some of the problems, and some of my own feelings about where we are as a church.

Richard Quebedeaux: I thank all three of you for handling an extremely difficult topic with skill. I would like to raise a few questions to begin with and then I'd like to throw it open to discussion.

Discussion

Richard Quebedeaux: I hope that we will be able to respect each other in this discussion. That is, I hope no one person will attempt to dominate the conversation and that each of us will attempt to understand and respect the opinions of others, however different the opinions expressed may be from our own.

My impression from listening to the three of you is that, for the most part, you spoke about an ideal rather than about the facts. I have been working for the Unification movement for two years and know that the kinds of issues that you have been talking about are major problems within the movement. Many people in the movement have come to me, as an outsider who will listen to them, who have very difficult sexual problems. They feel they have no one to talk to about their problems and that if they don't talk to somebody about them they will have to leave.

I have talked to too many high officials in the movement not to know that the attitude you express of real openness is not always there. I asked one high-ranking person about birth control who said, "We believe just like the Pope: it's our policy that artificial means of contraception are not permissible." Another person said, "Sex is only for procreation." Also, in respect to the separation periods, I have the impression that the only times when it is acceptable for a woman to leave her mission to spend time with her husband are those in which she can become pregnant. I do not sense that sexual enjoyment within marriage is always looked upon as good. Also there is the problem of homosexuality—people in the movement have told me about their struggles in this area. Some of them are engaged and are planning to get married. They are worried and don't know whom to talk to.

Unfortunately, I have read speeches by Rev. Moon in these areas and I have heard other talks that really puzzle me. I think that this is largely a cultural problem. Rev. Moon, however, is gradually coming to understand the American way of life better. I have seen some evidence of this. The Korean and Japanese cultural baggage that is floating around the movement is very harsh for Americans and reminds me of the same white American cultural baggage that the nineteenth-century missionaries took overseas. Now I know why American missionaries are often no longer welcome overseas, and I see the same mistakes being made by the Unification leaders, particularly those from Korea or Japan. Now, I'm not going to charge them for that—we are all subject to our own cultural conditioning and to the inability always to separate our cultural baggage from the truth of the message we proclaim.

I gather that in Unification life there is this ideal and I guess I've been around too long to think that the ideal necessarily predominates. Maybe it does in a way, but at some point these harsh issues come to the fore, and I think that unless they are resolved, persons will probably leave the movement. I have seen very little interest on the part of the leaders of the church to employ persons with psychological/psychiatric competence to deal with these problems—to make trained counselors available and to encourage church members with problems to admit the problems and seek psychiatric help.

I think that in many ways Unificationists often treat outsiders better than they treat each other. Perhaps part of the problem is the feeling that once you are an insider you must be sacrificial—that's expected—and also that it's more important to treat outsiders better than insiders. Now it's just the reverse in other groups. So far as the Unification Church is concerned, as an outsider I get benefits and don't have to work sacrificially. So I have mixed emotions there. Again, the Unification Church does have problems in the area of interpersonal relationships, including sexuality in general and guilt feelings about prior relationships that are unresolved, and I really have not seen much indication of an interest in the leadership and the movement in helping people, in telling them, "We recognize you, we love you, we're not going to put you down because you have this problem. We'll be honest with you. Please be honest with us."

So when Arthur speaks about affirmation of a person's self-worth, I think that in certain areas, and particularly in the cultural relationships between the Orientals and the whites, this is a problem of major proportions. I do, however, see a gradual improvement, even in Rev. Moon himself, who I'm sure has the best intentions. Yet I am somewhat dismayed by the persistence of some of these issues. So with that I would like to open the discussion.

Wellington Nyangoni: Does the leadership of the Unification Church realize that these are problems? Whether the church realizes the problems exist and whether the church is willing to help are different issues.

Richard Quebedeaux: I think that the white leadership understands the problems of white Americans. But at the present time the white leadership appears to be subjected to the Oriental leadership; and, furthermore, the white leadership finds it hard to communicate with the Oriental leadership about those problems.

As Arthur said, the cultural background of the Koreans makes it difficult for them to understand some of the problems Americans have with Korean views. For example, I gather that in Korea women most often have no public or professional roles at all. So it is very, very difficult for both Americans and Koreans when the Koreans have to be told, "Women are basically the same as men and ought to have the same professional and service opportunities." Yet I think that gradually the Americans are convincing the Koreans on this point; but I do not think it is happening fast enough for us. I think that this is the major reason why the Unification Church in America does not get as many members as it would like.

I do not say that the Oriental leadership has the wrong intentions. I think their intentions are right. They have a great deal of difficulty, however, in understanding why something should be a problem in America when it is not a problem in terms of their own culture. I think that any one of us has the same type of problem if we are educated and our parents are not educated. Then we have a much broader and more complex cultural experience than our parents. We try to explain to them why we have different values than they have, and they can't understand us. I see the same sort of thing between Americans and Koreans.

Steve Post: One aspect of the cultural difference is very interesting. Richard alluded to the question of the purpose of marriage: is marriage only for procreation or is it also for the cultivation of interpersonal relations? In Roman Catholic marital ethics there is a natural law tradition which is teleological and goes back to Ulpian. This tradition treated marriage as a physiological function: marriage was intended for procreation. They de-emphasized its interpersonal aspect. Now Roman Catholic ethics has moved toward balancing the procreative and the relational aspects of marriage. An example is the work of Charles Curran at Catholic University. The Protestants have done the same thing: Paul Ramsey, who wrote *One Flesh*, also saw a kind of balance between the two.

I think we are struggling with the same sorts of difficulties that other traditions have always struggled with. What is the purpose of marriage? For us, procreation is an essential element in marriage; but the relational element is also essential. Our theology of marriage includes the belief that the ideal marriage reflects the give-and-take relationship between the masculine and feminine aspects of God. True, this theology of marriage that stresses personal development, relational, and procreational aspects of marriage is still emerging and becoming clear within the church. And, as is to be expected, some persons, both within and outside of the movement, bring their own hang-ups and problems to the consideration of marriage.

Don Jones: Then how are you answering the charge that Richard made that you regard human sexuality not as redemptive but as preventative?

Steve Post: I want to refer that question to the Spurgins. I am saying that a true, objective account of the ideal Unification marriage would emphasize the fact that there is a balance among the aspects of the marriage relationship.

Richard Quebedeaux: Would the Spurgins like to respond to that?

Hugh Spurgin: When I asked Rev. Kwak (a Korean leader) a few of these questions, one of the points he emphasized was that Rev. Moon teaches that we can and should control our biological urges. The spiritual should dominate the material. That doesn't rule out physical pleasure—it doesn't negate the material—it simply says that ideally the spirit should be stronger than the body, and therefore we can and should control our sexual passions and desires.

Nora Spurgin: I'd like to add to that. Definitely you're going to find leaders who say the kind of things that you just said. But there definitely are others who do not say that at all. And I know that Rev. Moon has said that within marriage, especially when you've gone through this restorative process and when you reach a certain point of maturity where you are really capable of taking responsibility for another person and loving that other person, then there is no limitation. You and your spouse are one body, and so there is no need for feeling that the other part of your body can't be part of you. I know that certain Korean leaders have said this, too.

On other occasions Rev. Moon has talked about birth control. I know that many of his speeches are situational. Then he is talking about certain situations, and what he says depends on the problems and questions he finds in that situation. Basically our attitude is not to use birth control. However, I don't feel at all that it's a sin if anyone does. This is my personal feeling. And I think the majority of couples would say we have to take responsibility for what we do.

Also there is the question of periods of separation of husbands and wives and of their getting together. People are missing the point here. These Unificationist couples want to have children, but they also want to serve the movement—even through their separation if that is necessary or helpful. So they want to be sure that when they do get together, it is during a time when conception is likely to take place. Still, there is a positive side to the separation.

Richard Quebedeaux: Then do you have another question, Don?

Don Jones: Added to the sexual questions, do you have a theory of romantic love that is part of the theory of marriage?

Richard Quebedeaux: Someone, I guess it was Hugh, said that there is a romantic element in marriage. Could you explain that?

Hugh Spurgin: OK, but I didn't want to dominate this conversation. With regard to what Richard was saying, before we discuss the romantic element, I would like to say that a leader or an individual here or there might make some statement, but that doesn't make it official church policy. Even Rev. Moon's informal comments are not on the level of official church policies.

But with regard to romantic love, Unification people are not automatons. Of course they have a love life, but they just put the priority on the spiritual. You pray before you enter your married life. Indeed, you can make prayer a most important aspect of that life. That's what is important. You'll find very few statements by Rev. Moon about the detailed personal marital life of couples. He seldom gets so involved. He gives long sermons and talks about what one's attitude could become. But he doesn't provide all kinds of restrictions.

Don Jones: Let me tell you what I'm thinking. I'm thinking of a Unification student who I think is romantically in love with his future wife. He shows all the signs of this. He can't study because he is thinking of her. I think he's going through exactly the same experience that I went through, and I know that you can spiritualize this. You can use religious language, but you can also use ordinary language. His heart palpitates, his hands get sweaty, and he looks forward with great longing (laughter) for her visits on weekends and that sort of thing. What I want to know is this: Is that kind of feeling and all the experiences of romantic love—a heightened consciousness of the self and sense of generosity and self-sacrifice for the other person—is that permitted and understood theologically? Or am I misreading the situation?

Diana Muxworthy: Of course these experiences are permitted theologically. I think romantic love is even essential to the theology. I'll be specific about my fiancé but first I'll give a little background.

There are two things: the heart of restoration and the heart of the ideal. As far as restoration is concerned, we talk a lot about struggle and we spiritualize a lot. We talk a lot about pain, and it often seems that Moonies are very sadistic and possibly masochistic and that through this pain they will receive joy. To me that *is* part of restoration. The fact is that we believe that the Unification Church, and each one of us, is in a providential situation. We believe we are more than just haphazardly alive and living our lives, and that each one of us, as well as every human being on this earth, has a project and a mission at this time in history. There is a certain mission, there is a certain responsibility that we are carrying.

In a sense that plagues us—I don't enjoy it, let's put it that way. It does plague me that I have to live this kind of sacrificial life, in the sense of not being able to live with Franz at Drew University. That is not joyful, but at the same time I'm inspired by it. So there's the paradox of being plagued and being inspired. I'm inspired by it because I do believe that something historical and very good for the sake of the world is taking place in my willingness to not run down to Drew. Now at the same time, for instance, I just went to Drew this weekend (laughter) because there was an ethics conference. There was an ethics conference, but it was also a chance to see Franz.

On the other hand what I saw this weekend was that Franz had not been able to write a paper during Christmastime because we were supposed to get together for Christmas. Now that was the romantic part of him which was very inspiring for me to see, and I was feeling it too. Classes at Harvard were to get out on the fifteenth; and I had convinced myself that I was going to work until the twentieth, then meet Franz and run down with my mother to North Carolina and go on through Christmas. The fact was that on the fourteenth, classes were out. There was no way I could wait five days and work on my paper. Because of the situation, Franz's professor excused him from turning in a paper until after Christmas, which meant we could meet on the fifteenth or sixteenth. It was much earlier than it could have been otherwise. Now that was the romance, and it was very beautiful to be able to enjoy it. And we did enjoy it.

Now this weekend I saw the other side. Franz is so inspired by what he feels is the mission of becoming a very good student at Drew that when I went there, his roommate said that it's like Franz is chained to a chair. He really is working hard. I can't work the way he works. Discipline, discipline, discipline in his work. So there are both sides of the picture. There are two concepts that you see throughout *Divine Principle: happiness* and *indemnity*. They are constantly juxtaposed. I realize that this way may seem to be something of a problem in *Divine Principle*, because you can emphasize one or the other. In our growth in the church, however, we learn that there is a balance between happiness and indemnity both in the community and in the life of the individual. It takes time, but through the years we do come to see the balance. It varies from person to person, which is stressed at any one time or in any one situation.

Leonard Lovett: Someone made the point that marriage, the Blessing, is a passport to the kingdom. Also, the suggestion was made that salvation begins with marriage and that with marriage one is freed from one's sins. Yet there appears to be a simultaneous surrendering of one's volition. The choice of one's marriage partner seems to be a mediation of the will of God by revelation and inspiration through Rev. Moon. I am wondering how you resolve this conflict: through marriage you find freedom; yet in the choice of a marriage partner, you surrender your freedom to Rev. Moon.

Hugh Spurgin: From my perspective one aspect of that is that there's a greater Mind in the universe. God knows more about me and my potentiality and more about my future mate than I do and I have to be open to that divine inspiration. But that does not negate one's response. When Rev. Moon makes a choice, then one makes a personal, individual commitment, or decision based on that choice. One can say "yes" or "no" to Rev. Moon's choices. But the important point is that you accept the belief that God knows more than you do about what would be good for you in your life.

Leonard Lovett: He may know more, but you say you open up to the response of God because this mind out there knows more than you. Does this knowledge about you have to come through Rev. Moon?

Hugh Spurgin: For me it did.

Nora Spurgin: Maybe you could say that ultimately we are responsible for what happens. You know, if we don't like this marriage, we can't go back and say, "Well, it was all your fault, God." Rather we go with a feeling of responsibility. We take responsibility for putting ourselves in that situation. I think if we maintain that kind of faith, then it works. There is a problem when there is a loss of faith. Then the marriages start to break down. This has happened.

Leonard Lovett: Loss of faith in whom?

Nora Spurgin: Well, you can lose your faith in God. You can lose your faith in Rev. Moon as a mediator. Then you start losing your faith in yourself as a Unification Church member. Next you start losing faith in your husband or wife. And then the breakdown comes.

Richard Quebedeaux: The other part of his question has to do with salvation by marriage.

Hugh Spurgin: Let me bring in the concept of freedom. We may compare the dating and romantic love pattern that's common in Western culture with this kind of arranged marriage. As I look back on it, I now see that for me growing up in America in the 1950s and sixties was very unhappy. I was frustrated with the dating process. Regardless of whom I was dating, there was always someone else. I was always looking for someone better and for a different experience. I never deeply understood the concept or the feeling of commitment to one person because I was always looking for greener pastures. For me, then, there is more security in knowing that God has chosen my wife and that, if I respond in a faithful way, this can be a secure, stable marriage in a way in which if I were deciding by myself, it might never be.

Richard Quebedeaux: I want to ask Arthur Eves to pursue Leonard's point that marriage is the point of salvation. Arthur stated that a single person could find total acceptance in the movement. How is that possible? You are not matched yet. Do you believe that you, Arthur Eves, can have salvation if you choose not to marry? Do you believe that any person can find salvation if he or she chooses to remain single?

Arthur Eves: According to Unification thought there are three blessings. The first blessing is that of perfected individuality in the God-centered life. The single person can achieve the first blessing. But a qualitative step is taken with marriage which is preparation for the remaining blessing and, thus, for full salvation. I do not think that the person who achieves only individual fulfillment has full salvation.

Richard Quebedeaux: So essentially you are backing up a little. It seems to me that if I were in the Unification Church, and if I decided that I valued my singleness, as many people do now, and if I felt that, for whatever reason, I didn't want to marry, I would have to get out, if I had any integrity at all. In terms of what you've said and in terms of the Unification theology of marriage, I don't see how you can avoid this conclusion.

I hear you saying on the one hand, that marriage is central and very important and that there are three blessings we have to go through in order to gain the fullness of restoration. This means that if you go through only the first blessing, as a single person does, then you really can't achieve full salvation. So you are ultimately a second class citizen within the movement. I was a second class citizen in fundamentalism and I never want to go back to that status. You say that *Divine Principle* talks about the worth within each person and his feeling of self-worth. How can a single person feel he has any self-worth if he doesn't feel that he needs to get married? Are there other alternatives?

Ernest Stewart: I'd like to reply to that. I think there are alternatives. It depends on the degree to which the individual really wants to work at it. As St. Paul said, those who feel called to marry, marry. If you think you can do without marriage, then maybe you will choose to remain single. I think there is a sense in our movement that some people want to work at marriage and there is a sense that some people do not. I know three or four people who didn't want to be married. They wanted instead to devote their time to various other things. That's quite possible. They believe that after they die, they'll be matched to somebody in the spirit world. They don't have to marry now. If you do not wish to marry, you don't have to feel uncomfortable. To be sure, you may feel some pressure, because some people may say to you that marriage is everything, and you may fear that some will look down on you, but that's not necessarily so.

I'd like to add some other things, because I want to throw the argument back to you a little bit. Because of my own background of having been married before, I'd like to say something more about marriage. I worked very hard at my first marriage, which lasted for seventeen years. I think that in some ways it was quite successful, although I always felt there was something missing. Even though I tried to center on God, even though I prayed a lot and worked very hard in the church where I was, I felt that something was missing. At one time I was not very involved in the church, but what ultimately drew me back (into the Baptist Church at that time) was that I wanted to find the answers for my marriage, to find fulfillment, to find the depth that I really felt should be there.

Ultimately my first marriage did break up. But I found that after being Blessed and uniting with my wife here, in just a matter of weeks, I achieved a much deeper relationship than I had ever been able to have in seventeen years no matter how hard I worked at it. So I'm very grateful for the foundation I did receive through Rev. Moon and for the experience of preparing myself for marriage through the church.

Richard Quebedeaux: First of all, I want to say that we have one hour left in this discussion. I want to be as fair as possible in bringing you all out, but I think this is the kind of situation where we have to understand that not everyone is going to be able to ask his or her question in this period. I encourage you to continue the discussion informally. And if necessary we can at the appropriate time bring up the questions of people who will not have an opportunity to speak during this session.

Paul Sharkey: It is one thing to have faith that one's marriage was made in heaven or faith that one has a God-given mission in bringing about restoration, but how is that related to one's faith in Rev. Moon? After all, according to you it is through Rev. Moon that the revelation about God comes. Rev. Moon chooses one's spouse. He decides what one's mission is to be. Now, I see several questions here. Does one have faith in Rev. Moon or in God or both? If both, how is one's faith in Rev. Moon related to one's faith in God? Also, it seems to me that Unificationists attribute to Rev. Moon a kind of extreme infallibility. I am a Catholic. And I would say that even the Pope does not claim that kind and degree of infallibility. No Catholic that I know would attribute it to him.

Then there is what I see as a very large question. I have never understood exactly what *true parenthood* means. The notion of true parenthood seems to presuppose that there is some other kind of parenthood which is non-true. In the four years that I've been observing the movement I have never been able to get clear about the criteria or characteristics of what counts as true parenthood. Are these characteristics spiritual, biological or sociological? What are the necessary or sufficient conditions that distinguish a true parent from a non-true parent?

And with that, one last little comment. I can very easily see how biological parents, a Moonie's progenitors, might be hurt and mistrustful of the notion of true parents when they are told that Rev. Moon and Mrs. Moon are the Moonie's "true parents."

Richard Quebedeaux: One issue is the nature of Rev. Moon's authority, in particular his authority over the life of the individual Moonie. Is he regarded as having higher authority than even the strictest

Catholic would give the Pope? Secondly, what about true parenthood? Who are the true parents? Are Rev. and Mrs. Moon the only true parents, or are all Moonies aspiring to be true parents? How does the notion of true parents relate to one's biological parents? Comments? Steve.

Steve Post: I think there is an egalitarianism in the concept of true parents. Right now, of course, it looks as though great authority is vested only in Rev. and Mrs. Moon. Yet as time goes on we will see that everybody will be a true parent. This will mean that everybody in a society will hold the same position of authority in spiritual matters. What we see now is an interim situation.

Richard Quebedeaux: Here we see Unification thought at the societal level. Is there to be a democratization of the role of true parents? Do any of you want to comment on this?

Nora Spurgin: We're put in that position now. Before God we're put in that position to take the responsibility, to develop ourselves to become true parents. The reason we say we're becoming true parents is that we have not yet worked out all of our imperfections at all. Therefore, before God we are put in that position. You understand what I mean? It's like God forgives us and allows us to be in that position but we still have the responsibility of working out all the things that make us less than true parents. So as we develop, we're in that position but we don't deserve it. Future generations deserve it. We don't because we come from the fallen world.

Mary Carman Rose: One of the things that attracts me most to the Unification Church is that you are bringing back to us universal themes of tremendous significance that we in the West have never known or have forgotten. Three of them have been mentioned this morning.

First, there is the reality of the next life and how there will be opportunities for progress and creativity there, too. Second, you have reminded us that a particular person can be uniquely a channel of spiritual insight and power. Rev. Moon is in that position. I do not think that he should be compared with the Pope. Rather, he is very like the Catholic, Hindu, or Zen spiritual director who has the gift of discernment of the spiritual needs and potentialities of others. And third, there is the work of indemnity, or the spiritual work that is done by our giving up our own desires for the sake of great ideals.

Also, Unification thought is still in the making and we must never forget that. We mustn't act as though things were really firmed up because somebody in New York once spoke dogmatically.

Finally, I would like to see more real give and take between Unification thinkers and those of us who are also committed to particular religious paths. For example, as a Catholic Christian I, too, have first-hand acquaintance with what you call indemnity. I know how good is accomplished through my giving up my own desires. The Wise Men, the Magi, in Christianity are extremely important. They brought their individual gifts to Jesus. They had the good sense to realize that many gifts were going to be needed. All of us here have gifts, and I would like to see us share our experiences so that we can all work together for unification.

Wellington Nyangoni: I want to preface my statements by a sociological observation. There is nothing new in the matching of couples. People have been matched for centuries. The history of free choice of whom you want to marry is relatively recent in modern history.

And there's no evidence that those who choose individual partners necessarily have successful marriages. There is also no evidence to suggest that those who are matched have less successful lives. So it depends on what vantage point you are coming from and I think we have to be open. I was one of the people who was very angry about why people were being matched. In fact, I went to the New Yorker and questioned the people who were being matched. Then after a while I realized I had been Americanized. (laughter) My own parents were matched. (laughter) And a greater part of Africa was matched. They have been matched for centuries. Jews do matching. There has been matching for centuries even among Catholics. I was raised as a Catholic, and in fact I still feel very guilty because before I went to marry, I ran with God only knows how many women. Then when I started dating a particular woman whom I sort of liked and wanted to marry, I never made love to her until I got married to her.

I have an additional question about the Unification theology of sexuality—where does homosexuality fit into the theology? I interpret *Divine Principle* as a testament against homosexuality because central to the Unificationist view of restoration is marriage, procreation, and the family. I could not understand, then, how Arthur could say that how the homosexual issue is solved depends on the individual. Doesn't homosexuality stand outside the movement?

Richard Quebedeaux: Would any of you like to respond?

Patricia Zulkosky: I'd like to. I would say that basically there is no active homosexuality in the church. I think Arthur said that a homosexual in the church may legitimately choose not to marry, although there is no place for active homosexuality in the church. I know of a couple of persons who entered into a homosexual relationship and there has been a "case by case" dealing with this problem. Sometimes the persons with homosexual inclinations will be under a leader with a very narrow perspective on that situation who will try to kick them out of the church. Sometimes you will find homosexuals under a leader who is much broader and who, recognizing that this is a real problem that needs working with, will take the time to try to guide these individuals toward normal sexuality. So homosexuality is not seen as a legitimate choice within the structure of the Unification community, but there is a wide range of ways it is dealt with, depending both on the views and experience of the particular leaders and on the extent to which the individuals themselves seek guidance.

Kurt Johnson: I just wanted to address this issue of whether Rev. Moon comprehends the problems in the movement. My answer is yes. We went through a period in the movement where it seemed like the East-West culture clash was creating some pretty dismal casualties. A loss of perspective and vision was causing people to leave. Rev. Moon invited the leadership of the church up to East Garden (his home) and talked to them for about four hours on Christmas Eve. I was amazed at his comprehension of the problems. I'm like every other person in the movement, I'm human. I imagine all these things that he doesn't know.

Anyway, he knows the breadth of these cultural problems. But just like any of us he's caught in this dialectic between what the ideal is and what and who he has got to work with. Now anyone who has ever been in a position of authority, whether as a division head or whatever, knows that people are constantly in that trade-off situation. When one is a leader in the movement, and a lot of us are responsible for a lot of people, one is caught in that situation. On the one hand, one is trying to lay a certain historical foundation, and on the other hand, one is trying to care for individual people. And this play-off between concern for individuals and concern for laying the foundation is always a conflict.

A good example is the handling of homosexuality within the church. Pat said that under some leaders, at least, this problem would be met on an individual basis; and someone said to Diana that he didn't believe it. I have to say that in some respects that person is right. But the reason is that a leader in the church really doesn't have much time to be reflective. We are always playing a trade-off between the needs of individuals and the needs of foundation-laying. We don't always have time to be reflective in making the choice of how we will invest our time and energy.

Finally, I think it says a lot that Rev. Moon personally chooses the people who come to this conference to represent certain issues. I don't think he chooses us because he thinks we can tell you "what you need to hear" about the movement. He chooses us because he believes that the way we think is somehow close to what he thinks about the Blessing, about social action, or whatever job he's given us. Even in the movement we have people who will say, Johnson doesn't really represent the Principle. You see, so we're always in that dynamic. Believe me, if I didn't think that the doors were still open for the whole development of the movement toward a really genuine, authentic whole life, I wouldn't be around.

Marianne McGowan: Does *Divine Principle* teach that when you are ready to marry you have achieved individual perfection?

Hugh Spurgin: Ideally, yes. But not in today's reality. Rev. Moon is a pragmatist. He is a scientist as well as an idealist, and everywhere in *Divine Principle* you'll find the kind of dialectic that Kurt's talking about. Our Blessings now are conditional blessings, which means that we are not perfect.

Marianne McGowan: But you must be perfect to have perfect children.

Hugh Spurgin: No, we didn't say we had perfect children.

Marianne McGowan: I thought you said that your children would be free of sin.

Hugh Spurgin: When Rev. Moon explained it, he drew a chart on the blackboard. You've probably seen it: formation, growth and perfection. He told us that each of us who have received the Blessing was near the top of the growth stage. Ultimately we hope to achieve perfection at the individual level. But we have not yet done this.

Nora Spurgin: The belief is that we parents still have sin and are a part of the old world which is passing away. We are all now in a period of transition between the old world and the new creation which is being brought about right now. Because we parents have not yet attained perfection our children will suffer a little. Because we have not completely matured, our way of raising our children will be somewhat imperfect and in a sense they will suffer from that.

Marianne McGowan: But perfection is possible for you?

Nora Spurgin: Yes, it's possible for people, but we're in a transitional stage.

Patricia Zulkosky: We do not think that even in an ideal world that a child will be born perfect. Everyone has to go through a growth stage. We believe that a child can be born sinless, without original sin. Then, if he or she grows up in an environment without fallen nature, he or she can grow up to be perfect.

Judith Simpson: Nora, on the same subject, how do you as a woman with children deal with the possibility that one of your children may decide not to be in the Unification Church? What would your relationship to that child be if he or she decides not to?

Nora Spurgin: It's my responsibility to raise them to the best of my ability, to give them the quality of love that's necessary for them to have a deep relationship with me, to give them intellectually the truth that I believe will guide them. But then I have no choice other than to let them make their own decisions. We believe that our children are in the same position as Adam and Eve were before they fell. Adam and Eve fell, and they didn't even have the kind of environment that we've got—with a lot of sin in it. There's nothing to guarantee that our children wouldn't make the same mistakes. But I have to let them go. The only thing is that we are at least giving them a better start. And our hopes and our prayers are that also the work that we do will provide some kind of spiritual merit and protection for them.

Judith Simpson: Do you mean that you would then give up all of your parenting responsibilities towards them? Would there still be communication?

Nora Spurgin: Of course I don't have this experience at this point, so I don't know what I would do. But definitely I wouldn't write them off, because certainly God didn't write man off. He's worked with man and struggled with man throughout all of human history. So my answer is that I would act in respect to my children as God has acted in respect to man. It's just that I couldn't force my children. I have to let them have free will just as God has let us have free will.

Thomas McGowan: Sometimes I find it helpful to discuss historical precedents for groups even though I recognize the danger involved in this. Once I have tentatively labelled a group I can work out other things about it. So I have been trying to decide whether Unificationists are Pelagians or Augustinians. I find strains of both in what you claim. On the one hand, you say God chooses the person you are matched with. And, on the other hand, you say you have free choice in the matter. Your matching is not only a sociological event. It is also a theological event because, unlike other cultures in which there is matching, the belief is that God does the matching. But then in addition there are church criteria for receiving the Blessing and being matched: number of years in the church, a specific number of spiritual children, and so on. Isn't this a confining of God's choice? On the one hand, we are told that the matching is God's will. But also we are told that there is romantic love, freedom of choice, and the possibility of choosing one's own mate. Are you Pelagians or Augustinians?

Wellington Nyangoni: I think he is off the mark here. We can learn much from the African view. There is no distinction in it among the sociological, theological and economic. All these are parts of one undivided whole.

Francis Botchway: I want to examine Wellington's point. If I had heard this lecture in Africa, the question that I would have posed to my Unification friends is this: all that you have said is now being practiced in traditional African society, so what's the difference? In the traditional African sense, before one marries there is an investigation done by women. And the data collected is passed on to the men. And before the marriage is consecrated, there is an invocation of the spirits, and the deified dead ancestors. So we can say there is a religious meaning and significance attached to the actual process of marriage. The only thing missing in the African case is the presence of Rev. Moon. In the African case, the ancestors may be said to play the role of Rev. Moon. My question then is, what is the fundamental difference between the traditional African process of which I am a part and the Unification process? What would Unificationists say to people of African descent who come out of these socio-religious experiences? The only perceived difference, it seems to me, would be the centrality of Rev. Moon in the whole marital process whereas in the African case there is no one central figure. When we invoke the ultimate deity, we invoke him through the *deified* dead ancestors. But in your case you are substituting Rev. Moon for the role played by the ancestors and I'm seriously wondering if this whole process is not conditioned by the cultural experience of the Koreans. Is it really a divinely ordained process?

Richard Quebedeaux: Kurt has experience with various intercultural situations. Would you like to respond, Kurt?

Kurt Johnson: What is unique in our situation? It is that a man, Sun Myung Moon, came out of Korea with the concept that God has been guiding history towards some homogenization to a final idea of what the true culture is. The difference between that and all that has come before is that he is preaching about a restoration that needs to be done and can be done on a worldwide level. Now obviously someone could have come out of Africa in the same position. I think it's just an historical situation. He has come saying this and offering it as an idea of what the world culture will be. And by its very nature it will homogenize many, many things and offer new things. And that is in the Bible. That is in the treasure chest, old things and new things.

Ernest Stewart: There are a couple of concrete differences. When my wife and I were matched, it was with eighteen hundred other couples. Rev. Moon was making decisions. But there was also a great deal of individual, personal input on the part of church members. A friend of mine came along and said, "How about this one?" And Rev. Moon looked over and said, "Oh, very good." That is, people were asking, "May I have this one or may I have that one?"

George Exoo: Acorns when they grow up, if they operate correctly, become oak trees; and there are other kinds of seeds like maple and elm that grow into maple and elm trees. I am very much concerned about heterogeneity and pluralism within society. I'm concerned with the possibility of those maple trees growing into maple trees and the oak trees growing into oak trees. And I hear some very strong sentiments saying that in some cases maple seeds are expected to become oak trees and act as acorns and that elm seeds also should grow into oak trees.

I am particularly concerned about this in the attitude toward homosexuality that has been discussed thus far. From what I have heard, these people are unacceptable. They could not create a Blessed marriage within the movement. They could not, for example, form a couple relationship and adopt children and fulfill even more than one blessing.

And that's all right if you want to create a small community and say, we are going to realize some absolute natural law. We're going to live in our little commune someplace in the world. We're going to exclude all others. But what I hear you saying is that you are harbingers of the new age, that you propose to provide a pattern of living that is going to be good for all humankind. But what about homosexuality? I could take other descriptive categories, I'm certain. But in regard to homosexuality, what are you going to do with that ten percent of the population in the new age? Are you going to build a new gas chamber and play Hitler and put those people in it? Where are they going to be?

Steve Post: It is important to affirm that there is particularism in *Divine Principle.* It is not the case that we are attempting to relate to all concerns of all people in a pluralistic society in modernity. We are sectarian. We are sectarian in the same sense that the Hutterite brethren were sectarian. They formed certain kinds of communities. They had an ideal. In marriage there was a matching. They had to go out and do missionary work someplace in the world. There was no homosexuality in the Hutterite community.

George Exoo: Well, you don't know.

Steve Post: We don't know that, right. But we have an ideal as a community, and we try and live up to it. Now I think that necessarily at this time in history—and here I would go a little different direction than some might—we are being particularistic, in that we are talking about heterosexuals in the Unification Church. It's not that we would ever conceive of violating the human rights of people who are not heterosexuals. But we have a faith in God that if we establish the kinds of relationships which we see as theologically justified, this has integrity in itself. Our prime purpose is to create those families. To me, that's the essence of the church.

What is happening in the world outside? We live in a secular, radically pluralistic society. But my faith is (and, of course, this is just my position, because these are ambiguities that have not been clarified and articulated in any Unificationist text) that eventually through God's providence the world will become aware of our fruits—of the harmony of our marriages and of the beauty of our children. People will then see that, indeed, the Unification Church has some sort of solution. Then voluntarily those who want to come can come; and those who don't, won't. And God bless the latter. But it may be that in the future, in the ideal world, there will be a normative pattern, a certain image of human fulfillment and that is the perfect marriage.

George Exoo: And that begs the question of acorns and elm seeds. I would like to hear you respond to it, Mr. Stewart. You have articulated a view that has been more liberal and kind of free of restraints than anybody else here who has spoken. How would you respond to that question?

Ernest Stewart: My understanding, too, is that we hope that *ultimately* everyone will have an ideal marriage. We feel that some of our problems today exist because we do not have ideal marriages. People become unhappy with their spouses. They become unhappy with many things. And they do not find fulfillment in anything. So we are trying to build a better mousetrap. If we do, maybe everybody will like the mousetrap, and that may solve part of the problem.

George Exoo: Do you think that could encompass a female-female marital relationship or a male-male marriage relationship?

Ernest Stewart: As far as our faith is concerned, we believe that God's ideal is that marriage should be between male and female, that God created man for woman and woman for man. This doesn't mean that people are always going to fulfill what God wants of them. Who has? And we don't intend to "put people in gas chambers" because they don't fulfill the ideal. Otherwise I'm afraid all of us would be in the gas chamber.

Patricia Zulkosky: Theologically, our stress on the heterosexual relationship derives from our view that God has both masculine and feminine elements and that God has given more masculine and feminine elements to man and woman respectively. So a woman in and of herself has an experience of the nature of God but not a male experience, and vice versa. Then, man and woman brought together become a more complete representation of the nature of God to their children than could happen in a homosexual relationship. That is why we stand so strongly on the male-female relationship.

George Exoo: Is there anyone here who would argue from the Unification side that the Bible was conceived also in a cultural context and that perhaps some of the seeming heterosexual chauvinism inherent in the Bible is also part of Korean culture and part of American culture at the present time, and we maybe ought to be able to stand back from those cultural contexts and view them in another light? Is there any Unificationist here who would make that statement?

Steve Post: I'd like to respond. The basic presupposition of George's question is that there are acorns and there are elm seeds, right? Recent research on homosexuality claims that sexual instincts are *not* object specific. That is to say, our sexual urges can go in one way or another. But the point is that with a thorough understanding of the kind of natural law that's embodied in the Unification Church tradition, our sexual drives, which are not object specific, can be directed the way God wants them because they are malleable. And that's the import of the division of God into masculine and feminine. If we can understand that internally in its value and meaning, then we can direct ourselves.

George Exoo: I just hope that God-directed isn't culture-directed.

Richard Quebedeaux: OK. I think in fairness we should go on to Andy and Leonard; we can take up these issues later publicly and privately.

Andy Smith: What is the effect on your children of your involvement with the movement? Is there pressure from the other kids' parents? Do your kids interact with the other kids outside of the classroom in the normal way that happens when kids go to the same school? What of your concern in terms of bringing them up within the movement?

Nora Spurgin: Well, it's harder to answer your questions because our children are still pretty young. We have a son in first grade and a daughter in second grade. However, we do want to expose them to as much of the "outside world" as possible. For example, my daughter is a Brownie and goes to Brownie troop meetings. She goes to the birthday parties of the other kids and they are invited to ours. Some parents know and some don't. In general the kids are still so young that they don't have any prejudice. So there's not so much of that. I'll just give you a little story as an example of things that happen.

My daughter was in kindergarten when she did this. She came home from school one day and had, pinned in the middle of her sweater, a big button with Rev. Moon's face on it that was used for one of the rallies. I was a little shocked when she came in proudly wearing it. I said "Did you wear that to school today?" "Oh yeah," she said. I said, "Did anybody say anything?" "Well, on the bus on the way home from school the bigger kids said, 'We don't like him.'" But she was still wearing it and she was going to wear it the next morning to school. I said, "Why don't you not wear it since everybody knows who he is? (laughter) But not everybody really loves him because they don't know him." And she said, "OK." But she would have worn it and she said, "Well, I was going to wear it, because in my class nobody said anything about it." So to her it was just an artifact. It was just a thing to wear.

This is the kind of thing our children are going to face. And as they get older they will face some prejudice against our movement and against being Moonies. We're trying to raise them in such a way that they will have an internal integrity, that they will be proud of themselves as individuals, that they will be well-adjusted, happy and capable kids. That's the way I was raised. I was a Mennonite and I was raised very differently. Everybody knew I was a Mennonite, much more obviously a Mennonite than our children are obviously Moonies. And I felt like I had tremendous strength and I could handle it. And I hope that I can do the same thing for my own children. We can't protect them forever, and I'm sorry that they have to experience it.

Hugh Spurgin: One point is that Unification people are not trying to escape from the world. If anything we are thrusting ourselves on the world with such intensity that it frightens people. There is this thrust into every aspect of the world: business, politics, education, everything. And that applies to Andy's question, too. As a matter of fact that's Rev. Moon's desire, for the children to go to public schools, to live normal lives and interact with other children.

Richard Quebedeaux: OK, Leonard, one more question.

Leonard Lovett: I keep coming back to something that appears to be somewhat morally ambiguous as well as possibly leading to contradictions. By taking part in the matching you surrender your responsibility in the choice of your mate. How, then, can you maintain your responsibility for your marriage, its goals, and its uniqueness? Where is the responsibility regained which you abdicated initially?

Esteban Galvan: When I was matched I felt like I had died and I came to some major realizations when I was first conversing with my fiancée. One realization was that in 1971 I was to be ordained a priest. After many years of seminary training, I had theologically and sociologically been prepared to live a celibate life, "married" to Christ and the Church. So I was oriented to thinking that marriage was second best to celibacy. You got married if you couldn't make it as a celibate—a chosen one. I talked to many of the brothers and sisters who were matched and they said that they had accepted out of faith in God and God's will and also out of trust in Rev. Moon. I mean it looked great, everything was happening so fast and people were getting engaged.

But I couldn't follow the crowd. In fact, my fiancée said to me, "You know I just knew it had to be you." I said, "Now don't tell me that right now." (laughter) I couldn't even talk. I was shaken, because I realized the situation I was in. I felt like I was hanging. So I realized that I didn't accept myself as getting married, even though I had been in the church for six and a half years.

Another realization I had was what I shared with my fiancée: I told her that much of the Latin culture is immoral, with a double standard between men and women. Suddenly, I felt the pressure and tension behind the responsibility that I providentially was representing the restoration of Latin culture. So I felt then that not only was I cutting off from my past theological training, but also that I was being confronted to act against the immoral aspect of my Latin culture and stand for righteousness and a higher standard of marriage. I said to my fiancée, "My indecision has nothing to do with you personally." And she replied, "You don't have to decide to become engaged to me. I wouldn't force you to do it." And I said, "I know you are not going to force me." But of course, I could see that she herself was worried and wondering about me and our potential relationship. (laughter) Then I said, "I've got to get outside, I've got to breathe, to get out in the street and get a coke." So we sneaked out the back door, although we thought that we weren't supposed to do that.

Then I said to her again, "My attitude has absolutely nothing to do with you personally. I could ask Rev. Moon to match me with another girl, but I'd go through the same thing with her too. So either it is you right now or no one. So, let's try it out." And that is what we've decided to do.

Now the point is this. By my struggling so much that day, I actually experienced the engagement as a personal decision of mine. I struggled a great deal, and this helped me to take responsibility that it was my decision. I am sticking to it. When I made this decision I took full responsibility for it and for my engagement and future marriage. I am very vertical and at that particular moment I experienced a separation from my confused ancestors who wanted me to be a priest instead of a family man, the poor standard of man-woman relationships in Latin culture, and my narrow theological training of celibacy versus marriage. And I decided, "I am going straight ahead." To develop a relationship with her and with her family will be demanding and complicated, maybe one reason is because she has a Jewish background, while my background is Catholic. She and I have to work at that relationship ourselves in time and with God's blessing.

Nora Spurgin: I understand how it may be puzzling to some of you to hear that we believe that we have to take responsibility for our marriages and for our own lives. So I just want to add that we have to take responsibility for knowing our own limitations. If we think that we do not have the ability to handle a particular person, we have to be aware of that. We have to ask to be matched with someone else. That is one very important aspect of our personal responsibility.

Richard Quebedeaux: Thank you all very much for a very tough, heartening discussion.

Piety and Spirituality

Patricia Zulkosky

Richard Quebedeaux: This evening we are going to talk about spirituality and piety in the Unification Church. Patricia Zulkosky will give us a presentation and after that we will enter into discussion and dialogue. I met Pat when I convened the first evangelical conference in Barrytown in June of 1978. I remember this event. There is a place called Jack's Place near Barrytown, a drinking establishment. A number of us evangelicals wanted nothing more than to go there afterwards. Pat just couldn't believe it and got really upset. She just said, "Oh, I didn't know that evangelicals did this." Now of course there were a few Moonies that went with us too. She didn't seem to see those. (laughter)

But at the next conference Pat brought the key to the car and said, "Here's the car ready for you." Pat is now at the School of Theology at Claremont. She's really getting into simple lifestyle and is about ready for the Sojourners community, I feel. She's a pietist in the true sense of the word. Piety has really been misunderstood in our generation, but piety and radical Christianity have a lot in common. So I asked Pat to deal with this topic of spirituality since I think, of all the people I know in the church, she knows more about it than anybody I've talked to and has a very interesting way of presenting it. With that I would like to introduce Pat.

Patricia Zulkosky: I have to admit that Richard's story is true. I was shocked and let people know that I was shocked.

The issues suggested to me by Richard tended to cluster around ritual and worship more than piety and spirituality. In thinking about them, though, I was moved to consider two questions: Does the Unification Church have a unique spirituality, and what is the theological foundation for our spiritual practice?

It is difficult to say how our spirituality differs from other traditions because there is a lot of diversity in spirituality in general and in the Unification Church in particular, although there is a clear theological underpinning for our basic spiritual practices. Our common spiritual traditions are taught in seven-day and twenty-one-day workshops, as well as in day-to-day community living, but each spiritual life is also greatly influenced by a person's previous religious tradition. For instance, my Catholic background emerges through my love for the saints and carries over into deep regard for modern personalities like Ruth Carter Stapleton and Mahatma Gandhi. This combination of Unification Church traditions, previous religious experiences, and inspirational models results in the many nuances of personal piety. Yet despite the variety, there are common themes that influence all Unificationists.

The first and most important theme is the desire to understand and experience the heart of God as expressed in the Bible and *Divine Principle*.

The heart of God in the creation process is thought of as one of great vision and expectation as humankind grew toward fulfilling the three blessings or purposes of creation. Second, we learn the sorrowful and grieving heart of God resulting from the fall of humankind. Finally, we strive to understand the heart of God through restoration history as God works with hope and perseverance in the restoration process. Unificationists try to understand these aspects of God's heart in many ways, but the primary methods are study of the Bible and *Divine Principle*, and prayer. Study and prayer are often combined into what is called "providential prayer" in which people recount the *Divine Principle* understanding of God's heart in conversation with God. This kind of guided imagery can bring us to an encounter with different aspects of God's heart. This personal connection with God can inspire us to make the kinds of sacrifice God is making.

In addition to providential prayer we also stress prayers of gratitude and petition such as might be found in any religious community, except that our emphasis is more focused on praying for the whole purpose and the providence than on individual needs. The first thing we might try to do is to connect with God's concerns on the largest scale possible—God's concern for the world situation, national issues, or foreign missionaries. Then finally His concern for my family and me.

Our manner of prayer can be silent, representative, or unison prayer (in which everyone in the room prays his or her own prayers in an audible tone at the same time). Some individuals are very subdued in prayer while others become highly involved and pray in loud tones with sweeping gestures. A more unusual characteristic of our prayer is what I call "fatheritis." Prayers are frequently punctuated with the word "father"— sometimes to the point of distraction. This may be due to trying to keep an emotional connection with God, but also the word "father" is one of the first English words learned by foreign members when they come to America and the over-usage has been contagious.

Prayer, then, is an important factor in the building and maintenance of personal and corporate spiritual life, but it is not our only act of spirituality. Prayer in action is just as important as spoken prayer. Prayer in action to accomplish a goal is called a condition. A condition is an offering an individual makes to God for a specific time period and reason. For instance, everyone in the church does a seven-day fast. This, much like baptism, represents dying to the fallen world and being reborn to God. The first step in making a condition is to determine the goal. If the goal is to understand the historical providence then perhaps a fast with meditation on God's work in history will help. Let us say a person's goal is to meet a spiritual child but he or she is afraid to start conversations with strangers. A condition, such as overcoming this fear enough to witness to at least three persons each day for twenty-one days, would be the offering made to God as a foundation to meet that special person. It is a specific contract that we make with God toward fulfilling our portion of responsibility in meeting a goal, still recognizing, though, that we can't accomplish any goal purely on our own merits or work. It's our understanding that completing a condition doesn't guarantee results, but it can show God that we are sincere and can be trusted by him to do at least a certain amount.

Young members often go through such a legalistic condition phase that they are always doing at least one or more conditions. This external dependency on conditions eventually transforms itself into a deep attitude of constant offering and gratitude and facilitates the development of a sacrificial heart and a connection between God, my life and my mission. In this way laying a foundation for the messiah to come to us becomes a more internal process as we grow in faith, though we would still do specific external conditions on certain occasions. In every case the goal is always to connect my life and activity with the heart and will of God.

Making an offering of attitude, prayer, and action is a continuous process of restoring our relationship with God. At the time of the Fall of Adam and Eve, patterns were created which were inherited and which continue to separate humankind from God: (1) failure to see God's point of view, (2) leaving one's proper position, (3) reversing dominion, and (4) multiplication of evil. These patterns must be reversed. Conditions act as aids in laying the foundation for the messiah who then shows us how to restore our vertical love for God and horizontal love for each other.

The discussion of conditions up to this point was focused on conditions which help restore our vertical relationship with God, but some conditions are to help us to restore our horizontal relationships with each other. Based on the story of Cain and Abel, one person in the position of Cain may follow conditions set by the central figure. This can serve both spiritual and practical functions. Spiritually the central figure should stand in the position of Abel (or relatively closer to God), so Cain's connecting with Abel by reporting his conditions allows the central figure to support the person making the condition. This is relating to God through the central figure in much the same way that Catholics go to confession before a priest representing God. Practically, a person often lacks the wisdom that the central figure may supply in terms of making appropriate and reasonable conditions. For instance, a person's timing may be inappropriate—such as wanting to fast when a fundraising campaign is coming which requires a lot of physical effort—or the condition may not be appropriate to the goal. Conditions are not easy—they always involve a sacrifice, but neither should they be impossible or interfere with activities of living. It is better to succeed in an easier condition and to use that as a foundation for a later one than to fail. Conditions need to be possible to accomplish since they are agreements between God and ourselves through a central figure.

There are special conditions such as pledge which have become church traditions. Pledge is a prayer recited at 5:00 AM every Sunday, the first day of each month and on the holy days (Parents' Day, Children's

Day, Day of All Things, and God's Day). The five main points of the pledge affirm our determination to become true children of God. They can be summarized as follows: (1) affirming our determination to become children of God, (2) affirming our willingness to sacrifice and take responsibility to do God's will, which we understand as accomplishing the ideal of creation, (3) reminding us of the difficulties of our mission by saying that we will sow sweat for earth and tears for humankind with the tools of sacrifice, (4) restating our determination to become children of God and responsible lords of creation, and (5) affirming our pride in our tradition. Pledge is a time of rededication to God and to our missions as we remind ourselves why we joined the church and what we hope to accomplish.

Pledge is not only a condition but also one of our main rituals. We all gather shortly before 5:00 AM to prepare ourselves in an attitude of prayer. Men and women sit separately on different sides of the room. The service begins with three full bows to the floor as a sign of humility and respect to God. The Pledge leader—generally an older Blessed member or center leader—begins the prayer and everyone recites the pledge together. This is followed by a representative prayer usually given by the leader, unison prayer and finally a closing song or greeting to God and brothers and sisters.

There are other rituals in the church such as the wine or engagement ceremony, the wedding, or the dedication of newborn children on their eighth day of life. Though I imagine there are ceremonies surrounding death, I have not yet experienced them.

A less formal tradition is daily worship held once or twice a day. The order of the service varies and leadership often rotates among all of the center members. Nearly every service includes song, prayer, scripture, or inspirational reading, and an interpretive message. The songs are often traditional Christian hymns or holy songs (original compositions written in the early days of our church by Unificationists that reflect the spirit of that early church) or popular songs with new, more spiritualized words. The evening service often consists of song and prayer following a community sharing meeting. Sunday service is more formal and is open to the public. In every case the worship is flexible and tries to meet the needs of the particular community.

In Unification spirituality there is also an awareness of spirit world and of the fact that people and angels in spirit world can help you. They can, however, also hinder you depending on the nature of their inspirations. This is not to say that this awareness of the possible interrelationship leads to a stress on developing spiritual powers or spiritual communication. In fact such activities are often discouraged since they may distract a person from his mission. However, the living person can always be in control regardless of the number or nature of inspirations; we each must take responsibility for every decision. The restoration of the people in the physical world is most important—as the physical world is restored, the persons in spirit world will also be restored.

In summary, it is clear that the spirituality of the Unification Church is built on our theology and the goal of relieving the suffering of God by fulfilling the ideal of creation—namely the building of the kingdom on earth. The challenges to this life of faith are many as we try to be in the world but not of the world. Only time can speak to how these traditions will develop and change in the coming generations.

Discussion

Richard Quebedeaux: Thank you very much Pat. Any questions or comments?

Mary Carman Rose: I want to thank you, Pat, for calling attention to the fundamental role of love in our stewardship of creation. Also, I am grateful to Unification thought for telling us about the suffering heart of God, the Father. My own Christianity has been enriched by that. And then, as a convert to Roman Catholicism, I, too, believe in and emphasize what Unificationists call *spirit world.* I pray to and count on the help of the Catholic saints. And every day at mass I join in the prayers for the souls in purgatory who are in need of further spiritual development. Your interest in spirit world is not the least of your gifts to us, and I look forward to the day when we can all benefit from the knowledge that you have of this aspect of creation. You do, you know, have much to offer contemporary psychic research.

Kurt Johnson: I want to make a comment deriving from my Catholic religious life before I came into the Unification Church. Since I come from another tradition, there are many things in the Unification Church that I recognize as unique. One is the large family celebrations where everybody from the church in one area, a hundred or maybe a thousand, come together and put on an entertainment for each other. Rev. Moon enjoys singing; he likes to hear individuals, couples, and groups sing and he likes to sing. But he's not concerned about the quality of the singers. It's the exchange of the offering, brother to brother, sister to sister, singing each other a song. Something else that's absolutely unique and I think very beautiful is the spontaneous dance. Many, many times at the end of a celebration when Rev. Moon and others in the church are very happy, and there's music, there's an expression of that happiness just in dancing around in a very childlike, beautiful way. It has no form, but just that feeling of elation of here we are in the world, isn't it great? That's something I've never seen anywhere else, and I've found that very, very nice.

One other thing in Unification spirituality which is different from my training in the Catholic Church and religious life before, is that the Unification Church has a clearer understanding of Satan. It's one of the few churches that clearly understands the reality of Satan and teaches it. Also it has a number of models in which it casts the reflections of satanic behavior. It does this with behaviors of individuals in the sense of selfishness, greed, etc., down to very intricate things which are very perceptive. It does this also in its analysis of history and of certain ideologies. That is, the Unification teaching identifies the extent to which all these can display a satanic quality. I think it's a very unique aspect of the spirituality of the Unification Church.

Thomas McGowan: Just a question. Could you explain the holy wine ceremony? I've heard of it a couple of times. And also, have these practices like the pledge and the special church holy days originated in America or do they come from Korea?

Patricia Zulkosky: The pledge and the holy days were formed in Korea before Rev. Moon came to America. So they have come to us from there.

What is the holy wine ceremony? At the time of the matching there is a sort of confirmation of that matching in what we call the holy wine ceremony, where the couples exchange holy wine.

George Exoo: In every community of faith there are uses and norms of language. The Christian Scientists are always grateful to Mrs. Eddy, and the pentecostals are praising the Lord. Are there idioms of speech that a figure of authority would use to try to influence the behavior of someone who is a novice by inculcating the macro forces of the divine world or the satanic world in the form of a series of should's and are's? Are there norms of speech like that that are used to chasten and hasten?

Kurt Johnson: Someone will say that an act is "really archangelic," meaning that it shows utter disregard for other people, which is a characteristic that we feel is inherited from the fallen archangel. Or someone may say this person is "Adamic"—available, giving, generous. There is an equation of behavior with those types and symbols to a degree which many times is very perceptive.

Mary Carman Rose: Also *heartistic.* I think your word "heartistic" is a tremendous gift to both the philosophical and theological communities.

Richard Quebedeaux: Then there are Cain and Abel. Are you in the Cain position or the Abel position? It's used quite regularly. Are you "principled"? It can refer to certain kinds of behavior. Somehow you are a principled person or you are unprincipled. That has more than just the normal meaning. Also there's—I hate to say it—pidgin English. It is always *Unification Church.* It's never *the* Unification Church. The article is omitted, and there is a sort of reverence for the Korean or Japanese style of speaking English to the point where pidgin English is used in the course of normal conversation.

David Simpson: I don't know how to start saying what I want to say, but I have a need to get some things out on the table that probably don't have anything to do with tonight's discussion. They have a great deal to do with the anxiety that I feel mounting in myself and perhaps in other people about a continuation of what I was frustrated about in the Virgin Islands. You said, Richard, that this was not going to be a continuation of the sort of theological discussion we had in the Virgin Islands, but we were going to get down to practical aspects of what Moonies do, how they behave, how they practice in their real lives their religious convictions.

I came to this conference very excited about that, because I raised some questions in the Virgin Islands about the same kinds of things. My frustration has to do with the fact that what I've experienced so far in this morning's presentation and tonight's presentation is basically a continuation of the same style. I'm not criticizing the content; I'm criticizing the style, and I want to make my point very clear about that. We are hearing "lectures" that have to do with what I would call an exegesis of *Divine Principle.* In other words, everything that is discussed or referred to always comes out of some kind of philosophical-theological discussion of what

Divine Principle means or how one would address oneself to that particular issue as interpreted by Rev. Moon or in some way by *Divine Principle*.

My frustration has to do with the fact that I came here believing that we were all going to get together in a small-group session and talk about what we do when we get up in the morning, and what I do when I get up in the morning—the very first thing I do is go to the bathroom. Nobody has gotten down to the level of just talking about life, and I'm getting really anxious about the fact that I think we're going to continue to get diagrams about *Divine Principle*. I made three pages of notes this morning and my wife and I went over those notes and they referred constantly to the fact that there was a discussion about doctrine, about Principle, about the ideal, about what one ought to do, and there is no real down-to-heart discussion about behavior.

Patricia Zulkosky: We are presenting the principles which govern our behavior.

David Simpson: That is fine. Let me finish making my speech and then you can either throw me out or we can get serious and have a real discussion. I have to say that I'm not an academic. I'm an Alinsky-trained organizer and I have to do with changing people's behavior as it has to do with social justice. That's exactly where I'm coming from, and I need to have some questions answered about those issues; but I'm not getting anywhere near a hint that those questions are going to be answered. I came to the Virgin Islands last summer as a newcomer, invited by Richard. My board was very nervous about my coming. I work for an interfaith organization that is very tied into national organizations. This time my board would not even allow themselves to know that I was coming. (laughter) And I think that's cute, but it's that serious. And the president of my board said, "Please don't tell the other members of the board where you're going. Just take a vacation, take your wife, come back with a suntan and don't tell anybody what you did."

I think that's a very serious commentary on what we're up to this week here, and not getting a suntan and enjoying ourselves. I need to come back with some answers and some answers for myself, personally. I don't want to hear any more doctrine. I don't want to hear any more speeches about what *Divine Principle* means or how it might interpret George's issues about homosexuality. There are many issues that I'm going to raise when we get into more serious kinds of things having to do with social action, politics, fundraising, and the whole business, and I really feel that we evaded the question this morning about the family. When Janie and I were walking on the beach this afternoon we said to ourselves, "Maybe the one thing that might answer it would be to get together some families who are not Moonies with some families who are Moonies and talk about how we raise our kids." Maybe that way we would come into some real live conversation. I didn't hear that happening this morning.

Richard Quebedeaux: OK. This is a perfect introduction to my next point. First of all, there are some reasons why what happened happened. And as you know Unification more, you'll know why. It is very hard for a new movement to circumvent the ideal in favor of the real. I find that among Moonies. For instance, when people make an exit from the movement, they're not even mentioned anymore. I can't get people to talk about it. Even my closest friends in the movement won't talk about their leaving. One person said, "I don't want to be invaded by Satan as a result of this."

David mentioned the possibility of a conference in which some families get together and talk about family issues in concrete form. I think that it is a good idea. It is possible for you to seriously suggest conferences, even those conferences that you yourself may wish to convene. Darrol and I are in the position of having to think up and seek advice on future conferences. I know that there are some people who feel that their interests are also concerns of Unification and that mutual benefit can be derived from the conferences. I would say first of all, that if any of you have suggestions for conferences, be sure to let me, John, or Darrol know and we can take it from there.

Another "problem" is that many of you keep getting invited to conferences. We who are on the organizing end of conferences feel somewhat guilty inviting you to gatherings that may be repeat performances, even when we ask you to take leadership roles in those conferences (despite the fact that you may not agree with Unification theology or politics). I've never known another movement where people seem so ready to come back when they have such strong disagreements, but this is a fact of life.

So we are interested in your feelings. As a matter of fact, we have prepared a statement asking for your suggestions which we are going to pass out. I will read it to you now:

You are among a number of scholars who have shown
interest in the Unification movement. We would like
to continue our relationship but realize that it cannot
be a matter of simply coming to more conferences.
We therefore would like to suggest that a scholarly
organization be started in which common issues and
problems can be addressed in a mutually beneficial
way. What kind of association would you propose?
What would you call it and what do you see as your
relationship to it?[*]

I would also like to add the word *nonthreatening* in the development
of this organization. There are many people at this conference who come,
as David has done, at the risk of their jobs and reputations. We do not
want to establish an organization where, if it has your name on its P.R.
material, you're really going to be in trouble.

Unification is interested in the idea of conferences and is also
interested in the restoration of the world. I think that it looks at scholars
and church leaders as people who are going to help restore the world. If
you have any ideas about how you might help in the work of restoration
or about conferences we might have, write them down. We are certainly
open to good ideas.

Now I would like to respond to what David said. I'm sure it is not
quite as simple as some of us guests would like to think for you Unificationists
to come out with personal matters in this context. Many of you are
rooming with Moonies; I suggest that you share experiences with them.
And if you are not rooming with a Moonie, I'm sure that one of them will
be willing to stay up all night and talk to you.

Mary Carman Rose: I would like to respond to David, too. I
appreciate his concern and his honesty. But clarity and pretty thorough
understanding of what we mean by justice, of our moral principles, and of
our views of reality and our relations to reality are essential for firm
commitment and action in the world. One of the most worthwhile
aspects of Unification thought is its stress on philosophical understanding.

Paul Sharkey: I want to ask a question about the spirit world and I
want to lay my cards on the table first. I'm a philosophical skeptic, which
is to say that I don't have any knowledge of spirit worlds one way or the
other, so I don't want my comments to be taken negatively. I come out of

[*]Following this conference, New ERA (New Ecumenical Research Association) was
formed in New York City in March, 1980.

the Humean tradition. It's not that I *deny* or *affirm* it. I just don't know.

I have a number of acquaintances in the movement who are not seminarians. They're people who are working in various other capacities in the church in Washington and in state centers and this sort of thing. And I get letters and phone calls from them and at least once in each of these there is some mention about communication with the spirit world, and about their dreams. They tell me of things that they've learned about me through the spirit world and want to communicate to me. You, Pat, said that this is a very minor part of Unification and only a minority of people are concerned about it. Yet it seems to be a big part of the spiritual life of the average Moonie.

Patricia Zulkosky: I know that some members of the church get inspiration and personal revelation in dreams. I know also that some get an intuitive, gut-level conviction which they attribute to a source in spirit world.

Esteban Galvan: For me there is a very definite connection between the spirit world and practical issues.

Before I met this group I, too, was trained by Saul Alinsky—in Chicago for two years. This was urban training and I learned things about power structures, etc. I was proud that I was practical in my fight against injustice. Since joining the church I have experienced the practical value of applying spiritual knowledge to social systems. For example, there is the power of the trinity. The trinity is symbolic of Father, Son, and Holy Spirit. It is also connected to the fact that Jesus had three major disciples. Three people who are close to each other and really united in wanting to do the work of restoration can move in a heavenly direction. They can change a community and a city. I have seen that happen. There is also my decision to support and unite with the person chosen, perhaps by Rev. Moon, to be a central figure for me. If he and I—an Abel and a Cain, so to speak—really come to understand each other in a heartistic way, then the two of us can generate a magnificent power which can also effect great change internally and externally. I have seen that happen, too.

Wellington Nyangoni: I want to dissociate myself from the criticism of this morning's session. I found it very exciting. I love ideas, disagreement. By training I am a social scientist and we play with models, create them. Some of these models end up being bombs that kill you, some of these models end up being thousands of millions of dollars of taxes given to old people. Practicality doesn't just mean when to shovel, it is much more than that. But I think that depending on how you conceive totality, this morning was very productive.

I'd like to ask a question. I'm intrigued by the idea of evil spirits. The Bible talks about evil spirits and demons. The Catholic Church does also to some degree. What role does this play in the Unification Church? I know you said you de-emphasize it, but de-emphasizing it doesn't mean it doesn't exist.

Patricia Zulkosky: In the Unification Church there is an awareness of both the good and evil in the spirit world. We attribute a lot of inspirations that we get to influence of the spirit world. Those inspirations might be to do a good thing like picking up all the garbage on the street. Or they might be evil, like to steal the purse of a little old lady. It's up to you to recognize what comes from better realms in spirit world and what comes from the evil realms in spirit world. However, I don't have so much direct experience with spirit world as some other people and am not the best person to answer in detail and give examples.

Hugh Spurgin: I want to return to David's point. I do not consider myself mystical, and I was not very religious when I joined this church. My interests have always been sports and politics. I am a product of the social concerns of the 1960s. For instance, I was deeply involved with Eugene McCarthy's campaign for the presidency and supported LBJ's Great Society. But I was disappointed by all that. The bottom fell out of the social legislation, as well as the peace movement of the sixties. I now realize that legislation and money are not enough. We must change attitudes; we must affect the human heart. And that is more difficult than demonstrating in the streets, making laws, or demolishing slums. For instance, regarding racism, it is necessary to focus upon changing attitudes towards Black and other minorities. Laws have a certain value but they are limited in their ability to affect intangibles. When we're discussing attitudes we're talking on a different level; and at that point, a Higher Power is needed. The Christian notion of God as a parent and of all people as His children is great. If we can just live that Christian ideal, then, we can solve problems of injustice and bigotry.

But what I want to say to David, or to whomever, is: be patient with us as Unificationists, we're still young. Even today many Unification people are naive about economics and politics, and such was even more true in the early days of the movement. When I joined the church, I couldn't believe how uninformed most members were about world affairs.

Few of them read newspapers. Many early members were psychic people who had had spiritual experiences (such as clairaudience or clairvoyance) which I didn't know much about. They had, for instance, direct spiritual communications with Buddha, Jesus, and various Christian saints. And apparently such was even more the case in Korea and Japan in the early days. I only know about *this* world; hence, what attracted me to the Unification movement was the social thrust of the *Divine Principle* teachings, not the mystical aspects of the church. However, that social aspect is not worked out even yet and you can help us—you can help to sensitize us to the realities of the world.

Let me conclude by commenting that when I joined the church in the 1960s the first thing I did when I got up in the morning was read the newpaper, but Rev. Moon has taught me to pray first; that was a change for me that I'm still adjusting to. And it takes a lot of determination not to run for that newspaper first. (laughter)

David Simpson: I want everybody to know that I was not being critical of the presentations. I was very sensitive to Arthur's presentation. I really felt, though, as I was sitting next to him that sometimes he was trying to find himself in his notebook. I don't say that in a critical way, because I know the pain you must feel trying to share yourselves with this whole group of strangers. I don't want to be critical about people's presentations and about where you're coming from. That obviously is a very sensitive and important thing for you in terms of how you see yourself as a human being.

Let me also give you an immediate reaction to what Hugh said. I think we can help each other grow. We both came out of the movement of the sixties and we both understood all that process and all that craziness. We were both disillusioned about the Great Society and the myth and failure of all that—I think we've been through that.

What I think we are still oblivious to are the kinds of behaviors that we continue to go through that I've just experienced in the last three days here. When I came down here, I asked myself, why is the Black staff so arrogant and so hostile towards me? One of the things that came across to me like a two by four at the side of my head was the fact that the management and the ownership of the hotel is white and all the staff is Black. Need I wonder where this hostility and arrogance comes from towards all of us rich white people who are down here enjoying this luxury? Both as Unification people and as a whole religious community we need to look at these issues; I just raised that as an example. I don't want to say we ought to leave here tomorrow, because I really enjoy all the sun (laughter), the food, and everything else. I'm just as sinful as everybody else, but I think that we're not naive about certain basic issues in our society that have to do with the way in which we hurt other people. Perhaps we'll hurt each other here in the next three days with our frankness, but I hope that that comes out of a compassion for each other and a desire to do God's will, because I think we all believe in the same God.

I think we know a lot and I think we can have a tremendous insight into what God's will is, and we ought to use that in the best way we can.

Myrtle Langley: Just a quick question for Pat. I take it that your central figure is what in other spiritual traditions we call a counselor or spiritual director. Do you ever choose your own central figure? Do you have any choice about whom you go to for guidance?

Patricia Zulkosky: The central figure is the person in charge of the particular mission that you are in. If you are on a fundraising team, the central figure is the captain of that team. In that case you have not chosen your central figure. On the other hand, there are instances where a person couldn't relate to a central figure and asked to be moved to another place.

Kurt Johnson: I have had experience as a central figure for about eighty people. This means I've had to take care of a lot of people, love them, and try to help them be happy, productive, successful. I honestly don't think the major or unusual problems that have been suggested in the press have ever come up. This has been my experience of the entire Unification Church. I know that there are people who have left my Washington center or, more recently, my International Relief center, who might try to convince you of terrible things I or someone else did. Yet I know as an honest human being that these things did not occur. I know there are problems, but I have never seen anything that is any worse than you would find in any religious community.

And I want to answer David here, too, by saying that I can't separate my belief in the Principle from my actions. The longer I am in the movement the more I don't want to separate them.

Also, I am grateful that I never met my fiancée before we were matched. I begin that relationship with an understanding of what I want to achieve, and that is the cleanest personal feeling that I have ever had. I have an ideal that I believe in, which I see articulated not only in Rev. Moon's life but in what he has written. And because I didn't know Marianne before, I am more clear about my understanding of the ideal.

Thomas McGowan: First of all, I'd like to comment on David's methodology question and second I'd like to share something about spiritualism. I find what's happened today is extraordinarily practical. I have none of the anxiety that Dave has about the practicality of what I heard this morning and this evening. If I know how people pray, I think I can learn a lot about the way those people live. I was very happy with this. The thing I'd like to share is that during the past summer I gave out a questionnaire with the cooperation of Kathy Lowery of the Public Relations office of the church to seventy-four Moonies, most of whom were going to the seminary. I asked this question about spirituality: "Since your association with the Unification Church have you ever had mystical experiences such as visions, dreams, etc., which you interpret as being revelatory? If so, please describe your experiences." My comment is really a follow-up to Paul Sharkey's earlier observation. The survey showed that seventy-three percent of the seventy-four did have such experiences. So it was quite high. I have some excerpts which I'm not going to bother with now, but they refer to dreams about Rev. Moon, Mrs. Moon, Jesus Christ, dead relatives and so on. Anyhow, the point is that spiritual or mystical experiences are common in the church.

Patricia Zulkosky: Yes, that's true. When I said that we de-emphasized these things, I meant that our behavior is more important than spiritual experiences. I would have included dreams and visions and other forms of Unification mysticism in my presentation if I had thought of it.

Thomas McGowan: I didn't mean to be critical; I just want to share the information with the group. I think that it's good to have some kind of statistical information about spirituality in the church.

Myrtle Langley: In any case, it's a common experience anyway in a lot of religious movements all over the world.

Richard Quebedeaux: Such as pentecostalism...

Rod Sawatsky: I want to respond to David and Richard on their criticism of action and theory in the Unification Church. Their perspective seems to be more of a Lutheran dualism in which there are distinctions between the individual's secular work and spiritual work. In the Roman Catholic tradition, however, there is a unitive perspective in which the two are never separated. Unification thought is more like the latter.

Patricia Zulkosky: You would never fundraise or witness without praying constantly.

Rod Sawatsky: I want to pursue something which I see as a problem. These central figures are very important in the Unification movement. Do you find that there is a problem of imposing this hierarchical structure in the North American church? Are some Americans uncomfortable with it? For example, if you are unhappy with your position in the church and start complaining about it, isn't this interpreted as revealing some lack in spirituality? When things get bad, are there mechanisms to handle that? I am wondering whether there is not a structural problem so that there is not really a way to release one's frustrations.

Patricia Zulkosky: This is a problem, and there's no getting around it. We do have some way of dealing with these problems. For instance, when Nora acted as an itinerary worker, she was in a sense one of those safety valves. A person who is in real distress can bring his concern to the itinerary worker, who then is in the best position to mediate the situation or to facilitate a change of mission. So, the itinerary workers have a lot of missions. They provide leadership in the field, they are safety valves, and they facilitate the kinds of changes necessary for people to come into a situation they can handle. I do know a few people who deal with that problem simply by moving themselves. That is looked upon by some in the church as unprincipled. But when they get to where they function well, then eventually they are congratulated for having had the vision to move to where they could succeed.

Steve Post: I think it might be worthwhile to introduce a few distinctions and a view of Cain-Abel relations. When I first joined the church I went out on a fundraising team, and I think of that as my period of noviceship. I mean this in the sense that the Catholics might have a period, depending on the order, of some years, where there's really a kind of radical obedience. After all, Martin Luther spent three years cleaning toilets before he studied any theology. When I look back over my first couple of years in the church I see that I worked hard and maybe I didn't develop a lot of breadth in my thinking, not a lot of creativity. But I was going through that period in order to separate myself spiritually from my old life, which was a life without God, without understanding God's heart. So in that context, the structure made a lot of sense. But after a while, I think if we're faithful and if we do well in the things that we get involved in in the church, whatever they might be, then life broadens out. We still have central figures, of course. I write David Kim a letter a month from Chicago. Here you have a Cain-Abel relationship, but it's a different sort of Cain-Abel relationship than if you were running a twenty-one-day or a one-hundred-twenty-day training program.

Kurt Johnson: Right. Our situation is different, too, because we're experimenting with a new model which is successful, and which I think is going to become more widespread in the movement. I would call it a simpler and more Western understanding of the Cain and Abel relationship. Here the leader is the facilitator. The leader exists to give to the people in his care at that time whatever they need to fulfill their potential, to surpass their own leader, to become happy, to become productive, to become stable, to become successful. His job is to help them find a cluster of relationships that they can both have now and continue through their whole lives, a place where they know their lives are whole and that what they are putting into their lives is genuine. The leader is that responsive role model. Now the reason that I feel that this kind of leadership is close to the Principle is that I think this is Rev. Moon's relationship to God. God has not been authoritarian to Rev. Moon. Rev. Moon is in a responsive relationship to God, in my understanding of how I have seen him operate. And yet I have a central figure too, David Kim. I've never had a problem in that relationship, because I work in a responsive way in that sense, too. So what's happening there is very organic and very dynamic. The membership in our department has quintupled since the beginning of the year. It's something that's attractive, and I think it's something that can work very well.

It's inappropriate to other things in the church. You could not run an MFT* the way we run the departments I'm in charge of. Probably you could not run a group of younger members that way. All my people are over thirty and married. Most are educated, they are interested in something of real quality and vision, and I learn from them, believe me. That's how I function. I find out from the people what's going on, what to do. It's always that type of relationship.

William Shive: Let me get back to David's point. It seems to me that we're missing a little bit of what he's saying. The format, not the

---

*MFT is the name used to designate the mobile fundraising teams that raise money for the Unification Church.

substance, is the problem. It seems to me the problem is that we have presentations by people from the Unification movement and then we react to that. There is no way for us to initiate the concerns that we have, all the problems, the questions, the things that David is really upset about in the Unification Church and the problems of his coming here. There's no way for us to get those things cleared unless it happens to come out of somebody's presentation. I have a need to react to one thing that Rod said. I think he expressed a mistaken assumption about Protestants with respect to spirituality and the so-called secular world. I know where you're coming from, but my own old New England Congregationalism says to me that there is nothing that we do in the secular world that makes any sense in terms of a religious community's involvement in social change, or whatever you want to call it, that is not deeply rooted in spirituality. One of the real gurus in Protestant communities right now among the so-called activists, happens to be a Roman Catholic priest. He has said a lot to many of us about the relationship between spirituality and the ministry. I think that there is an assumption that liberal Protestants have discarded spirituality—this is not true. It means everything to us. I'm taking a sabbatical later this spring just for the purpose of trying to get back in touch with my own deeper need for a spiritual relationship between myself and my vocation. That's a very serious thing to Protestants and I think that it may be something that may have been overlooked in the past. But it's a very serious matter.

Renée Bakke: I can agree with the Unificationists about spirituality in regard to worship. I'm Pentecostal, so I'm involved in worshipping, raising hands, bowing whichever way. People ask me how I keep slim and I tell them I dance in church. So, Kurt, it's not new. But to me that is not spirituality. I love it because I love God. But spirituality to me is life and I'm concerned first of all with my home and my children. This young man here was saying that he has someone he can lean on; that's fine. But how often do we have anybody to lean on in a given situation? And that's the whole point. I can't run to somebody when my children come home because they're Christians and say, "Mummy, we've had some terrible things done against us because we have defended Christianity." My children had to have something in their heart that was so spiritual that it was beyond human resentment, something they could grasp quickly when a situation came up and put into practice. Now if anybody asks me whether I am spiritual, I will say, "Go and ask my children." I want you to know from them how I behave. That to me is being spiritual. When others can say, she knows the heart of God, she knows what God requires of her, not only towards Him, the Creator, but towards people, non-Christians and Christians alike, that to me is spirituality. God knows that there is an ultimate lifestyle that we can attain and that to me is spirituality. We must attain it, first of all in our homes so that our children won't call us hypocrites, and then in the world. If people can see Christ's light in us, then they'll know there is a living God.

Hugh Spurgin: I'd like to address Bill's concern with format. I have no doubt that the organizers of this conference are open to changes in format. Unificationists are amazingly flexible. I also want to comment on Rod's point about leadership and church polity. I remember a speech of Herb Richardson's in which he said that ecclesiologically Unificationists are seeking to reconcile Protestantism and Catholicism. There exists an incredible variety of leadership styles within the Unification Church. There is a stress upon obeying one's leader and an emphasis on egalitarianism. The egalitarianism exists because each individual has a direct personal relationship with God and with the Messiah that transcends his relationship with any earthly leader.

I'd like to give you one example of how things operate within the Unification Church. One of the most incredible things I ever saw Rev. Moon do occurred in 1975. At that time he'd been in America approximately three years and had developed a very successful evangelical organization. Prior to 1972 there had been members only in a few American cities, but by 1975 there were members in every major city. In the period between January 1972 and May 1975, membership in our church dramatically increased. But in May 1975, Rev. Moon sent the best leaders overseas to one hundred and twenty nations to be missionaries or assigned them to such national missions as fundraising, the seminary, News World, etc., thereby taking the backbone out of the church in America. The only people available to replace these middle-management leaders were young, inexperienced people. Newly converted members, often nineteen-or twenty-year-old kids, were suddenly asked to become local church leaders.

I'm trying to point out not only that the polity of the Unification Church is evolving, which it is, but also that Rev. Moon avoids institutional stagnation by encouraging people to find new horizons, thereby opening positions for enthusiastic young people. He took a big risk when he asked so many church leaders to go overseas, but by his doing so, many enthusiastic young people were given opportunities to lead. Moreover, although in the short run the Unification Church in America made a great sacrifice by sending its most experienced members overseas, in the long run it will most likely gain because people from other nations no doubt will have greater respect for America once they realize that it was because of the sacrifice of these missionaries that people in the Third World nations had the chance to hear God's message for the twentieth century. Sometimes our church seems to have bishops, at other times it seems to be congregational in its polity, but more likely than not it possesses both simultaneously.

Richard Quebedeaux: OK, we are now coming to the close of the evening. As the central figure (laughter) of this conference I would like to say we will see you tomorrow at 9:00 AM, when we'll get into the nitty-gritty of social action and communism and all those things with Kurt Johnson. Good evening.

Social Action and Politics

Kurt Johnson

Richard Quebedeaux: I'd like to read a portion of scripture again before I introduce Kurt, who will give a presentation on social action and politics in the Unification movement. I'm reading again from the Phillips translation of the New Testament, which I think a lot of you Unificationists don't know about. It's not really a literal translation but kind of a paraphrase, and then I'm also using my own paraphrasing. (laughter) But essentially it's very good. I'm reading from the Epistle of James, Chapter 2 beginning with verse 14.

> Now what use is it, my brothers, for a man to say he "has faith" if his actions do not correspond with it? Could that sort of faith save anyone's soul? If a fellow man or woman has no clothes to wear and nothing to eat, and one of you say, "Good luck to you, I hope you'll keep warm and find enough to eat," and yet give them nothing to meet their physical needs, what on earth is the good of that? Yet that is exactly what a bare faith without a corresponding life is like—useless and dead. If we only "have faith" man could easily challenge us by saying: "You say that you have faith and I have merely good actions. Well, all you can do is to show me a faith without corresponding actions, but I can show you by my actions that I have faith as well."

To the man who thinks that faith by itself is enough, I feel inclined to say, "So you believe that there is one God? That's fine. So do all the devils in hell, and shudder in terror!" For, my dear shortsighted man, can't you see far enough to realize that faith without the right action is dead and useless? Think of Abraham, our ancestor. Wasn't it his action which really justified him in God's sight when his faith led him to offer his son Isaac on the altar? Can't you see that his faith and his actions were, so to speak, partners—that his faith was implemented by his deed? That is what the scripture means when it says:

And Abraham believed God,
And it was reckoned unto him for righteousness;
And he was called the friend of God.

A man is justified before God by what he does as well as by what he believes. Rahab, who was a prostitute and a foreigner, has been quoted as an example of faith, yet surely it was her action that pleased God, when she welcomed Joshua's reconnoitering party and sent them safely back by a different route.

Yes, faith without action is as dead as a body without a soul.

It's interesting that in this passage, the author talks about God being pleased and working through Rehab the prostitute. It's interesting applied to the church and the situation of the gay person, especially the gay minister. It's very difficult for most denominations to understand that possibly God could be working through these people. But I think that if God can work through a prostitute and a Mary Magdalene, who many people look at as an ex-prostitute, then perhaps God is bigger than a lot of us.

With that I'd like to introduce Kurt Johnson. I met Kurt for the first time at Barrytown and we sort of walked around the grounds and he started to say, well I'm sort of a heretic in the movement. I didn't know what a heretic in Unification would be and he started talking and I thought, "This guy is what's going on here, he's really into social action," and then I discovered where he hangs out in New York and what he does, and it sort of blew my mind as it probably will a number of yours, since you may not be aware of what Unification is doing, concretely trying to change the world. I've asked him to talk about social action and also discuss the issue of anticommunism in the movement because, as most of us know, this is the real objection of many of the religious liberals and social activists in this country. They look at the anticommunism of Unification as an attempt to keep the fat cats fat and the poor people poor. Kurt has another idea about that which I hope he will share with us, and I'll give it over to him at this point.

Kurt Johnson: Thank you, Richard. We have a short amount of time to cover a vast and complicated subject. I want to discuss the relationship of social action and political awareness to religious commitment and to the particular teachings of *Divine Principle*. I want to explore whether there is an approach to social action and a political awareness that could develop uniquely from *Divine Principle*. Then, I will cite organizations which have been founded by or through the movement to relate to social purposes and describe what each is doing.

Please understand that the contents of this presentation, though aimed at representing the movement, is my own point of view. One thing I have found in the Unification movement is that it has considerable integrity. There is room within it for the development of many platforms and a very pluralistic base for understanding and action. Further, there is considerable dialogue within the movement itself concerning different areas of social action as they develop. No one in the movement has tried to impede any point of view and we have always been encouraged, especially by Rev. Moon, to pursue the development of our thinking. Therefore, much of what I will cover is developing in the dialogue and action of the movement itself.

I have always been surprised when people ask, "Is the Unification Church interested in social action?" What is social action anyway? Obviously, evangelism is a form of social action. But social action tends to mean how a group uses its resources to address particular social ills. Obviously, one could hardly read *Divine Principle* which has as one of its most important topics the subject of "restoration," without realizing that our point of view must involve tangible action. If we think of the "restoration of the world," we become awfully aware that we must do something—perhaps even something drastic or revolutionary—if we are to authenticate restoration. Restoration must be liberating—it must not only involve man becoming liberated from the various external and internal tyrannies of the world, but pragmatically, how solutions should be approached and executed in the real world of particular political situations and social complexities.

Obviously, you are not going to *restore* anything unless you are really interested in finding genuineness and wholeness in life. Then, the movement must think about authenticity. The movement must address the meaning of the Incarnation. The movement must continually ask questions like: "What is humanity?" "What is mankind supposed to be like?" "What does it mean to be sons and daughters of God?" "What does it mean to follow Jesus?" "What does it mean for people to serve each other?"

In the long term, the movement wants to achieve the restoration of the whole world. Let us think about it. This is a substantial claim. Historically, we believe that something is going to come of the movement. We think that hundreds of years from now, people will look back and see that with the beginning of this movement and many others and the coalescing of these, something began to improve in the world. We believe history will prove the beginning of a new era, a "quantum leap" that began, roughly speaking, at about this time in history. We must recognize that such an historical event would run counter-current to any other model for restoration which is fundamentally different and has a substantial base in the world. Therefore, such a movement has to understand its relationship to other claims. This is why a part of my topic today inevitably concerns the movement's various approaches to Marxism.

There are certain unique attributes of *Divine Principle*'s understanding of reality, God, and humankind. This has practical consequences. Let me enumerate some of these. First, when you join the Unification Church, you are taking a step out of the secular world. Though our life is not much different from the religious life of other religions, Unificationism accentuates that that stepping out of the world is also stepping back *into* the world in a different way. The Unification movement is large, economically well-grounded, and is interested in change. When you become a member of the movement, you begin thinking about how to fully mobilize manpower and resources toward a practical goal of restoring the world. Since such a concept is not a guise under which Rev. Moon is trying to do some other "ugly" thing in the world (as much of the media or other detractors have suggested), social action in the movement is a question of how these persons can mobilize their lives to social service. Such work cannot be carried out by spiritual inspiration alone or by public relations gimmicks.

Nor can it be carried out simply within the context of the secular world where such attempts have failed because the structures are restricted by secularity itself.

Since social service to the Moonie is an effort to help find some way out for mankind from what seem to be ever more complex problems and eventual consequences, persons within the church evaluate their lives in terms of how they are contributing to this goal. The interracial or international couple, for example, have a unique opportunity to use their lives to aid in the restoration of unity among people. Social action also comes from the individual lives of the people in the movement who are living within areas of social concern—particularly now, the inner city. They are trying to find clear inspirations and ways of working within the view of *Divine Principle* which can bring help to their local communities. They are praying and looking for methods. The organizations and works I will mention later in this talk have grown from individuals' projects.

Within the above context, Unificationists have been able to envision and substantially begin a network of nonprofit organizations. These are run by persons not primarily interested in the fulfillment of their private lives, but who are trying to be unselfish and serving at a high level of freedom and authenticity. Service has to do with reaching out to the genuineness of humanity and human nature. It exists to address the human condition. Service must be unconditional.

The practicalities of service are, of course, on another level. We have found that to achieve success, one must be able to mobilize some essential expertise in three areas: money, manpower, and mission. One must have money and resources to give and utilize; one must have man-hours to give and coordinate; and one must have a vision, a direction, a model and a sense of plan. Then, a deeper understanding of whether a particular methodology of social action actually has developed from *Divine Principle* emerges.

I want to give you some introduction so I can address that issue. At the level of methodology I think substantial dialogue can be developed between not only Moonies and other Christians but also with the adherents of other world faiths. From this question of how different faiths relate to a model for social restoration, I feel that developments and dialogues through these and other conferences can achieve practical results. Let us begin to look at some models now in a way that can embrace most of the considerations raised so far in this discussion of social action and politics.

If you read Marxist literature, for instance many of the shorter writings of someone like Angela Davis, you see a distinct form of analysis. There is a distinct methodology of exegesis and apologetic from which the Marxist addresses and analyzes a social issue. This is because a Marxist not only has a particular view of how reality is structured, but a Marxist also has a particular view of history. *Divine Principle*, quite distinct from other writings coming out of Christian history, also has a unique view. It has a view of the ideal, of how reality is structured, and a distinct view of history. Obviously, from *Divine Principle*, just as from the early articulations of Marxism, a methodology must emerge. I want to point out to you that the Unification movement is now in this germinal stage: its view and particular methodology are only beginning to be articulated.

For instance, within the methodology of Unificationism, the Moonie may think of a problem he wants to solve in the context of the Cain and Abel typology through which *Divine Principle* illustrates the path of restoration. Abel is the brother through whom God wants to serve mankind (in the symbolic position of Cain) in order to bring both through unity to the ideal relationship that God originally envisioned.

Therefore, if God desires one to be an Abel, how shall one act and how shall one learn from the past? First of all, if Abel is to succeed, Abel must always have more to give than anyone else. People come to the person from whom the most is to be gained. But how can Abel give what he has without creating resentment or jealousy in those he is trying to serve? How can a person truly serve from the position of an unconditionally loving brother or sister? The Moonie must analyze his or her motives and methods to see if they are truly pure. How is one an instrument of God and not just one's own ego? Also, if a person has come with resources, how can he make sure that the resources are not misused? Any social activist who understands the problems of administering resources in the area of socially and culturally deprived situations will understand the predicaments.

Because of training in the Principle, the Moonie may also ask, what kind of action should I take to please the spiritual world so that people there will participate invisibly in restoring a particular problem? How can this invisible world be motivated to work with those to whom by ancestry or personal attributes they are spiritually connected in this historical problem? Then, how should I proceed at the social level to create relationships with people that can bring about a pragmatic unity within a community or neighborhood and achieve some substantial goal? The Moonie will be aware that *Divine Principle* requires a time period in which satisfaction of the internal purity of motivation will in practical ways emerge to create a spirit for the unity and cooperation desired. The Moonie knows that the external quality emerges from the internal one, as in Jesus' words, "For out of the abundance of the heart the mouth speaks."

Another question which is part of the *Divine Principle* perspective concerns the relation of Unification social involvement to the work of various churches and faiths. According to the historical analysis of *Divine Principle* the Unification movement comes in the position of little brother to the big brother, established Christianity. Unification social action or ecumenism must consider how the movement can humbly communicate its vision and hope for unity to the bigger brother. This is another question that relates practically to the Cain and Abel typology. How does Abel speak his inspiration without incurring the anger of Cain? Because persecution is a reality, the Moonie must consider what kind of unconditional service will convince the big brother that *together* they are to solve major historical problems; that the insights brought by the younger brother combined with the sophistication of the older brother are God's plan to influence history in a new and positive way. The Unificationist, therefore, sincerely analyzes how he can achieve a partnership between his "New Age" religion and traditional Christianity such that together they can move toward restoration—God's actual goal.

The Moonie will try to analyze, as has the Marxist, the patterns in historical relationships that will finally lead to the goal of a liberated and truly whole mankind. He will look for the individuals and peoples who are in the Abel position today. Who is most truly like the standard of Jesus? He may come to note that Black and white Christianity may represent a key Abel/Cain typology through which God is trying to work. He will note that it is in the Black church that the most pure reflection of Jesus' standard is most often found. The Black church exists at a level where faith and social concern are one. The Black has suffered and forgiven more. White churches are in many cases more self-serving, detached from social concern, and teaching spiritual salvation without regard to the need to liberate the brother. It can be noted that it was Black and white Christians *together* who brought about the civil rights movement. The Moonie will see that as consistent with the teaching of

Rev. Moon: the movement began with Abel and was joined by Cain. The Moonie may analyze current sociology and conclude that the route of restoration for American Christianity will begin from the Black community and spread into and mobilize the white. Then, he will hear Rev. Moon mention this in a speech and feel that his spiritual insights and analysis of *Divine Principle* have been correct.

Obvious to my comments so far must be the observation that the concept of unity between brothers which is central to Unificationism is a counter-proposal to Marxism since Marxism condones the destruction rather than the restoration of what is in many cases the Cain position. To evaluate the Unification position on Marxism, one must consider the content of the Principle and think about it in relation to the basic claims of Marxism. Our movement is distinctively *for* something, not just against something. The dialogue about how to approach Marxism is a hot one within the movement itself. This is healthy and good. How have some of the more destructive conceptions of the Unification Church approach to Marxism come about? I am sure that many of them are the result of the misunderstandings and mistakes of the movement and others as well. I am also quite sure that our detractors have tried to spread as much of the "bad" word as they could.

Within the movement you will see a proliferation of tensions between many cultural backgrounds trying to articulate together the Principled counterproposal to Marxism. You will find all kinds of political leanings in the movement, and people trying to find a harmony by centering on *Divine Principle* and its ideal of the one family of man. One thing is certain: in Rev. Moon's own teaching and speeches there is both criticism of communism for its extreme violation of human rights and criticism of Christianity and the West for selfish usage of resources and other abuses.

The articulation of an approach to social action by the movement is one of the exciting things in which we can ask your participation. We feel this process is occurring through the development of *Divine Principle* as theology and ideology. The movement is those who are in it. Its ideas are articulated by those who have become its adherents. Though its formulas are in one sense fixed within the teachings of Rev. Moon, their applications and explanations will be a long historical process.

On the handout, I have listed the kinds of organizations that the movement has nurtured to address political and social questions. Some of these organizations are independent in constituency and structure and should not be confused with the church itself. First I've listed organizations whose primary work is in relation to political awareness.

New World Forum: The New World Forum deals with the ambassadorial and United Nations communities trying to foster a religious view of values and concern for mankind. It is an educational group trying to offer a perspective. It is one of the early groups working in relation to education about communism. It is now, I would say, in some tension with other approaches like that of the Freedom Leadership Foundation.

Freedom Leadership Foundation: It has traditionally taken a very conservative approach to Marxism and has focused on human rights abuses, but it may be growing now in its perspective. The fellow who is in charge there is finishing his master's degree at George Washington University in political science and he has his undergraduate degree in political science from Brown. It will be interesting to watch this group's future development. It has won many awards, principally from groups representing those who have fled from Marxism.

Society for Common Insights: This group has tried a different approach to Marxism, a liberal, more nonreactionary one. It has stressed what we are for, not what we can be against, and tried to build an alternative. It has done conferences on racial and cultural issues. It has a publication series. Some of these books are in the back. It is doing a book now on American foreign policy in South Africa, and it has done a series for the University of Pennsylvania on dialogue between Black and white social scientists. This is an independent foundation founded by members and nonmembers.

Capitol Hill Ministries: This group works in Washington, D.C., in relation primarily to the Congress. Its interest is First Amendment rights and also countering the slanderous actions against new religious movements by the deprogramming and antireligion organizations and lobbies. It is interested in instilling an idea of religious character in politics.

Professors World Peace Academy in Japan: I have been particularly impressed by what this group has done. They are an older group and have done high-level strategic studies on the economic future of Japan and the strategic future of Southeast Asia. These are serious works, well thought out, not at all reactionary in approach. You can order their publications. I think there are about eighteen hundred Ph.D.'s in the Professors World Peace Academy of Japan. It is a large and effective organization, inspired by the church's founder but independent in its actions.

I've listed next the social organizations. Most of these are independently incorporated, nonprofit organizations. Some are completely Unification people, others are mixtures, others authentically non-Unification but substantially funded or helped by the Unification Church.

Project Volunteer: This is a social service entity of the California Unification Church. They have distributed tons of food and are involved in recycling, vocational training, and many other community projects. They are innovative; they deal with networking resources for the benefit of local community needs. They have won many awards and are well accepted in the West Coast community.

National Council for the Church and Social Action: The National Council for the Church and Social Action is an ecumenical group, formed by us and our friends in about eight other denominations. We guard the authenticity and integrity of the organization, and as an ecumenical organization it is growing quickly. We have chapters now in New York, Philadelphia, Washington, Norfolk, Jersey City, Denver and Atlanta and eighteen affiliate corporations. This year we surpassed the three million dollar mark in services rendered. We're proud of this organization for two reasons: it's successful and authentically interreligious.

International Relief Friendship Foundation: The International Relief Friendship Foundation is young, only a year old. It is an independent public foundation founded by members and nonmembers. IRFF is now working in twenty-seven countries, and will hopefully grow to others. It works with various organizations through which it can render social service overseas. This year it produced a third of a million dollars in services, a five to one ratio of money invested. That was a very good start, I think.

New Society Social Programs: New Society is an endemic Harlem project. It's run by Unification people from Harlem and elsewhere who feel that God wants them to help in that particular situation. They are absolutely realistic about what's involved in trying to do restoration in Harlem. Their services are very successful and include food distribution; they are widely recognized.

D.C. Striders Track Club: This program combines a scholarship program for minority students with the opportunity to compete in major athletic programs during the year. The D.C. Striders qualified numerous Third World students for the Olympics in Moscow. The program was initiated by members and non-members and functions as an independent foundation.

World Medical Health Foundation: This is a testimony to Rev. Moon's interest in social work. He's very interested in medical service, specifically the implications of *Divine Principle* for wholistic health, the relationship between acupuncture, chiropractic, shiatsu, traditional medicine, etc. It holds conferences and seminars and will be opening a clinic in the future. It is a private foundation formed by church members.

International Cultural Foundation: The world of the ICF is well known through the International Conference on the Unity of the Sciences. It is so well known, and well regarded that I need not further elaborate it here. It should be considered social action in the context that it serves to bring the work of scientists to a consideration of values and the application of scientific knowledge to the betterment of the human community.

Before I go to slides, because I can go through them fairly briefly, I want to emphasize that it has been a distortion of the truth by the media and others who oppose us to list these groups as "front organizations." I can assure you that our detractors will comb the proceedings of this conference for information about these groups so that they can attack them. I ask them now to question their motivations and open their minds to a fairer understanding of the movement and its objectives.

The last consideration I want to address is what is the source of these organizations and their work? There is, of course, the inspiration of the Rev. Moon and the Principle. Inspirations are also flowing now from a large constellation of people who are gifted people. The secret of everything I've talked about today is a lot of gifted people who are seeking answers in prayer and in their personal lives, within the racial and cultural admixtures they represent, as to how as adult human beings drawn to this movement they can find a way to practically achieve the goal of restoration. I want to conclude with some simple observations. We are a young movement in America—not only young historically but youthful in membership. This is something that must be considered. We're beginning. We're discovering, and we are also making mistakes. That is life—that is what it is all about. We have to deal with both sides of Rev. Moon—inspiration on the one hand and practical life on the other. We win some, we lose some; but there is an overriding surety about the character of the work we are about. What, then, is our vision for the future? Will social action grow or diminish in the movement? It is simple enough to say that social action will become as big in the movement as there are gifted people to make it big. It is so simple. That is the way the Unification movement is. It is who is in it. It is their vision added to that of the movement's founder. The future of the movement will depend on their energy and what they can build. Where the energy is—there also will be the result.

(This talk was followed by a slide presentation.)

Discussion

Richard Quebedeaux: OK, do we have questions about Kurt's lecture?

Andy Smith: What are the eight denominations that are participating in the National Council for the Church and Social Action?

Kurt Johnson: That number may be too low now. There may be many more. On our boards of directors we have Lutherans, Presbyterians, Methodists, Catholics, Baptists, AME, AME Zion, Pentecostals of every kind and variety, CME, a member of the United Church of Christ.

Andy Smith: You say those are members of those churches. Are there churches participating or denominations?

Kurt Johnson: No. These are nonprofit corporations that have people participating as individuals. The chairman of our national board is AME. The president of the Harlem board is CME. The president of the Washington board is Baptist. But they are all participating as individuals. Of course, they take flack from some members of their churches. Also, there was a problem in Washington, D.C., with the National Council of Churches. But that's been basically resolved by the fact that we're doing good work there. When we got our grant from HUD, the National Council of Churches did not vote against it. They just abstained.

Thomas McGowan: Let me start by saying that since I've met you, Kurt, I have been absolutely convinced of your sincerity and dedication to this kind of work. But I'd like to get your reaction to this. You would obviously be very offended if there was a front in the church that was out to proselytize and was using a community organization for that purpose. But in my survey of Unificationists, at least ten percent admitted that they joined the church through such a group in California. As far as I can ascertain from talking to them and reading their responses, there wasn't any community activity as such. It was really a front to proselytize. Now I know you said we should ask Dr. Durst about this, but I think it has to be asked to you also. How do you feel about this? Is it a front? And does it injure the work you are doing here?

Kurt Johnson: If Dr. Durst feels that types of community outreach can attract people who can then understand the Principle and join the movement, then I am not in any position to interfere or to infer anything bad about that. That would be his decision. I know that there is substantial service work done through Project Volunteer. They have a staff that just does that. I've been there and I've spent time with them. But I also know that Creative Community Project has served as a way to approach people for joining. So in that sense *that* could be called a front. It depends on how you define a front. I think that there are groups that could be called a front, but are those any different from groups that other people use to either recruit, do PR or anything else?

Thomas McGowan: How do you feel about it? Wouldn't this injure your work? Is there any friction between you and Dr. Durst?

Kurt Johnson: It bothers me in one sense, but in another sense it doesn't. After all, we are a family. And a family may have this internal diversity and that's fine. The East Coast social action people are seriously interested in the methodology of service. We don't think that the West Coast people are as exclusively interested in that particular target as we are. It's just not where their thinking is. And that is why we are sometimes conservative in our relationship to them. We certainly don't want to become dominated by their paradigm because we feel that our mission is a specialized mission to serve and one which Rev. Moon has given us.

Richard Quebedeaux: I live in Berkeley, and I know the Creative Community Project is not to be judged as a social action organization. It is set up as a model community. Actually it is the camp where people are introduced to Unification ideas, but it is conceived as a group of people who live there as Unificationists in order to show those who come as guests that there *can* be a community of fellowship and love. It is a recruitment device one hundred percent. It is distinct from Project Volunteer which is primarily a social service agency related to other ecumenical agencies. Project Volunteer has a weekly church service which is usually run by local elderly Black people who have their own revival meetings, and it's not specifically designed to recruit people into the Unification Church. However, I believe that people from the outside who attend Project Volunteer services are invited to evening workshops at the centers and then to Camp K. As far as I know, the Oakland family members are very single-minded in their belief that their primary mission is recruitment and that pervades all their concerns.

How many liberal youth ministers, however, use devices to recruit people who would not otherwise go to church? Youth for Christ often uses a more inclusive name, Campus Life, and Campus Life has social gatherings for evangelistic purposes. The Berkeley Christian Coalition, which is now a radical organization, was started as a front for Campus Crusade with the aim of appearing like radicals in the Marxist movement but opposing the Marxist Third World Liberation Front. (It later became radicalized itself.) It is true that this kind of deceptive intent does not necessarily justify front organizations. But let us be aware that many of our own denominations use them.

Myrtle Langley: I want to reinforce what you're saying. In the history of Christian missions such a debate has been going on since the last century. Take, for example, Uganda where the doctor, Albert Cook (later Sir) was taken out and about by Bishop Tucker as an 'arm of evangelism.' The Church Missionary Society spent a great deal of time debating the issue in its committees. The first missionary medical and educational work were thus undertaken to give credibility to the gospel. The debate concerning the method's justification is still going on.

Stillson Judah: I'm in full agreement with what was stated. The only problem as I see it is that because of the bad press, there has been resentment against the Unification Church. Take, for example, the case that was in the news about a building that was bought in Northern California. It was a very old building and had been a very fine building. So the sale had to go through the city council to determine whether it could be used for educational seminars. The question was asked, "Are you connected with the Unification Church?" And the answer was, that there was no connection with the Unification Church. Yet the buyers were the Creative Community Project. But the distinction which they made then and which they always make is, that they are independent of the Unification Church but affiliated with it. Then all of a sudden when the seminars were given there, and people discovered that this was the Unification Church, there was a big uproar. They say they don't want the church in their community. It's unfortunate that this happens. And I don't know what the answer is.

Kurt Johnson: I don't either. I don't want to minimize the fact that people misuse things when they have a goal they are trying to reach. But I also want to appeal to process and development. We have to carry this baggage—people's fear of how our organizations are being used by Rev. Moon.

George Exoo: I have had some contact with the Creative Community Project and I will be very specific about it. When I left the Virgin Islands' conference I flew to San Francisco and as a part of my experience in San Francisco and Berkeley went up to Hearst Avenue as a naive newcomer, coming in off the street, just to see what would happen. And it was pretty ugly. I judged it extremely negatively, because it was so much in contrast to everything that I'd experienced in the Virgin Islands. I think that some of what went on, if it were publicized, would be an embarrassment to the Unification Church.

Richard Quebedeaux: Could you explain?

George Exoo: Well, I will give you one very simple example. It reminds me of the things that one business I know of used to do to sell land up at Tahoe. They would invite you to a dinner and then pump you full of the land sale, try to get you to go up and see the land. Only at least the firm knew who was interested and who wasn't, and they didn't put pressure on the people who weren't interested. Finally I told the church members who I was, and I even said that I had been to the Virgin Islands. Then I said that I had a funeral to do in Charleston and I could not go up for the weekend. And a young lady looked at me and said, "You don't have to worry about that funeral, you just call them up and tell them you have something more important to do."

I had a gut feeling about that meeting being a front organization, because there was no mention of the Unification Church. It was only Creative Community Project and it was clear that it was being used as recruitment for Unification Church. They were not up front about it until I turned to this young lady and said, "Could I see a Unification hymn book?"

You know, I have a singles group in the Unitarian Church in Charleston, and we bring hundreds of people into Gage Hall every two weeks. And is this a front organization for the Unitarian Church? When I sell that to my vestry, I say that this is going to serve these people, and it's going to bring people into the church. And it does. But I don't invite anyone even from that singles group into the Unitarian Church in

Charleston, although everybody knows that that organization is sponsored by the Unitarian Church. It meets on Unitarian Church property but that kind of up-frontness just was not there with the Creative Community Project.

Kurt Johnson: Well, I'm no authority on the California situation.

Richard Quebedeaux: I believe that Dr. Durst is arriving today and we can discuss the Northern California church beginning at 6:15 this evening. We only allow fifty minutes for him, but I'm sure that he'll be willing to stay up all night as he always does to talk to any of you as long as you wish.

Diana Muxworthy: I sense that Kurt has been thinking a lot about his projects as long-term counterproposals to Marxism and I want to ask him what he thinks and how he thinks Rev. Moon is thinking about the future of the world. I'm asking this partly because I want to understand why it is that many people in different denominations are seeing you and your group as people who really care. I have also been disturbed by what I perceive to be a narrow view in our church. I would prefer to see our church through *action* get more involved in positive constructive critiques of Marxism.

Kurt Johnson: Well, besides me, you could talk to other people in my department who are getting direct inspiration in relationship to the Principle. What we're talking about here, of course, is a long, long-term thing, which you have to compare to the history of Marxism. In other words, in understanding Marxism you have to start out with its background. The Feuerbachian idea of liberation is definitely not the type of liberation we want. And Nietzschean liberation is analogous to what Satan said to Adam and Eve in the garden. Both Marx and Nietzsche told us that their prayers for liberation and justice were not answered because there is no God. So the Marxist tells us to stop praying and to take responsibility for restoring the world. They tell man he is the only boss. That's why when a Marxist has that experience, he has a revolutionary insight. He'll give his life, he'll give his energy.

The problem is not that there's no God. The problem is that man has not taken his responsibility in relation to God and man. So we are not to get up off our knees and become atheists. We are to discover our responsibility, within the context of religion. When you talk to a Moonie and you talk to a Marxist, you get the same testimony. What does a Moonie say? "For the first time in my life I understood my responsibility."

The church made his responsibility clear.

So, you start with Marx and you get a scientific apologist, Engels. Then you get a political apologist, Lenin. Then you get a cultural apologist, Stalin. And then you get a culture, which is the whole Marxist world and now all of its variations. The same thing ought to happen with the Unification Principle. You have a prophet, and a vision, you start getting people who build social models. Then you finally deal with a political idea of how that can work and finally you get a culture. We're talking about a long haul.

Don Jones: I want to go back to the question of fronts, but I don't want to use the term "front." I think the term is misplaced and pejorative. I suggest that we should be more precise about how all these different groups function in the overall mission. Let me give you two types of organizations. One is the current United Methodist Church type who are antiprosyletizers. They are even embarrassed to suggest that the reason they go to South America and help in liberation movements or support the ERA is to gain new Methodists or even Protestant Christians. They clearly do not intend to do that. They don't mind new members, but that is no longer the goal for most liberal social gospel Methodists. On the other hand, during the mid-nineteenth century the Methodist Church was absolutely clear that, when they built hospitals and schools and they struggled for the freed man, their ultimate goal was the Christianization of the entire world. And that meant de-Catholicization of the Christian world. They knew very well that they wanted more Methodists. They were competing with the Baptists for membership. I would say that the Church of Jesus Christ of the Latter-Day Saints is more like the nineteenth century Methodists. Their fundamental task is, in their phrase, the upbuilding of the church, and by the upbuilding of the church, the renewal of the world. Now my guess is that you would see your projects more on the model of the Mormons or the mid-nineteenth century Methodists.

Kurt Johnson: I think I can give you a clear answer. You'd be amazed that there really isn't a clear agenda in Unification activities, because the situation of being a person interested in *Divine Principle* and whatever is ahead, is always an innovative situation. We're never sure of what that answer is, so we're doing a lot of experimenting. We're caught in the paradox that restoration obviously is not exactly the same as getting people to join the Unification Church.

Don Jones: But don't you think it would be easier if more people were members of the Unification Church?

Kurt Johnson: Yes, this is the paradox. We have to ask ourselves, is there something unique to the Principle which is really essential to achieving restoration? And then we end up thinking, unfortunately yes. Because our experience is that the Principle helps to create a vision that gets things done. But I'm very clear on one thing: I will not violate anyone's integrity to get them to join this church. There are others who might. I won't because that's the way I was taught. For example, chastity means you don't manipulate people. That's the way I was taught. OK, so the way I look at it is this. I'm willing to discover what's out there. I believe Rev. Moon is genuine aside from whether he's a prophet or whatever. I believe that we're serious, but I'm not sure we know what that means. So it's going step by step in this paradox, letting the thing grow and then within that, actually seeing what happens.

Don Jones: As just a little dividend, do you hope that this helps to establish legitimacy?

Kurt Johnson: I'm not worried about legitimacy.

Don Jones: I should think that you would want legitimacy because that makes your work easier. You don't have to spend so much time fighting off the dummies.

Kurt Johnson: Yes, that is a practical consideration but to me the issue is clear. Legitimacy is sometimes a fog that people throw up, but restoration is still restoration.

Richard Quebedeaux: I want to comment on this from the evangelical point of view. We Christians would not be here if the first century Christians had not recruited people. Imagine this: Somebody gives you a gift of a million dollars tax free and says, "I have ten more million to give and I want you to recommend people to whom to give it." And what are you going to do? Are you going to tell your friends or are you going to keep it quiet? I think that any person who has experienced something that has changed his or her life is going to want to go out and share it. They are going to hope that people will accept it.

Don Jones: That is why I like the nineteenth century Methodists.

Andy Smith: I want to follow this up in a somewhat different way. I want to contrast the Unification attitude toward anticommunism with what's happening, say, in Latin America and liberation theology. There Christians are affirming Marxist perspectives to a certain extent, because they see Marxists as the ones that are more involved in the action side of it than anyone else. Therefore, they are cooperating with Marxists and bringing about what they see as the restoration. In other words, their visions tend to bring them together, cooperation in terms of action. In fact, in one book I read, the author reported asking clergy and seminarians, "Who do you think is the most Christ-like person you know?" A frequent reply was "Che Guevara, because he is the one who is acting in the most Christ-like way in terms of what he is trying to do." Others in response to this question mentioned Ernesto Cardinal who spent time in Cuba and now is very much involved in an attempt to restore Nicaragua. So I wonder what your perspective is on how the anticommunist ideology fits in with this cooperation in terms of action.

Kurt Johnson: Our understanding of that would be very, very simple. The Marxists definitely, genuinely, are looking for liberation. The problems with that from our point of view are two: One is that in our view of history, Satan uses his knowledge of the Principle to create a model which is close to the Principle but can leave God out. It is in that situation, then, that we see the crucial difference between Christian-Marxism and Unification thought. The Principle insists on theism. And second, with the Principle you do not have to worry about a hidden agenda. This is a worry that I have for Christian Marxists. What is the level of control they have, given where the money will come from, and what about the role of arms, and so on? If you have no alternative as an indigenous liberation group to the terms of the Marxist, then what is your ability to keep your own indigenous control? I feel that a lot of American Christian Marxists are naive because they don't understand that complication. Is that helpful?

Andy Smith: That's helpful, but I'd like to pursue it further at another time.

William Shive: Are there annual reports on the work done by all these organizations and are they available to the public?

Kurt Johnson: Yes. I have the annual reports here of International Relief and the National Council if anybody wants to look. I just didn't want to spend the money to run them off.

Evangelism and Witnessing

Jaime Sheeran
Diana Muxworthy

Richard Quebedeaux: Obviously people are not going to witness or do evangelism until they have their spirituality straight. It's interesting to note that both of the witnessers and evangelists who will speak now happen to be women, so perhaps this will flow very freely into the next hour which is about women's roles in the church. I'd like to introduce Diana Muxworthy and Jaime Sheeran who will be giving us a presentation about witnessing and evangelism. Both of them have been and are involved in this process.

Jaime Sheeran: I graduated from the Unification Theological Seminary in the first class of 1977. At that time, I felt very excited about going out to the field to meet people and to witness about Rev. Moon and the Principle. It is ironic in a way that this was my desire because when I joined the Unification Church in 1973 I had no idea what the term "witnessing" meant. In my Catholic background there was very little focus in this direction. In the Unification Church, though, witnessing is very much a part of life.

I moved into our "family" while still a student at the University of Vermont. I'll never forget my first exposure to witnessing. One day it was announced that we would all be going out to the streets to speak to people about the Principle and invite them to come to our church center. The whole idea was overwhelming to me and even sounded religious! While everyone else was out witnessing, I ended up sitting in a restaurant for three hours trying to get the courage to actually approach someone. My new-found faith was just barely beginning to form at that time.

Needless to say, there has been a great change in my feeling and my understanding of what it means to witness and evangelize. Presently, I am directing our church activities in the state of West Virginia. Upon graduation in 1977, all of the seminary students went on fundraising teams for a couple of months, and by September 1977, Rev. Moon had asked several of us to go to various states to direct the church activities. If I can, I would like to paint a picture for you of what it has been like to witness on behalf of the Unification Church in West Virginia. You might wonder what it is like to go and visit people, to knock on their doors as a Moonie. What kind of reaction do people have to us, and what kind of experiences do we have meeting them?

Recently, a new aspect of our church witnessing has begun. In about the middle of 1978, Rev. Moon began to speak to us about something called home church. Our focus in witnessing up to that time, basically, had been to meet people in the streets, stopping them as they walked, and asking them things like, "What is your purpose in life?" or "Do you believe in God?" Then we would invite them to come to one of our evening programs to hear a lecture about the Principle. Also we would often go to campuses setting up lectures, discussions and workshops. So, for the most part our focus had been what we call "street witnessing" and the greater portion of the people who responded seemed to be young people. Our experience was that young people were more open to new ideas and more interested in actually changing the world.

With the coming of home church, though, everything seemed to turn around and take a completely different focus. Instead of approaching people on the streets or on campus, we began to visit people in their homes. Rev. Moon has asked each member of the Unification Church to take an area of three hundred and sixty homes in which to witness, serve and love the people with all our heart, all our soul and all our strength. I was very excited as Rev. Moon began to explain to us the meaning of home church. For myself, I felt it was very close to what I had been prepared to do and had been interested in doing my whole life. It was exciting to me because I could see in a more substantial way than before how God would bring the fulfillment of His ideal of the kingdom of heaven on earth.

In college I had majored in social work. I wanted to do something that would involve working with people and would improve our society; there seemed to be many problems especially in the family life of American homes. While still in college, I worked with elderly people and families in low-income housing projects. Before long I began to feel disappointed in my studies and in the work I was doing. There seemed to be a lack of real depth in understanding the core of the problems people were facing. No matter what solutions were being offered, the real situation in the field was not improving at all. I found that by providing material things for people you could solve their problems temporarily, but you couldn't give them a sense of pride or value. In housing projects there was little respect for property and often it would be vandalized. I could see that the theories I knew were extremely limited in their capability to improve our society, so I began to search for more answers and turned to religion. Up until that time I had not seriously considered religion as a way to solve the world's problems. I had viewed myself as an agnostic and sometimes as an atheist. My interest in religion began to grow, though, until I finally decided to make it a dual major along with my studies in social work.

I can see how home church is a fulfillment of both religion and social work. In home church, we visit homes with people of all ages, occupations, attitudes and economic brackets. It is our hope not only to teach people about God and spiritual life, but it is also our desire to serve people by helping them in many various ways. For example, in West Virginia our church center is actually a small house located in a residential section in a town called Huntington. It is a middle-income area with quite a variety of folks. There are many old people, young families, students and professors. In the area I have chosen, one side of my home church area is mostly people of the lower income bracket, while on the other side it begins to have people who are more wealthy. There are very few Black people, unfortunately, or people of various nationalities. In visiting our homes we have tried to approach people in as natural a way as possible. At the same time, it is very much our desire to be as out front as possible about Rev. Moon and the Unification Church. In fact, one day we set up a table in the park near our church center where we wore tee-shirts which said, "Make friends with a Moonie" as we gave away balloons, watermelon and church literature. So we have tried to be out front, and because Huntington is a fairly small community, people easily find out what's going on.

The first thing we do when we go to people's homes is to approach them by taking a survey in which we gather their opinions about such things as moral issues, the future of America or their goals in life. What do you think can help the world more today, religion or technology? Do you believe in God? What makes you happy? These are examples of the kinds of questions we ask. In this way, we can quickly orient the discussion toward meaningful issues; also, if we first are willing to listen to people rather than just tell them our own ideas, a more natural and comfortable relationship develops. Through the survey, we can also find out what their needs are and how we can best serve them. Sometimes, that means we end up cleaning people's homes or washing their cars, baby-sitting or doing an errand. Recently, I have been learning how to cut hair, because often people find it is very expensive to go someplace to have it done. Home church is our chance really to do service for people with unconditional love. We have made it a policy not to accept any money for the things that we do; instead Rev. Moon has often reminded us that through serving people, we can learn the meaning of true love. In a way, without these people to serve and to love, we could never become citizens of the heavenly kingdom. For God will speak through them, guiding us, whispering to us, teaching us how to love His children.

You might think we would encounter a hostile environment as we visit and talk to people, but actually we find there is very little hostility towards Rev. Moon and the Unification Church. People seem to be quite open and curious, and if they are not interested, they are usually very polite saying, "No thank you. I'd rather not be involved." In general though, they seem to be curious and interested.

One experience I had as we began to visit people's homes was with a Baptist woman. I knocked on her door and told her I was with the Unification Church. Immediately she asked me to leave, saying she wasn't interested in talking to me. I said, "Well, ma'am, I'm not trying to force any ideas on you. I just would like to meet you and find out your opinions on the Unification Church." She looked at me very carefully and said, "OK. You come back a little bit later and we'll talk about it." Well, I did come back, and after a fairly short time we became very close friends. She is a divorced woman who runs a beauty parlor and has raised her two sons by herself. For hours and hours we would sit and talk together. She eventually felt as though I was one of her closest friends, like her own daughter. She offered me a place to stay in her home and really wanted me to live with her family.

In providing service to people you have to be very flexible. Sometimes you can do something for them, and sometimes it may mean just having the willingness to listen and the heart to understand. Not everyone will respond with interest to the teaching of Rev. Moon and the Unification Church, but everyone can respond to the love of God. Some people as a result of our service do become interested in hearing more about *Divine Principle*; they may attend our workshops and actually become full-time members. Others may just become our friends. The least thing that happens is that people's opinions of what a Moonie is change very much. For the majority of people, the only contact they may have had with us was probably through the media or through one of our fundraising teams. Finally, through home church, I believe they can begin to understand the real heart of Rev. Moon and the Unification Church.

From a providential viewpoint, according to Rev. Moon, home church should have begun in the Garden of Eden with the family of Adam and Eve. It was God's intention that Adam and Eve reach individual maturity and oneness with God and establish the first God-centered family. As you visit homes you find out very quickly that most homes are not God-oriented and are often filled with numerous complications and problems. Although everyone is searching for a happy life and home, it is often not easy to find or to maintain. So Rev. Moon says to us that home church is not just a method of witnessing, a way to gain members. Home church is actually one more step towards the accomplishment of God's original ideal. The kingdom of heaven on earth is very simply a world in which God lives within each home, in the heart of each individual.

The reason we each have three hundred and sixty homes is because the number 360 represents a complete circle. So each area becomes a mini-world. Since the concept of loving the whole world seems so nebulous, by having our home church areas we can at least give our hearts to this mini-world. When you go to your area even if no one seems to care if it is dirty or full of garbage, our church members think, "I will care. I will be the one to take responsibility to make this place beautiful." Often we plant flowers, or in West Virginia we have been getting up early in the morning, praying for people before they awake, cleaning the trash from the streets or shoveling the snow in our areas. If there is crime in our home church areas then we search for a way to help stop it, perhaps by organizing more cooperation among neighbors. In other words we try to create a family among our three hundred and sixty homes. The hope of home church is that not only will we as Moonies try to do this, but that each person we meet can also take three hundred and sixty homes and they, too, can give love and service to others and expand further God's kingdom on the earth. In a way it is beyond denomination or religion; it is simply learning how to love. We, as members of the Unification Church, feel that God has given us a responsibility to pioneer a model of success, going through all the stages of human history and establishing a kingdom of love in our home church areas. Others, then, can follow that pattern as a model in their three hundred and sixty homes.

As I mentioned in the beginning, through home church, I could see more substantially than ever before how God could actually establish His kingdom on earth. At one point Rev. Moon mentioned that as we visited our homes we would experience going through six thousand years of biblical history. First, through the Old Testament age, we would be like a servant of servants or a servant. Then, we would go through the New Testament age as an adopted child. And finally, we would become like true sons and daughters and true children of God. I actually experienced something like this as I was working in my home church area. One time I visited our next-door neighbor who is suffering from arthritis. It was Christmastime and she was having a difficult time because when she had taken down her Christmas tree many of the dry needles had fallen off and become embedded in her carpet. She had tried to pick them up with the vacuum cleaner but it didn't work. The only way to do it was to get on her hands and knees and pick them up one by one. Because she had arthritis, though, it was too difficult for her to do. I therefore offered to pick them up for her, and on my hands and knees, I picked up each needle one by one. In a way I felt as if I was God and each one of the needles represented us, so brittle and dried up. As carefully as I picked up each one of those needles, I thought, in the same way God picks up each one of us. Then at that moment I heard a voice in my heart which said, "Servant of servants." A few minutes later the woman's son came in. She asked him if he would please take some chairs up to the attic for her. I was still on my knees gathering up the needles. Her son began to argue with her and complain about having to help her. Again I heard a voice in my heart which said, "In some ways you are more of a child of hers than her son." Finally, I felt as if through all of this, I was actually becoming more like a true child of God.

In conclusion, I feel very grateful to have the opportunity to do this kind of work. It is very exciting to try to practice high ideals and hopes. As I was growing up I could never understand why in Christianity so much emphasis was put on spreading the Word. If we are humble, though, and we approach people with the heart that Jesus had when he washed the feet of his disciples, then our words will have meaning and weight as our actions substantialize what we feel in our hearts. The kingdom of heaven is a place not only where we speak the truth but where we live the truth, and that is very difficult to do. But the great thing is that through all the joys, tears and struggles, we find God in a real way and it is very exciting.

Not only do we visit our home church areas, but we also try to visit public officials, ministers and professors to explain more about Rev. Moon and the numerous projects that we are initiating throughout the United States and the world. There is probably a lot more I could say about this but Diana also wants to share something. If you have questions, I'll be happy to try to answer them.

Diana Muxworthy: I'm going to add to that. I realize that there are a lot of questions, but I'm asking you first to listen to just a bit more on witnessing. I will gladly respond to your questions later. I would like to give a brief story of what I've done in terms of witnessing in the Unification Church and then refer to my being at Harvard and how I now look at witnessing.

I joined the movement in June 1974 at the beginning of the Madison Square Garden campaign. That was my first taste of witnessing. Then, my next chance to do witnessing was at the seminary, when on Saturdays and Sundays we would go into New York City to give away tickets for the Yankee Stadium celebration which took place in June 1976. I remember standing on the street in sun and rain for hours and hours, some days giving out over a thousand tickets. That was one way of witnessing: tickets to Yankee Stadium. My next chance to go witnessing was after seminary when I went to Rhode Island and was asked by Rev. Moon to be the director of the Unification Church in Rhode Island.

At that time witnessing was more of what I suppose most of you imagine witnessing to be—on the street, talking to people, bringing them over to the center, taking them to a workshop site, and on from there, helping them make personal decisions. In 1978, the home church providence was announced and in January 1979, I was accepted at

Harvard. So my taste of home church was brief.

At Harvard, I can't say that I'm witnessing in the sense that I used to witness on the streets or even when I was doing my home church. I'm at Harvard to learn what is there, to learn the heart of Christianity, to learn the problems that Christianity and other world religions have. My witnessing now consists of my learning how my life is to be a witness to *Divine Principle*, to Rev. Moon and Mrs. Moon, to Franz, my fiancé, and to my own family, and even to myself. I'm one of the few people in the church who at this point has been thrown to the wolves. I guess I can say that, but this has nothing to do with Harvard. (laughter) I've been to a certain extent a lamb, immersed in the life in the centers, in an environment which was cloistered in that I lived in a community of Unification Church members, praying, working, eating, waking with members of the church. Now I'm living in a dormitory with the wolves and with the lambs of other faiths. So I'm having to learn in this stage what it means in these circumstances to be a witness, what it is to be someone who believes strongly, not just in the theology of *Divine Principle* but also in the life stimulated by *Divine Principle*. What does believing in the Principle mean in reference to how I live my life? What does that have to do with the academic work? What does *Divine Principle* have to do with creating theology, studying ethics and dealing with feminist issues? How does the theology relate to what Kurt is doing with social action? I feel all this is part of my reason for being at school—that I may learn from what is going on there and from my own experience. From my belief in the Principle I hope to learn how to work out possibly new methodologies, new ways of intellectualizing, new ways of creating models of theology.

The other aspect of any witnessing is a very personal part. That is my personal life of being a witness to the Principle. My life obviously being quite different from that of a lot of the people at Harvard. I have been very touched, very moved by people's acceptance of Unification Church members. Yet intermittently I run into some unpleasant situations. The first week of this semester, for instance, a woman living across the hall came into my room and said, "Do you know that there are Moonies in this dormitory?" (laughter) I was standing with a very dear friend of mine who looked at her a bit in shock. I looked at her and said, "Yes, you're talking to one." The woman was very embarrassed. Her response was, "Well, you sure don't look like a Moonie!" And my friend's response to her (my friend is not in the Unification Church) was something like,

"Yes, she sure doesn't look like a Jew," mirroring to this woman what she was saying.

The woman was very embarrassed. But my first reaction was to pray for her and for this situation. This was someone who obviously had some preconceptions about what it was to be a Moonie. I determined within myself to see how this girl and I by the end of the school year could become friends. To me that's part of the testimony of what I have learned of what it is to live a Principled life, which I don't think I would have had the patience to do in the past. That means simply learning how to surrender a part of yourself for the sake of another, making conditions, praying, learning to live for the other before yourself. This woman and I are not now best friends, but certainly the preconceptions evident that day are somewhat cleared. She's asked me, for instance, if she could come to Barrytown to one of the student conferences to engage in a Unification dialogue. Much of what I'm doing at Harvard is simply to testify to the fact that Unification Church members are not what most people think we are. And when people do become interested in *Divine Principle*, they might be invited to come to Barrytown to participate in one of these dialogues.

Another manner of witnessing occurs during Franz's visits. There is a very interesting dynamic that goes on there because of the ways of the world. The ways of the wolves in a contemporary twentieth century U.S. dormitory, right now, would be that if your boyfriend or fiancé comes to visit you, it's rather unusual if he doesn't sleep with you. It's been many a night when poor Franz has had to grab a sleeping bag and walk down the hallway into Klaus's room and have people look at him and wonder what he's doing. (laughter) At that moment it's embarrassing for both of us. But when I go back to my room alone, I'm glad to be able to make a statement to these people and to my community of friends of how *Divine Principle* has helped me understand something about living a moral life, especially in relation to the other things that are going on on college campuses. Witnessing at Harvard then, is being a witness to Principled life. That's the new perspective that I've gained on what witnessing is. Home church has a lot to do with this—it's being a witness to the Principle, to the theology being actualized in our lives. This, though, is something that will be very gradual for the movement to embrace. It's even hard for the members of the church to understand. We're very hungry to find the resources and people to work with us because we believe that there's a war going on, spiritually and otherwise. The tactics that we use are sometimes shortsighted. But I think that the home church providence is something that we, the members of the church, are willing to struggle through in order to understand the deeper heart of what it all means.

I'll leave it at that and open it to whatever questions you have.

Discussion

Paul Sharkey: I have been thinking about this seminar, not just this one, but the one on theology which is going on in the other room as well. I think it is significant that we are separated. As some of you know, I'm a rather Humean philosopher, which means that I don't take occult metaphysics very seriously, especially certain kinds of metaphysics that I think are perhaps dangerous but which often are associated with theology. What I've seen in terms of witnessing here, the way witnessing has been described, is refreshing. I happen to live in the South right now, where witnessing often means telling you about theology. It seems to me, however, that Christian witnessing is not that at all, but is rather being Christ-like in relationships with people. Now, this is the sort of thing that I am not only hearing in this seminar, but that I know happens. I think this is one of the major attractions of the Unification movement. Definitely it will help your image, because if you're serving people and don't expect anything back from it, then they can't be threatened. And, as you've said, not only are they not threatened, but they become very attached to you because this sort of kindness doesn't happen in society. I think that something that needs to be thought about is the possible lack of wisdom of throwing the lambs of your religious life to the wolves of theology. I think Diana has done some good thinking on this. I worry about stressing too much to people in evangelizing the theology of *Divine Principle* as opposed to the practice. The theology of *Divine Principle* is "the book" as opposed to the practice of the Principle, which is not "the book." I think the latter is something that is needed and important. I'm not sure how much of the theology is needed, and too much theology can be a hindrance to the development of that other kind of witnessing for the Principle.

Mary Carman Rose: I'm glad that Paul made this sharp distinction between the direct Christ-like giving and love and the theological and metaphysical grounds on which the aim to be loving might be based, but I don't think that in the Unification movement these two can be separated. For me this is a tremendous strength in Unification thought. I've never heard members of the church discuss this; but, in fact, they are very wise in basing their actions on principles. They see their lives as constantly in a dialectic relation between their theological beliefs and understanding and their actions. Understanding without action is sterile. But action without profound and constantly developing understanding of reality, man, and his relation to God is without a fundamental raison d'etre. Such action could become mere naturalism and, hence, not God-centered at all. Once it becomes a naturalism, it could easily become egocentric and carried out for reasons of self-aggrandizement. I see the Unification insistence on a theological and philosophical basis as protection—and a necessary protection—against all kinds of dangers, spiritual as well as intellectual.

Don Jones: Yes, I want to make a witness to how graduate students in the Unification Church come over to me. There are two types, and I have a preference for one of the two types. One is Jaime's type, where the witness really is in just the ordinary life. I also think of Franz this way. When Franz is down, Franz kind of lets you know he's down. He doesn't have to always be up on top as a witness. That's more meaningful to me because I know that Franz is human like everyone else, and sometimes he feels lonely and sometimes he's down or frustrated because he can't finish his work or solve a problem or something. But Franz's sheer intellectual curiosity is a witness to the faculty, and that's very important. He will, for example, come in and ask what he can read. Steve, you come across that way too. But there is another type where there is a more intentional proselytizing kind of witness, not to faculty but to students. And I'm just not sure how appropriate that is. We may say to each his own, and yet it has been a little more off-putting. The second style appears to be combined with some deception. It may not be that at all, but to get students into groups and then six months later reveal that you are a member of the church is probably not very wise. I think there's probably more wisdom in Jaime's policy of coming out front immediately. But anyway, that is my experience.

Diana Muxworthy: I'd like to show you the other side of this. I have seen Andy Wilson, another student at Harvard, on his way to take a final exam, wearing an "I'm a Moonie and I love it" button. That's just Andy's personality. I guess that's one of the refreshing things to me about the academic community. There's something in the academic community that lets you be very up front and even be respected for it.

Stillson Judah: Is your home church a nucleus for meetings of the community where teaching can be conducted? Or is this all done in individual homes? In other words, will this eventually develop so that your homes will become a central place where worship would be carried on, and where perhaps some lecturing or preaching would take place?

Jaime Sheeran: That possibility is there, but it hasn't fully developed yet. In people's minds, because of the controversy surrounding the Unification Church, to associate with us involves a risk on their part. I find that quite a few people are willing to come over, to be our friends at this point, to visit and participate in our activities, but they will not come out openly in support of us. They may even tell you secretly that they are behind us, but in this community they may consider it a risk to actually publicly state that. I think that will eventually change though, especially if we continue to develop our service-type projects.

William Shive: Jaime, you said you visit city officials. What's that all about?

Jaime Sheeran: Yes, we not only visit our own home church areas, but everywhere we go is like a home in a way, including visiting city officials. So, for example, in West Virginia I have met people like the mayor, ministers and also the governor. Actually, so far I have met the governor here three times. When I first visit city officials, and other people of responsibility, I introduce myself as a member of the Unification Church and ask them if they have any questions about us. Secondly, I ask them if there is some way I can be of help to them in the community. Oftentimes, because we have visited so many people's homes, we get very much in touch with what is happening in their lives. Sometimes we have even helped people get back in touch with their own congregation. For example, one of our members, Kim Pickard, helped an elderly Jewish couple to recontact their Rabbi. Kim had already met the Rabbi because she had visited his temple. So those kinds of services go on because we're out there every day visiting homes.

George Exoo: When you spoke of visiting officials, I got the impression that you were doing advocacy work for the people in your communities. For example, if they had a problem with the city, you might go to the city and help them.

Jaime Sheeran: Yes, I might. First though, I introduce myself to officials as a member of the Unification Church because they have heard a lot of different things about us and may have questions.

George Exoo: As you said, your style of witnessing is really not a method. Its just your individual style, but I didn't find that to be very indicative of the Oakland family, because they deny their affiliation with the Unification Church. Now, of course, I didn't approach any large number. But I did approach some of them, and maybe it was because they were very young in the movement that they denied it and possibly you don't deny it because of the conservative area in which you live.

Jaime Sheeran: No, that's not the reason why I don't deny it. I can't speak for the California church, but I feel closer to God if I'm able to be honest and out front. By saying who I am, and where I'm from I feel more spiritual and more providential in what I am doing. Also, Rev. Moon encourages us very much to be up front. I find at times I have to counsel members not to hedge on that; they do tend to do that, especially when they're fundraising. I myself go fundraising. We have to support our church center and at times, when I'm with fundraisers, I find myself having to encourage them to have courage. Some of them haven't been trained in theology. They don't always know what to say when people criticize Unification beliefs, and it may cause them to avoid confrontations. But I think it hurts them in the end. They really want to tell the truth to people. They are very excited about what they're doing or they wouldn't be out there. As I am in a position of leadership, I feel I have to encourage members to go ahead and say who they are.

Richard Quebedeaux: Again, I'd like to remind you that Dr. Durst will be with us this evening and he is the director of the Northern California church and I do hope you'll address this question to him.

Jaime Sheeran: One thing to consider though, is that I haven't had great success in my own work. Maybe California (laughter) has been more successful. Of course, it all depends on what the criteria of success is. We haven't gained a lot of members in West Virginia. It may be because it is a conservative area, but I think primarily it is because of me not really living up to what *Divine Principle* actually says. That's really the primary problem, I think.

Kurt Johnson: I just want to comment on Stillson's question to Jaime. In Harlem, home church is really developed. It's even to the point now where people who have become home members of the church are moving in together to make communities. They buy property, not with church money, but with their own money. This is very similar to the Christian model. You meet in a home. Then you meet in a larger place. Finally you buy a place and form a community. The value of that is that it centralizes your people and you're really serving the community. You've got tangible personnel right there.

Jaime Sheeran: In larger church centers, members actually will live in with some of the families and try to be of help. Ours is so small at this point, it wouldn't really be worthwhile. But if we grew large enough then some of us could accept an invitation to live with a family.

David Simpson: I have a couple of questions. If they are too personal just say "no comment." I sat on all my feelings this morning, so I've got to get some of them out now.

First, Jaime, I have dealings with people in political office, and I'm curious about the statement that you had three meetings with the governor. One does not get into the governor's office without an appointment, and that you have had three meetings with the governor is of great interest to me. (laughter) I would like to ask you if you would be willing to role-play your three meetings with someone in the group. I won't do that, however, because we are not in group dynamics. But I do want you to comment on that.

I also want to ask you and Diana questions about how you live, in terms of some very mechanical kinds of things. For example, who pays the bills? Do you work at jobs that earn money? I guess specifically in terms of Harvard, who's paying the tuition? I just have a need to have some answers to those kinds of questions. I'm curious to know where you live and how you lived before you ended up in the dormitory at Harvard. By the way, if you do become disillusioned with people on the North Bank of the Charles River, there is a place in New Haven that you might be interested in.

But first, my question about what exactly is it that you say when you have meetings with people in public office? What is the real content of the conversation beyond, "I'm a member of the Unification Church and I'm here to let you ask any questions that you may have"? That would be about a thirty second conversation with most people in public office, so I'm curious about the real content of these conversations.

Jaime Sheeran: First of all, I just want to clarify one thing, I didn't say I had three meetings, I said I met him three times. The second meeting was actually an appointment I had made in which we discussed the Unification Church. The other two were more by chance. I had met and talked with his appointment secretary on a few occasions, and he was able to advise me as to where the governor would be during the day if I wanted to try and meet him. So, for example, after his dentist appointment one time, I was able to talk with him. For one thing, he happened to know one of our church members very well because they went to school together. The governor is Jay Rockefeller and he met Edwin Ang who works at our seminary now, when they were both students in Tokyo. I asked him about that to see if he remembered him, and he did. The second time I met him, it was a formal appointment in which I shared with him my point of view about the church as opposed to the way the media had presented us to the public. I felt that was important to do. The third time, I just happened to have an inspiration to go there. I stopped in the office at the right time, just as he was going out, and I was able to meet him once again and talk to him for a couple of minutes about his work and what he was doing, nothing much about the Unification Church. I feel that it is important to show an open door to begin communication. One of the meetings therefore was a planned one, the other ones were by chance. I felt they were valuable though, to me.

About our life, well it's kind of unusual. We have a three-year-old little girl there with us, and her mother who works at a regular job. One church member is a full-time student. They both contribute money towards rent. The rest of our finances are raised by fundraising done by me and one other church member, Kim. We often travel throughout the state with the MFT raising funds. Every month I have to do that for a week or two. Sometimes we receive contributions from people in our home church areas, but it's nothing really reliable. We try to conserve our money. Our budget is about one thousand five hundred dollars per month.

Every day we pray together in the morning and at night. At 5:00 PM we meet to have dinner and discuss our day. We try to study *Divine Principle*, too. If the student or the working person have time, they will try to come with me to visit homes. Or sometimes we may have guests coming over to hear a lecture and we all participate in that kind of thing. But Kim and I do most of the active witnessing in people's homes.

George Exoo: Do you have to account to anybody for your budget?

Jaime Sheeran: Yes, I send a monthly report in with my budget. Actually it is a thorn in my side in a way because it takes so much time to write down the money we receive, collect all the receipts, and write down everything we spend it on. I'm not very number oriented but we have to be careful. The IRS is interested in knowing what we spend money on, where the money goes. So we keep a good accounting of it.

George Exoo: Jaime, can you tell us something about your family? I know there is here a curious twist to the Jacob story, because I know that Jaime witnessed to her mother.

Jaime Sheeran: Yes, actually I have two sisters who are members of the church. My older sister and the next younger sister to me. I also have a brother and one other younger sister who are not members of the Unification Church and neither are my parents. My mother does seem to be taking interest in it, especially in activities like these conferences. Actually before I left to come down here, she was giving me advice about what she thought it was important to say. Last spring she came to visit me in West Virginia. She was able to meet quite a few people in my home church area who were very friendly and said some good things to her about us. So, she really seemed to be enjoying herself. She and I travelled around to different parts of the state together. At one time my mother had been very opposed to the Unification Church; both my parents were. I think at one time they even considered deprogramming, but changed their minds on that. My father is still far from supporting our work. My mother, though, seems to have had some kind of change now. My mother is a person who never was inclined to pray or go to church or speak about God. But now, she speaks a lot about the importance of God in the family. Recently, she said she watched the Pope speak on television. He was speaking about the breakdown of families in America and it brought tears to her eyes, she said. So I see a lot of changes occuring in my mother, at least in terms of her attitude towards religion itself.

Diana Muxworthy: All the Unification students at Harvard are on full scholarship from the Unification Theological Seminary. We do not go fundraising. When summer came, I was expecting to go fundraising with the attitude that I should fundraise because so much was being given to me. The tuition is quite high, and so are room and board. But we all stayed and did whatever we had to do—take languages or whatever. Then I receive work/study help because I'm in the M.Div. program which means that you have to do a certain amount of field work; and if you are eligible, you can receive work/study money from Harvard for this particular field work. My situation is different from Jaime's. I don't need to report to the seminary where the money goes. It's certainly generous, but it's not so much that I can spend it frivolously. It's enough for telephone, clothing, laundry, books and so on. So in a sense, I'm certainly free to buy anything I want and have dominion over what I'm buying and what I do. If I have extra money, I spend it on movies, presents or phone calls to New Jersey.

George Exoo: What about a bottle of wine?

Diana Muxworthy: The only time I've bought a bottle of wine was for a lawyer who had helped us out in a Rhode Island deprogramming case.

David Simpson: Diana, what do you see as your future goal in the church after your theological studies?

Diana Muxworthy: My future goals? That's a very good question, and I'm really trying to work that out. I'm having to work that out for myself, in terms of what Kurt said, in terms of what's in the future for social action. I think that's the situation for each of the graduate students. When Rev. Moon speaks to us, it's very open. I'm really amazed and impressed; but it also puts tremendous responsibility on us. My dream is to do something with Franz. Franz is German and is at Drew in a doctoral program. I'm in a master's program, but hope I'll be going on for doctoral work. I will have to learn German for my studies. I already know French a bit, and know Spanish fluently, so there is a lot of international potential between the two of us. What we do is up to Franz and me. We're being given the financial resources and the blessing of being at school. I think we're going to create our mission, and it's a tremendous responsibility. It certainly will be in service to the Unification Church, and it will be something new that hasn't been done before.

Hugh Spurgin: I want to say something about Paul's and Don's comments. There's a long-standing debate in the Unification Church as to whether the direct or indirect approach is more effective. On the one hand, there are those who have been effective by employing the direct or confessional approach, whereas others have been equally effective using the indirect or apologetic method. Let me give an example of the direct approach. If I knock on a door and say, "I'm Hugh Spurgin. I'm with Rev. Moon's Unification Church," I'm likely to get the door slammed in my face; although with a nice personality like Jaime's, that is less likely. (laughter) Although that approach may be effective, the problem with it is that people say, "I've got my own church. Don't try to impose your religion on me. I don't want to be proselytized."

On the other hand, by employing an indirect method one opens himself to the exact opposite type of criticism. In an apologetic approach, a person seeks to get to know another person before telling him he is a Moonie, trying to share what interests the other person and find out "where he is at." Some Moonies don't even mention God but talk only humanistically—even though eventually they are probably going to say they are a member of the Unification Church. The criticism that is often made is that in this manner, people can be deceived. However, such an approach can also be viewed from another perspective. It can indicate that a Unificationist is concerned about other people, not merely his own interests and opinions, that he is sensitive to others and not trying to "lay a heavy trip" on them. My opinion is that most—if not all—Unificationists employ both approaches to people, depending upon the situation, just as other Christians have always done. With some people they are more assertive, with others more passive. Indeed, all of us are both trying to find out what someone else feels and thinks, while at the same time expressing our own experiences.

Superficially Rev. Moon may appear to be an authoritarian leader, but those who know more about our church acknowledge that leaders, as well as members, within the Unification Church have considerable freedom and function quite independently. A dialectic goes on within the church between freedom and accountability. My observation is that the polity of the church is essentially congregational; leadership is simultaneously centralized and decentralized, but much more dispersed than most people believe. That's why there exists such diversity within the movement in spite of the commitment to the same overall lifestyle and goals.

William Shive: How does CARP* fit into evangelizing?

Jaime Sheeran: Well, it goes to college campuses and witnesses directly to students who are interested in world problems. I'm not involved in that, so I can't speak so much about what CARP is doing.

Kurt Johnson: I've heard that Rev. Moon wants CARP to make a lot of noise, because he feels it is very important that something make a lot of noise, to balance lots of other kinds of noise on campuses.

CARP (Collegiate Association for the Research of the Principles) is an international student organization which studies the relationship between various academic disciplines and the Principle. It also publishes a newspaper, the *World Student Times,* and sponsors programs on campuses.

William Shive: Organizationally, is CARP at the University of West Virginia at all related to you?

Jaime Sheeran: Supposedly by the end of this year, there will be CARP centers in every state, so I imagine we will have some relation with them. It's in the future, though, and I don't know what that relationship would be.

Stillson Judah: Since I have spoken about the Creative Community Project in a rather adverse way, I want to bring out something else which may help clear up some of the problems. When the church first started in the Bay Area, there were two missionaries, Mr. Sang Ik Choi and Miss Young Oon Kim. Mr. Choi worked in San Francisco, and he had an entirely different approach from Miss Kim. His idea was not to teach theology at all. Instead, he was interested in moral and ethical living, in teaching people to live the life of the kingdom itself. He didn't care about theology. Now this approach is the one behind the Creative Community Project. Presently in the Creative Community Project the first weekend, most people will never hear at all the name "Rev. Moon." Dr. Durst's approach is similar to that of Mr. Choi. But in the seven-day workshop following, they have Miss Kim's approach, which is entirely theological. At that time, of course, the name "Unification Church" is introduced. I think this explains this particular approach: there is one side relating to the experience of life itself, and the other side, the theological which follows.

Judith Simpson: I'm wondering if too much self-doubt is not as dangerous as too much discrimination. I'll explain what I mean by each of those words. Discrimination is present when a person makes choices, and sometimes arbitrary choices. He says that he likes one person but not another. Too much discrimination is a very narrow, streamlined, uncooperative, uncommunicative vision or position. It tends to be oppressive and narrow. At the other pole is self-doubt, which I would like to align with the Unification idea of sacrifice. What provoked this thought in me was Jaime's saying that her project hasn't been more successful because she hasn't done enough. That idea of self-doubt seems to go along with sacrifice, the serving but not having served enough. I guess I don't think that's as dangerous as too much discrimination, but there should be some middle-of-the road attitude that you could find more satisfying. Why should you always be doing more and more soul-searching about why you haven't done enough? I'm not really asking for a response.

It's just a remark.

Jaime Sheeran: Yes, sometimes you find out that it is not only you that is the problem. You find out that at times people are just not interested. They may not be concerned with world problems. In my area it's very easy for people to live within their own small world and not be interested in what's happening elsewhere. They are fairly happy people and may not be concerned with issues, yet here I come bringing them a sense of world responsibility. Still, within myself I try to keep a balanced attitude, realizing that I don't know everything. Maybe it is different in a place like California that attracts people who are searching. People in West Virginia who are searching may leave and go somewhere else. When I was in California at a conference once, I actually met a young man in a small restaurant there who had left West Virginia for that reason. I confess, sometimes I wonder if there really is anyone in West Virginia who is searching. (laughter)

Women's Caucus

Richard Quebedeaux: I'd like to introduce Lorine Getz who will begin the discussion.

Lorine Getz: I'd like to pose a problem that some of the women in the group have experienced in the conference and talk a little bit about it. The problem has to do with the participation of women here and the underrepresentation of women's views. What occurs to me is not a condemnation of our proceedings, but a question of what are we doing. Last year at the St. Thomas conference in the Virgin Islands we only had one conference. There we were all together in one group and women played a somewhat peripheral role. They gave a few presentations but their participation was a minimal kind of thing and it struck me as a concern at that point.

Here is a new religious group that has a theology which posits the possibility of the equality and liberation that women and other minorities have been searching for. I didn't feel particularly discriminated against in that conference, but I felt that I wanted more interaction and more searching in that direction. I voiced my concern about the minimal role of women in the dialogue at that time. Now a year later I notice two changes in the conference structure. The conference has a kind of mind-body split. And there was not one female Moonie mind presenting a paper in the mind group. I wonder if we are just recapitulating history. That is the way it has always been. In theology schools the thinking has been done by the men; in churches and communities the living out, the practice—*that* which women can participate in!—has been carried out by the women. That is more their field, and they *belong* in the lifestyle section. So I just want to posit this again not as a condemnation, but as a question. We women have talked about this with some of the men who are conference leaders. Their response was that to their knowledge, there were no women who were quite ready yet. There is a sense in which historically and culturally this is true. Women have not been in the forefront of theological education and your movement is not radically different from others. But shouldn't we be working on overcoming that?

Secondly, when we got a group of women together, we discovered that even in the lifestyle section women felt that their own concerns were not directly expressed and that they couldn't get to them. There is a problem of articulating authority and self-identity and getting those issues out in the open. But how can that be done in such a way as to generate a reciprocal, productive kind of relationship between concerned men and women? That is the question. How do we do that? How can we get the dialogue together? I would not like to see a separate women's section.

Diana Muxworthy: I have sympathy with most of what you are saying. My main concern is the positive side of this. We do have *Divine Principle*, something that we believe is new, revelational and can bring in the new age. The question for us women in the Unification Church is, obviously, what does that mean for women. This is something that we are struggling to try to figure out. What does the Principle mean for me, for women who are getting Ph.D.'s, or for women who are in more traditional roles. It is not a matter of trying to convert Unification Church women to become feminists, nor of trying to convert feminist women to become whatever. What is needed is an open dialogue between men and women to really open our hearts and minds to try to understand possibly what these new models are. We then can try to experiment with how we can live that out. We have something very good to do here. What I respect and like about this discussion is that it is a sign that obviously something could go wrong, and let's be aware. And I think the Unification Church women certainly are willing to say that some mistakes are being made. We need to stop and reflect and see where we go from there.

Richard Quebedeaux: In terms of the organizational process, to set up the conferences Darrol and I worked at the bottom level. Approval for people to be participants in these conferences must be made at the highest level. It is very interesting to find that even some of the allegedly chauvinistic leaders of the church are now absolutely insisting that everything be done to include women. Now, they don't know quite how to do it, but I think they are growing. I just wanted to make that statement to begin with.

Darrol Bryant: Just one other comment. The hermeneutics section is something for which I take total responsibility because the composition of that group was wholly in my hands. It wasn't because of something going on in the larger church. It was wholly my doing.

Lorine Getz: But it is to some degree because the church like the rest of society does not have a large number of women who are totally prepared to participate. I didn't want this to look like an accusation, because I think the problem is that we are all liable to recapitulate the pattern. And how *do* we deal with the problem that is already historically there?

Darrol Bryant: I am not doing apologetics about the situation. It was the best I knew how to do given the circumstances. The only reason I say that is just to make clear that there was no internal pressure from the church or from the seminary or anything like that that resulted in this situation. Quite the contrary, as Richard indicated, there is a desire from inside the church that these kinds of things don't happen.

William Shive: I would like to have some woman from the Unification Church explain to me what the male-female roles in the Unification Church are, particularly, what is right female action, lifestyle, what is right male action, lifestyle? Are they interchangeable?

Diana Muxworthy: The reason for the hesitation is that obviously we are still struggling to figure that out. The balance that I think we are really struggling with is, where does *Divine Principle* as a lifestyle come through purely, if that is even possible? There is the cultural conflict between the American version, the Korean version, and the Japanese version or whatever version. I am from Puerto Rico, so I have my version coming from Latin culture. I know within myself there is a real struggle to work this out: what is purely *Divine Principle* and where does the cultural part come into play?

I want to admit that role modeling goes on. Yet in a center for instance, where there are brothers and sisters, there is really not that much distinction. The women do fundraising and witnessing; the men do fundraising and witnessing. At the *News World* there is pretty much a balance. At the seminary when I was first there, (and some of the professors can testify to that) I willingly and gladly served the cookies, the coffee and so forth at the meetings. In time that changed. Now it is Arthur who does a lot of the food preparation from what I understand. There is obviously flexibility in here. We don't have any clear sense ourselves really to be able to determine, say, this is right and this is wrong. We are trying to work this out. That is why I appreciate the very strong, radical and angular critique of Lorine. She attacks us right on so that we are forced to confront ourselves. If we do come out and conclude in time or at least woman by woman that what we want is in a sense a traditional role, then I want to be given the opportunity to draw that conclusion, too.

Richard Quebedeaux: I think that there is a real problem in terms of my own experience. Quite often I stay at the New Yorker Hotel. When I ask where I can have my laundry done—and wanting to do it myself—the word is, we can have the laundry girl do it. And at the CARP center in Berkeley it is always the case as far as I have seen that the women do the cooking and generally function in the more traditional domestic roles. Even though all go fundraising and witnessing together, basically when it comes to domestic life you find the traditional roles. Some of the Oriental leaders of the church—I won't mention names—have told me that, yes, *Divine Principle* does teach the equality of men and women; however there are fixed roles and these cannot be changed. So there is that problem.

Therese Stewart: I'd like to say that I think that what is going on in the church as far as role definition, our discussion of and study of relationships between men and women, is very much a reflection of what is going on in the larger society. We just recently had the annual oratorical contest at the seminary. There were a number of suggestions as to what topic people would speak to including the role of women in today's world, but that wasn't an extremely popular topic with the students—President Kim then suggested that we ask the faculty what they thought the topic should be. It got only about a fifth of the votes when President Kim took a poll among the students during morning service. The professors felt very strongly that the women's issue should be addressed so we went back to the students with a modification and suggested the topic of the respective roles of men and women in today's world. Well, there were some interesting talks. I don't think the issue in those talks was addressed exactly in the way we are talking about it here today.

Maybe some of the students would argue with me on that.

Let me cite just one example as to the degree to which some women in the church feel that there is a problem. My secretary came to me a couple of weeks ago after having sat in with one of the male students in a small conference with a member of the Church of the Latter Day Saints of Jesus Christ who was working with us. The Mormon raised the question, what are the respective roles of men and women in your church? And the brother answered: the men teach, and the women cook. My secretary looked at him and exclaimed, "Tom!" This is a generalization but it was said more in seriousness than in jest. My own feeling has been, and is, that the whole question of the role of women in the church is very much in process, but I don't think it is going to be resolved very quickly.

Frank Flinn: In the past I have related several problems that I see in *Divine Principle* as it is written. As people know, I make a big distinction between the Principle and the book *Divine Principle*. In the book I notice on one level a relational language, a language of give-and-take, and on another level a language of entity, of substance, of hierarchy of superordination and subordination. Now I ask myself this question, which language is closer to the Principle? I think the relational language is closer. In relational language, if you take away one pole of the relation, you don't have a relation, so you can't say one is higher and one is lower, one is more important and one is less important. In substance language you can take away an accident and the substance is still going to be there. I feel the relational language is closer to the Principle but at the same time I see in *Divine Principle* an ambiguity about this. Maybe we are paying indemnity for the language we use. This is a theological question that pertains, I think, directly to the male-female question.

Patricia Zulkosky: Part of what I see happening is the fact that we are responding to Christianity which comes out of a patriarchal tradition. When you are responding to that kind of system then you tend to pick up that kind of language, so on one hand we have the relational which I would hope to be exactly what we are trying to do and work out. On the other hand we find this hierarchical language that has been absorbed. It is the same problem that we are struggling with at the School of Theology at Claremont—it is a question of language. Do you say "mankind" or "humankind," do you say "man" or do you say "person"? And I know myself, I have become extremely sensitive to even that kind of language, especially in the church. I know whenever I hear people talking now and

I hear the word "man," I feel excluded. Just excluded. And I have to translate to myself "people" in order to feel included.

Now this might be a more radical stance than ninety-nine percent of the women now in the church because we are not dealing with that kind of issue. However, in the context where that issue is one of the major issues on my campus, I can't help but become sensitized to that particular issue. This is just one small kind of thing, but even that kind of awareness hasn't yet surfaced within the movement as a whole in terms of the way we teach the Principle, or make our presentations here at the seminar or anything else as far as I can tell. This is part of the whole patriarchal tradition that we come out of. It is a struggle of women all over now to try to gain recognition in at least the language.

Durwood Foster: I empathize greatly with the struggle which Pat has just reflected. It has of course been going on generally as a struggle between tradition and modernity for most of us. I want to point out that in a sense the Unification community is under a kind of double-bind which hasn't yet been mentioned in this sitting. There is the inheritance of biblical patriarchalism, as you mentioned, and that is something which we are all struggling with in one way or another. In addition to that, as far as the roots of Unification tradition and lifestyle are concerned, there is the Confucian-Oriental tradition, which is extremely important and raises some very intriguing kinds of issues. In our hermeneutics seminar we had a very good paper from Andy Wilson expounding the Confucian background of *Divine Principle* and the Unification tradition. A couple of things in the Confucian and Oriental background deserve particular mention. One is the Confucian concept of relationality. It is a concept that, I would submit, synthesizes the antithesis of which Frank Flinn was speaking when he spoke of relational modes on the one hand and hierarchical modes on the other. In Confucianism relationality is hierarchical. There is a subordination of the junior to the elder and there is historically a subordination of the wife to the husband. The five different classical relationships establish a kind of hierarchy. Although in the West we come out of biblical patriarchy, in the post-enlightenment West, due in some ways to the impetus of the Christian faith, woman has been liberated to a degree that would be shocking, I think, to traditional Oriental sensibility. So there are cross-currents here that are very interesting.

The other thing from the Oriental background is the basic idea of yin-yang which was assimilated by Confucian tradition historically from the Taoist tradition. This idea plays a very real role constitutively in *Divine Principle*. Yin-yang or yang-yin is understood sexually from the very beginning. One way in which it is explicated is in terms of the contrast between male and female. The yang, or positive principle, is the male principle and the yin, or recessive or passive principle, is the female. This is worked out in a lot of different ways. Sometimes yin-yang is also expressed in terms of positive and negative without sexual reference. But nevertheless feminists have in the very roots of the Unification conceptual idiom something to struggle with. I wouldn't for a moment say it can't be overcome, but it does anchor very deeply a way of thinking of the feminine according to certain stereotypes. And that allies easily with Confucian hierarchical relationality and with biblical patriarchy. This is what I mean by the double-bind. I wish you well.

Jane Flinn: I was very impressed yesterday with some of the presentations. Especially Hugh and Nora Spurgin were showing us a sort of developmental attitude towards what was going on in the family, the sense that, "Here is where we are today, and maybe the next generation will be somewhere else." So I would like to relate that to this question. Are you thinking of the ideal of the traditional American family, the ideal of the traditional Oriental family or some other ideal that perhaps hasn't appeared? And, if the third, have you experimented with anything in your own family to help produce a generation that might be a little less constricted, a generation in which the girls wouldn't be the only ones who were compassionate and able to feel and the boys the only ones who could be president.

Nora Spurgin: You asked a lot of questions in there. I have been doing a lot of thinking about this personally. I don't want you to think that I am representing the church. Concerning the Principle and the concept of the yin-yang, I tend to think of masculinity and feminity as being names that have been given to certain kinds of energy. Masculinity is the kind of energy that is very focused, very pointed and very initiating energy. Femininity is the name given to energy that is more encompassing, more nurturing and those kinds of things. I feel that within each man and woman there are both of those energy forms. I also think that different people have different amounts of different qualities. And then I feel that as a couple within the church we work this out and there isn't a specific image imposed upon us. Personally my experience has not been a negative one in the church although there are occasions—recently my secretary was taken away from me—in which I have thought, "I wonder if I had been a man, if they would have done that?" (laughter) However in general I haven't had bad experiences. I feel that I have had a lot of freedom to develop. Basically I am not opposed to a domestic role although I would also like to do a lot of other things. I can be happy in a lot of different areas. Yet I never really have had the opportunity in the church to be very domestic. Usually I'm called upon to do other things.

Patricia Zulkosky: But aren't those other kinds of things things which feed into the traditional roles of women?

Nora Spurgin: I think they are, but I would say that I want to be a nurturing kind of person. I am not unhappy with that kind of role. But you know I have had many opportunities to speak, to study, and I haven't felt I was hindered because I am a woman. I know that there are some women who are more unhappy than I am. And I think that part of their unhappiness may arise out of the hierarchical interests which stem from the Oriental attitudes. My personal feeling is that Rev. Moon doesn't say this is the ideal and superimpose that on us in terms of our working relationships. Rather he throws people together, all the cultures, men, women everything, and lets us work it out. And out of that will arise whatever makes people happy and fulfilled—it seems to me that is what we will end up with. I can't believe that half the human race will ultimately be unhappy for the rest of eternity. I just don't believe it. That's my philosophy.

Lorine Getz: It seems to me that one of the problems is that *Divine Principle* itself does not provide many models for women. The models in the text are mainly male models. And so the question requires some kind of inventiveness. When we discussed it the other night and we talked about whether there is a good female model, I stated that a Lord of the Second Advent who is a male model like Jesus is no help. The rejoinder was, "Oh! but the Lord of the Second Advent is assumed to be a couple." If this is true, what is the identity for the other half of the couple? I mean where is the woman's theological model? That seems to me a real problem that still needs to be explored.

Jonathan Wells: I still have a brief theological point to make following Durwood's comment. Despite the patriarchal inheritance and the Confucian inheritance, I want to point out that *Divine Principle* is distinct from them and it has some quite novel elements to it. I will mention two of them. First, it is clear in *Divine Principle* and *Unification*

*Thought** that masculinity and femininity are secondary to a person's faith and character. Second, in this relational mode that we are talking about, subject and object positions and masculine and feminine positions can be interchanged, and often are interchanged. That is, once a subject-object relationship is established, in the language of *Divine Principle* it begins to "revolve," and there is no relationship that is static in the sense of one position always being subordinate to the other position.

Jaime Sheeran: From the position of being in leadership for a couple of years, it is interesting that, as I look back, I feel the strongest opposition I have had has come from women. I don't know what the motivation is or why, but there is a lack of confidence among women that a woman can actually do leadership things successfully.

Diana Muxworthy: My concern with the most extreme type of feminist critique is that it begins and ends with resentment. There is so much resentment there that it is very hard to come to an ideal. I think that the Unification Church is trying to struggle with this issue of historical resentment. It is interesting that Rev. Moon proclaimed the Day of Victory over Resentment. In the meeting with some of the other women last night Nora mentioned that it will be interesting to see if we will ever have a Day of Victory over the Resentment of Women. Beyond that is the very fundamental issue that when women get together this issue of resentment has to be dealt with. And then from there move on to an ideal image of what men and women can be. I hope that Rev. Moon can do something about this, and we can help him.

Herbert Richardson: I want to make three kinds of comments. The first one is on the general feminist point. As I view the feminist movement at the present time, I find it is absolutely divided on the following questions: should women have a special place and special tasks or should everybody have the same tasks? It is absolutely divided on this question. Is there a separate kind of identity for women or are women basically like men, that is, as persons? I think about the difference, for example, between Penelope Washburn who goes about talking about the bodily differences between men and women (women can have babies, etc.) and Elizabeth Clark who thinks women are persons and that bodily differences are about as accidental as you can get.

In terms of job placement I can give a couple of examples. We

Unification Thought (New York, N.Y.: Unification Thought Institute, 1978).

have all seen how women getting into all kinds of jobs has set the stage for men getting into jobs traditionally reserved for women. Now we have men telephone operators, men stewards on airplanes. It is a question whether women are better off or not from that perspective—this practical question is being debated at the present time.

And the third point is the question of hierarchy. An attack on hierarchy can become an attack on the family, and if the family breaks down, are women advantaged or disadvantaged? That is a practical question. The feminist movement is divided on that point too. To come at the Moonies as if they should be on one side or the other seems to me to be unfair to them. The feminist movement hasn't made up its own mind yet. I don't suppose any of us here could agree among ourselves what the position of women is.

On the question of women generally in the Unification Church, I am always amazed at our failure to talk about the real issues. We talk about yin and yang in the Godhead. (By the way yin-yang is not the fundamental character of God. The fundamental character of God is a person who possesses both masculine and feminine characteristics. Unification theology is not dualistic in this way.) What is really significant are things like the way the church organizes the relationship between men and women. Is it good to have both men and women active in the whole range of activities? Is it good to postpone sexual involvement and throw men and women together to live in a non-sexual way as brothers and sisters? What does that do to women? Is it good to select marriage partners or not to select marriage partners? Is it good or bad to put the very very strong stress upon fatherhood that the Unification Church does to try to make it coequal with motherhood. Are these things good or bad? These are very significant things that we can observe in the Unification Church. They seem to me to be much more important for judging its relation to the women's movement than speculating about a masculine-feminine concept of God or the Lord of the Second Advent being a couple. How one moves from those high level symbols into something that is going to affect behavior is always a big problem. But if you look at what people are doing that is different then we can ask things like this. I would argue with my friend Elizabeth Clark who says all this kind of yin-yang stuff in God is just more patriarchy. I don't think that that is the point. The point lies in such things as the way marriage is delayed and in the selection of marriage partners. In a society where traditionally men have selected their own marriage partners and women have had to make themselves attractive to men so that they would get selected, it is a tremendous advance for the situation of women to have a third party select and match. Women are in this fundamental aspect of life made equal to men. As to the decision of whether you will or won't accept the match, the grapevine tells me that many more women turn down the proposed person than men. That is very, very interesting.

I want to touch one final thing here. If we want to talk about the problem of women and why there is so much despising of women in our society, we have to get at the root of that. And I suggest that the root of many of the masculine attitudes of hatred towards women is their sense of being dominated and ruled by their mothers. There is resentment against mothers. Why is there resentment against mothers and what have we done to clear that up? Why I hate my wife in those moments of temper outburst that come up is clearly related to certain problems that I had with my mother. I don't think I am at all unusual at this point especially among a bunch of theologians. We male theologians are theologians because we are trying to please our mothers. That is why we became theologians. (laughter) There is plenty of empirical evidence for that: we were good boys pleasing mothers that wanted us to be good boys. That is partly why there is so much patriarchy in the church, because there is so much good-boyism among the male theologians satisfying dominating mothers. The resentment comes out in all kinds of ways.

Now as a practical kind of move into the problem, then, we could ask this: within the Unification Church is there some kind of alleviation of the problem of patriarchy, is there some kind of way of coming to terms with forms of motherhood that generate resentment against women? And my belief is that there is, because partly my belief is that the understanding of parenthood is basically a form of give and take between a husband and wife together. One of the critical points is that the children are wanted. One of the special things about *Divine Principle* is that you really want your children. This is going to fundamentally transform the attitudes of men towards women, because it is going to transform the attitudes of men towards their mothers. But I don't think there can be any discussion of the role of women in the Unification Church until we really face up to some of the origins of resentment in men against women. One can't do that without talking about mothers and family structures.

Nora Spurgin: This reminded me that I didn't answer Jane's question.

I would like to say that one of the patterns in the church has to do with the possibility of having nursery care for our children at times and also having a kind of an extended family feeling. The intensity of the relationship between mother and child, father and child is a bond of unity which is very strong. But in terms of education all is not focused on the parents and I find that very healthy. Sometimes I am relieved just to see other people handling my children. I am happy that my kids are having an experience that is apart from the intense emotional relationship they have with their parents. There is something that goes on between parents and children that sometimes is very unhealthy. A person who comes in from the outside and who doesn't have that intense emotional relationship with them treats them in a much more objective, matter-of-fact way. I am glad that my kids have this experience. I also want them to have experience with me but I am happy that they aren't limited to that give and take. The same thing is true with Hugh. They have his fathering, but then there are other men around that play a role with our children as models and people who give them something.

Myrtle Langley: This is a very brief comment following up Herb's. From the anthropological side, we need to consider not only the child-mother relationship but also the male-female relationship when it comes to childbearing and childraising.

Fundraising

Stephen Post
Esteban Galvan

Steve Post: Most of our guests here have questions concerning fundraising methods used in the Unification Church. Indeed, a number of you mentioned specific concerns prior to this meeting which I hope to address.

Before beginning, I want to state that my comments are derived from my own experiences in the church, and are mostly ad lib. They do not represent any universal view, i.e., one held by every member of the church, but they do correspond to my personal reminiscences. And finally, Esteban Galvan, formerly in charge of several fundraising teams before coming to Barrytown, will provide a more concrete description of fundraising lifestyle than I, with limited experience, could do. I estimate that I spent about one and a half years fundraising in the church, and this time was spread out over approximately three years. In general, I intend to provide what we, as members of the church, see as the theological justification for our obviously intense efforts.

The Principle is not a theology which denies the value of the material things of this world. We all heard Pat Zulkosky's careful and lucid presentation on the "three blessings" which are the core of the *Divine Principle* notion of human fulfillment, i.e., (1) to be fruitful, entailing individual perfection, (2) to multiply, entailing the nurturing of a family, and (3) to take dominion over the things of creation. By "dominion," we mean that our relationship with the things of creation should reflect the same attitude of love that God has toward the created order. Indeed, we teach that man is the connecting link between God and the things of creation. Thus, if a man or woman is one with God's heart, then he or she will use the material of creation in a way which is both responsible and condoned by God. Moreover, the proper use of the created order is a necessary qualification of the life of complete restoration. We teach, for example, that Jesus, who came not to die, but to create God's kingdom, would have established a family and restored man's relations to creation—thus fulfilling the second and third blessings—had he not been betrayed.

Sometimes people who take a purely external perspective on the church misunderstand our spiritual motivation for fundraising. In 1925 a book came out entitled *The Man Nobody Knows*. The twenties was an era of fundamentalisms, and this author suggested that if Jesus had been alive in 1924, he would be the president of an advertising agency. Well, on occasion, external observers think of Rev. Moon as a businessman-capitalist fulfilling the role of *The Man Nobody Knows*. All I can say is that this is a reduced perspective, and an unfortunate one. It is my view that Rev. Moon sees himself as a spiritual leader, and that his ministry in Korea in the early years testifies to his incredible piety. He has often said that the only reason he has allowed his living in a rather large house in New York is because people expect him to take care of his guests. But let me now continue to give my own internal perspective on Rev. Moon's relationship to the things of creation. I will try to limit my comments to personal experiences I have had over the last six years.

I can recall one time in 1974 when Rev. Moon came to Philadelphia. At the time, I had just joined the group of church members living in the local center. Rev. Moon and his party stopped by for a night. I remember Mrs. Moon washing Rev. Moon's shirt by hand in the kitchen sink—with great care, I might add—and hanging it on the line outside for him to wear in the morning. Indeed, although he had been traveling for some time, Rev. Moon was not carrying much extra clothing—just the bare minimum—and he and his wife were taking great care to treat something so simple as a shirt with tremendous respect. This account is significant because it shows me that Rev. Moon feels a responsibility to God which is displayed in his love for the things of creation. He is a caretaker. This is an ideal which we Unificationists hold up as central to a restored society.

I can recall stories about fundraising to help buy the Barrytown seminary. I was not involved in this, because it was just before my joining the church. But I heard many stories about the members all over the country joining together in a common cause. The huge acreage was not being bought for a selfish cause. It was not being bought for the personal use of Rev. Moon. Rather, it was bought for the use of the church in its effort to establish an ideal society founded on the three blessings. Some people cannot understand the power of a shared common cause which has no selfish motivational factors. Let me say that I was at Barrytown after it was bought, and I saw Rev. and Mrs. Moon *crying* in their public prayer while surrounded by fifty or so New York Church members as they were dedicating the land and the buildings to God and America. Again, our detractors may say that the spiritual teaching behind the use of material goods in the church is a farce—a front—but my personal experience is that it is very legitimate and real.

I can give a lot of similar anecdotes, but the point is already clear. Whether we are speaking of the dedication of the New Yorker Hotel, land in Westchester County, a new center in Boston, a new fishing boat, a new Chevy van, etc., it is always the same. Rev. Moon prays deeply, sometimes even with tears of gratitude to God, and asks God to accept the acquisition of created goods as one more step in the establishment of an ideal society based on the ideal of Christ-like families. It is my strong hunch that anyone who witnesses our church's use of material goods comes away thinking that there is something different—something out of the ordinary. There is—it relates to our understanding of restoration and thus, ultimately, to the heart of God.

You see, we teach that as a result of the fall, mankind lost the Christ-like relationship with God which everyone was intended to have. Moreover, love in the family, for instance, conjugal love, was misused because the original participants in that relationship were cut off from union with God. We have a notion of growth similar to that of the Eastern Orthodox Church, e.g., Irenaeus's three stages of growth toward maturation approximate the idea of *Divine Principle*. Conjugal love without piety and God is not meaningful to us. Because of the fall, such love was based on selfishness and sensuality, not on God. Thus, love within the family has been inadequate. Furthermore, our use of the created order has been centered not on the love of God but on greed. In a sense, then, restoration of the three blessings is the crucial metaphor which organizes Unification society, following the Augustinian notion of rightly ordered loves. God-centered use of creation is absolutely requisite for the restoration of the natural order originally intended by God.

Some of you have asked me about the church's motivation for "catering to intellectuals," and have suggested that this is an abuse of money. Well, this is an accusation which is commonly made and it is the result of a purely external point of view. First of all, when we have these conferences, our members know about them through our church newspapers, etc., and they feel that this is probably the best use of funds. Recall, if you will, the reference I made earlier to the spirit of a common cause which motivated our effort to raise money for Barrytown. Well, this is the same spirit which permeates all that we do. Every project is undertaken with prayer and sincerity, and our fundraisers, as well as myself, see this conference as a part of our ministry. We are catering to God and a cultural millennium about which we dream, and that is all the catering we ever have done.

I hope that I have provided you all with some notion of the theological justification of our use of money in the church, and the pietism which lies behind it. In a sense, my remarks have been more formal, and I hope that Esteban will provide us with more of a concrete perspective on daily life on the mobile fundraising teams (MFTs).

Esteban Galvan: I have fundraised a great deal since I joined this church. I was on MFT for four years before I came to the seminary. I fundraised for one year, was a captain for two-and-a-half years, was an assistant commander for half a year, and the commander of an education team for one year. Sometimes I held two positions at the same time.

First of all, I want to give you the feeling of what it might be like on a fundraising team. Surely some of you have been approached by a fundraiser? I am going to pray the way a fundraiser might pray to begin a typical day of fundraising.

> Most Heavenly Father, I pray that today, Heavenly Father, when I go out, I can really care, have a heart for these people. Heavenly Father, I pray I can really understand the providence here in America, what it means, Heavenly Father, for America, that so many of her values are so far away from you, and the people have too little care for each other. When I go out fundraising, I pray that I can have respect for this money, and for the people who worked so hard to

donate this money. I pray that I can respect, and really understand these people. Heavenly Father, I know that money can even be taken away from Satan, and used for a heavenly purpose. I pray that I can have an attitude, so that even when I get persecuted, and rejected, Heavenly Father, I can really understand, and have the heart of acceptance of these people, and then the next time, this person will probably donate to another fundraiser who comes along and I pray, Heavenly Father, that I can keep a good heart, have the heart of your son, Jesus Christ, the same kind of heart that he had. When he came, he lived and he sacrificed for this entire country, this world. I pray that we can unite all people whether they are poor people or rich people. I confess, Heavenly Father, in my heart, that many times when I go into rich communities and rich suburbs, it is really difficult. I want to have a better heart, and confidence. I pray that you can work with my captain so he can find a good area. I want to unite with him so that you can speak through him to me. I pray all this in the beloved name of our True Parents. Amen.

Hugh Spurgin: That was authentic.

Esteban Galvan: Yes, something happened to me on MFT. I will never forget MFT. It definitely changed me. The prayer wasn't planned; it wasn't written down.

Anyone who is on MFT changes. A lot of fallen nature is removed. Many people overcome selfishness, a low self-esteem, lack of confidence, lack of religious faith, and a lack of experience of God.

I want to share with you a passage taken from one of our church's books: it is called *The Way of Tradition.*

> Even in impossible situations, Father always . . . has room to plan, and room to think about the future. That same trait is absolutely needed in you. If anybody is sitting behind a desk trying to figure out how to save America, that will not work . . . . You have to be out there breathing with them in order to know the situation. *

The Way of Tradition (New York: Holy Spirit Association for the Unification of World Christianity, 1977), pp. 48, 49.

A team consists of eight to ten people. A region may have four or five teams; and the region may cover two states and center on one large city.

In the morning it is very important to wake up with a good attitude and start off the day with a good prayer. It is very helpful to jump up as soon as it is time to get up and have a positive attitude. Everyone shares in the responsibilities of getting ready, cooking breakfast, and cleaning the van. In order to understand what we go through in this part of our movement, I've been trying to give you the feeling of a fundraiser. (laughter) There is no room for Clark Gables; that is, people who are nonchalant about everything. You have to have a lot of zeal, a lot of spirit, or you cannot get everything done.

Before leaving for the area, the captain will meet with everyone to see how they all are. Each team usually also has a team mother. That means that we have two people who represent the masculine and feminine aspects of God, Adam and Eve, true parents, supporting the team. Both should know the spiritual condition of the members. The teams usually consist of both brothers and sisters. We'll sing some songs before we set out. We have holy songs like "Beautiful Morning Sunrise" that express a high spirit. Depending on the team that you are on, you might get into John Denver songs, patriotic songs like "God Bless America," the fighting spirit of "Rockie," and/or sing Christian hymns. We sing all different kinds of spirit-filled songs to make God the center of the team.

While I was in the van, I would keep a "centered" attitude. That means that I would do something to contribute to the atmosphere in the van. The MFT members keep a high spirit so that they can continue to work hard. The reason for that intense dedication is that we want to try to alleviate the suffering of God's heart, saying to God, "God, although mankind has failed you for six thousand years, I am going to promise you that you can trust me to do the best I can, one hundred percent effort today." It grows on you, after a while; you start thinking that way. You develop a close relationship with everyone on the team and communicate in prayer and love each other.

Then we go out into the area. The policy expressed from church headquarters is that we get permission in the area. When I joined the MFT in '74, we were not getting permission. We were being led by the spirit. (laughter) It was exciting. I might be dropped off in a city to fundraise for the day, and I might not know where I was. I would get left in a city and I'd go off somewhere on the sidewalk and pray like you just heard.

If I were the captain, I would pull up to an area and I might say, "Who wants to go here?" I would expect mixed reactions. I'll tell you why. Because the experience of MFT fundraising is challenging, spiritually and physically. There is always much persecution and not everyone has the same motivation in fundraising.

I always did my best by setting a goal. There are two kinds of goals that I would set. There is the spiritual goal and the physical goal. For example, my spiritual goal might be this, "Heavenly Father, I want to love these people. You know that I have a difficult time accepting persecution and having a forgiving heart. So I pray to overcome that problem." An external goal might be, "Heavenly Father, today I pledge two hundred dollars for you." That would be my mind-set for the day: to achieve those goals. Sometimes I would feel that all spirit world heard me when I made my declarations.

When I first came on MFT, I didn't have that kind of conviction. When I heard brothers and sisters pray in unison, it scared me. I had never experienced praying with such conviction and power. During prayer, brothers and sisters would be shedding tears for the people that they were fundraising to. I knew then that my personal quest for a meaningful and religious experience with God had been answered. Until this time my religious background had left me empty. I was to have been ordained a Catholic priest in 1971, but I had never seen a Catholic priest cry with God's heart for an entire city. I really felt that I wanted to have a new kind of determination, a new kind of heart, a new kind of feeling for people. The MFT way of life grew on me after being part of it for four years, but in the beginning I was partially committed and at least open to new experiences of finding love, faith and God.

Believe me, I'm trying to share with you the intensity of a fundraiser's life, so you can appreciate what is going on in one aspect of our movement all across the country. Brothers and sisters are out there fundraising, and it is a life and death matter to them. They never know what they are going to encounter during the day. Many times we find that the Black, hispanic, and the poor white people, whether you are in the ghettos of large cities or in the hollows of West Virginia, all these people are generous and loving. They helped me know myself better. I began to find myself as a missionary. In the early years of MFT, through the excitement and adventure, I experienced that doors were opened to me when I would conscientiously speak to God saying, "Please use me as your instrument of goodness and love."

I had a "memorable" experience with U.S. Steel in Pittsburgh, Pennsylvania. They complained and wrote to church headquarters about it back in 1974. What happened was that I saw this hard hat and I thought why not? So I put it on. (laughter) And I went through the whole place, and the results were fantastic. (laughter) I was caught, scolded and corrected. After repenting, I then went to a bar across the street from the factory to fundraise, and one of the foremen who had been instrumental in kicking me out donated twenty dollars, because he believed in our cause. Anyway, further down the street—you see I didn't know U.S. Steel was such a large organization—I fundraised in the U.S. Steel cafeteria (laughter). What began with a good intention became a mischievous event in my life as a fundraiser.

Also, in the beginning, to gain spiritual power, I would do forty-hour conditions, and forty-day conditions. Forty is symbolic separation from Satan. The number forty comes from the forty-day fasts of Jesus, John the Baptist and Moses. I still try to get spiritual energy by connecting my daily life with the lives of providentially significant figures committed to God. So I might do a forty-hour condition and stay out all night fundraising. But the condition aspect became too external for me; it became like a gimmick. I was learning that the heart was more significant. Having the right motivation was more important. I felt it was more important to have a good relationship with my captain. I wanted our relationship to be something that could be sanctioned, that could be blessed by God. I experienced my first joy of unity with a central figure while on the MFT. This came after much struggle and testing on both sides.

Later, when I was a fundraising captain (team leader) myself, I also learned and saw many things. I saw that a captain could make or break a person on the team. The people on the team are very influenced by the leadership of their captain. In many ways the captain is a key person to the team's experience of God and success in fundraising. In the beginning, to be very strong with the members was an effective method and brought results. Like some other captains in the early days of MFT life, I found myself telling them to grow, out of my good intentions, but also my ignorance. I judged them more than I loved them. I would also tell them that they had to unite with me. I began by not giving enough of God's heart to my brothers and sisters. But I was at least *learning* the heart of a father—I was learning to see the good points of my brothers and sisters before noticing their fallen natures. By growing in this direction, I eventually had many victories in my interpersonal relationships and financial goals.

A commander is responsible for eight to ten captains. He is the one who trains the captains. There is no uniformity about our styles of leadership. One thing that is uniform, however, is the desire to alleviate God's suffering, to love brothers and sisters, and to bring results, internally as well as financially. We have a lot of room for improvement, because I know some people have left our movement due to bad experiences with leadership while fundraising. Our movement is young and many of our captains are very young and lack the experience of understanding people and creating a family feeling, the conscientious application of vision according to *Divine Principle*. I am grateful to God for giving me so many lessons while on MFT.

I experienced being alone many times on the MFT. I was finding God in a new way. Many times while I was fundraising I would read from the works of Rev. Sun Myung Moon, Richard Wurmbrand, and Og Mandino. I would relate to these people who had personally experienced persecution and forgiveness like Jesus did. I've experienced personal confidence in God's love for rich and middle-class people as well as the poor people. I have passed through three levels: first believing I knew about love; secondly, understanding that I didn't know enough about how to love; and finally, feeling that I could love anybody at the end of my MFT experience. I came away from the MFT with a strong sense of personal worth. Through a hard life of shared sacrifice, I really came to feel that all people are like my flesh and blood brothers and sisters.

Discussion

Mary Carman Rose: I am sympathetic with everything you have said, but nothing in my background, nothing in my professional work, has prepared me for this understanding. I have gone off on my own tangent to find the truth that you have expressed, and I'm with you one hundred percent.

Thomas McGowan: I wonder if Esteban could just amplify one thing that bothered me a little bit. It was in your prayer when you said that you could take this money away from Satan. What did you mean by that?

Esteban Galvan: Since the fall of man, money isn't always serving its rightful purpose. Money we receive by fundraising is sometimes being used for things that hurt people. So Satan advocates the misuse of money.

Thomas McGowan: I mean, poor people have worked hard, and they are donating money, right? But you are talking about prostitution and gambling.

Esteban Galvan: Sometimes prostitutes and gamblers donate, too. On poverty—my background is that of a migrant worker and I have had to ask myself, what am I doing taking money from poor people? My father was working and only getting forty dollars in two weeks to raise a family of eight children. Therefore I really had to search and know that the money we solicited would be used for a good purpose. I'm not saying that people like my father have a satanic purpose in mind for their money. Still, people are giving me the position to use the money they donate for a purpose of building God's kingdom. It is not a black and white thing. Many times when a poor or *rich* person gave me a donation I have cried afterwards, because I realized how hard they had to work for their money. I feel the sweat and tears behind that dollar, and that money means a lot to them. Also I'm understanding God's spirit that inspires people to give to a religious cause. I know I cannot fundraise on my own powers.

Richard Quebedeaux: The widow's mite.

Rod Sawatsky: I can understand the motivation if you know where it is going, then you can say that person has really donated. But it is only you who knows that. You don't spend time explaining to those who give how the money will be used. How often don't those of us who give money say, "I'm going to give this dollar to get this person off my back"? There is no great sentiment about it.

Steve Post: I think the problem here is one we are going to get to anyway and it has to do with disclosure. Do people really know who they are giving the donation to? I hear all sorts of stories from around the country. This summer in Illinois, I heard some testimonies from some former members of the church who stated that they rarely identified themselves as Unification Church members. The issue of disclosure is probably the most controversial thing among the accusations that come against the church. I personally never fundraised without an identification badge. I always mention the Unification Church, usually I mention Rev. Moon and I always did well.

Mose Durst: I think there are many people who are not mature and who do many things. It can sound picaresque when you get into a factory without identifying yourself, but I don't think it is proper. Our church has changed in the last six or seven years, but the policy has always been to clearly identify ourselves and to clearly say what the money is for. Unfortunately, in the early days, like my experience in California before Rev. Moon came to America, members were working and throwing money into a pot and then spending it. Then all of a sudden you have a church structure, and you have buses and vans and accountants. Very few of us were trained to deal with the whole process of receiving and spending money in a formal way. Especially with young people in the early days. Somebody would want to start a sandwich company. He made sandwiches, took them down to the local school corner, sold the sandwiches, took the money, brought it home and threw it into the pot, and everybody used whatever they needed. I have been a professor all my life in the church. At one point before my conversion, I was a Marxist and later I wasn't concerned about getting a tax exemption from my donations to others. I just cashed my check, threw it into the pot and whoever needed money could have it. Later on we needed accountants.

David Simpson: The issue of fundraising, where the money comes from, and where the money goes really bothers me the most. So if I haven't said anything heavy yet, I am about to say something now. I think disclosure is very important, and I want to talk about a different kind of disclosure, which we discussed last summer in the Virgin Islands. Someone specifically asked whether there is an accounting of the financial resources of the Unification Church, as there would be for any other organization that has to give an end-of-the-year accounting. And the answer, as I remember it, was that you could get that information from the IRS. It was, quite frankly, a snotty response; and I didn't appreciate it and have been sitting on it for eight months. Now perhaps we can talk about it a little more.

I feel that it has been done to me again in this presentation. I thought we were going to talk about the issue of money and the concerns that the public and people like myself have serious questions about. Instead, what we got was a sort of personal scenario on two things: a theology about fundraising and a kind of personal witnessing to what it does spiritually. Maybe you can tell the rest of us how much money you raise, where it goes, exactly how it is spent, how the individual fundraising that is done by individual persons on MFT relates to the overall financial resources of the church, how that relates to the corporations that are set up. Kurt and I were talking earlier about a corporation that was set up that got into a commercial business and made a lot of money. A lot of the articles that people like myself have read in the press that are critical of the church always focus on questions, and may raise real criticisms about the whole financial empire of the Unification Church. If you want to talk about changing control of the world and getting into the business of competing with big business, then that would be a good straight answer.

I'm not sure that we are getting a straight answer. I don't know that there is a straight answer, but I am now even more uncomfortable than I was before about what seem to be unanswered questions. I am not interested in going to the IRS to get the answer. I want to get the answer from Unification people, and I want to get it as straight as it can be gotten. Somewhere there has got to be a statement which says this corporation made that much and it cost that much to do that, and this piece of land cost this much and what is being done with it. This is where the income is, and this is what the expenses are. I'm sure that it costs a lot of money to do things like this conference. Somewhere there is a tremendous feeling of uneasiness within myself and a lot of other people about that kind of disclosure. I don't even know if you know, but I think somehow we have got to figure out how we can get to the bottom of that. Do you know where the money went that you raised for four years?

Kurt Johnson: Everything that our department has done is based on our savings as individual people and as a cluster. We don't get funding from the national church. It is a cluster of seventy to eighty people pooling their resources like Dr. Durst said and doing our own thing to make our own financial base, the purpose of which is to fund our nonprofit organizations. We have a profit-making corporation that generates money for our non-profit-making corporations. But that is completely different from the concern of the national MFT.

Steve Post: My experience has been that members of the fundraising teams are well informed on what the church is doing as it tries to establish an ideal world. That is really our purpose. I knew that we were having

Science Conferences. I knew that we were funding a seminary. I knew all sorts of things. The word was out that we were getting a World Mission Center (the former New Yorker Hotel) and we fundraised for that. There were some national efforts. I know when Barrytown was being purchased, everybody in the movement made some offering. I think, by and large, our members are very well informed. The newspaper, the *New Hope News* clearly explains most of the general trends within the church, which way the church is going, what it is doing, that sort of thing. There may be an article in the *New Hope News* that we had this conference. So it is not that as a member out there on the street fundraising, you know exactly where every dime and penny is going. But I think that people are generally well informed about what the church is doing.

Esteban Galvan: I can be sympathetic with your question, because there have been times when I clearly knew and times when I didn't know what the church was doing. I have been a captain and I have dealt with the money. I would count the money at the end of the day. I had a team of eight members who maybe at the end of the day would have $800 gross; but the net might be $600 after personal expenses, after gas, after getting a permit, getting our product. I would have to order flowers from Denver. I might have to pay $300 for, say 1500 or 2000 flowers. I might have to pay for somebody who needed shoes, $20 to $40 for a pair of shoes.

But the reason I explained what I did at the beginning, what you called a testimony, is that I wanted you to feel what brothers and sisters on the MFT are experiencing. Fundraising experiences go beyond the realm of intellectual experience, and the level of sacrifice is very deep. One reason why I fundraised was because I saw that I was changing in my attitude, heart, and confidence. I was pleased because I was doing something of my free will and I was at the same time becoming a different person. I was involved with fundraising because I wanted to develop my faith as a Christian.

Before I joined this church, I was, as I mentioned earlier, working in Chicago as a community organizer, trained by Saul Alinsky's organization, working with people's issues. At one point, a source of funding was a large charity organization and we were being paid to organize troubled situations and keep conflict acute. There were conscientious objectors who were receiving as much as twelve thousand dollars a year who were staging demonstrations the effect of which was to keep Black people out of white communities. But for the church I have been fundraising hundreds of dollars for a better purpose because I can really see that this money is used to move towards a better end and more just society than I have experienced in other action groups and causes.

Judith Simpson: How can you say that we are here promoting real dialogue towards truth? You are building barriers to dialogue. My feeling is that I am "out there." I am being put in the ugly world while you are in here with your particular truth. Real give-and-take dialogue will begin when you start talking about your sense of justice and my sense of justice. We have different views, and you are building walls.

Esteban Galvan: Quite honestly, I feel there is some resistance to understanding the good aspect of fundraising. I sense that some people don't appreciate what is going on behind the scenes as far as fundraising is concerned, from my point of view, or how much good is being done.

Richard Quebedeaux: I am going to conclude. For a year and a half I worked as a consultant to an established mainline denominational agency in this country. I found out some things about how the parishioners' money was spent and what the church told people in the pews about how money was spent. In fact, Doubleday offered me a contract to write a book on the issue, but I decided that I had made so many enemies among my evangelical friends through my other books that I didn't want to lose all my liberal friends too. If any of you would like to ask me the same sorts of questions you ask the Moonies about what that group does with its money and what it tells or doesn't tell its people about where the money is, do so. I'll tell you that the local churches are giving less and less money to the national for very good reasons, because the national group doesn't necessarily hold itself accountable to the givers themselves.

I think we are all guilty of some misuse of money—whether it is the United Church of Christ, the Billy Graham Association, the Unification Church, the Catholic Church or the Mormon Church, which is a wealthy church in this country, and I think that we *all* need to confront these things. We do have different ideas about how money should be spent. As a result of Watergate, as a result of the vast amount of money that is going to television evangelists and their ministries, many Americans are concerned. There is very little that riles us up more than money. Yet, I think that what we need to understand is that there are different ways for different people in terms of raising money, in terms of what they use the money for. It is a very complicated issue. We all need to be into the process of wanting to restore the use of money. At least the Unification

Church is stating a way that they hope will enable them to restore the world with money. I think that we can all cite specific examples of ways in which money is not being used properly or is not being raised properly, and we should do that. We should respect each other and each other's opinions. We should also let the Unification Church criticize our churches if they feel that the way that our churches are raising money and using it is wrong.

Life in the Northern California Church

Mose Durst

Richard Quebedeaux: I don't know how appropriate this is—but it must show that I am an evangelical, because I have been reading a lot of Scripture. I want to read a passage before we begin with our discussion of life in the Unification Church in Northern California with Dr. Durst. I would like to read a passage of Scripture that is well known to all of you, and is something we have been talking about, and I think is something that we really need to remind ourselves about as we proceed this evening on a very hot topic. It is from Paul's first letter to the Corinthians, Chapter 13, and I am reading from the Phillips translation:

> If I speak with the eloquence of men and of angels, but have no love, I become no more than blaring brass or crashing cymbal. If I have the gift of foretelling the future and hold in my mind not only all human knowledge but the very secrets of God, and if I also had that absolute faith which can move mountains, but have no love, I amount to nothing at all. If I dispose of all that I possess, yes, even if I give my own body to be burned, but have no love, I achieve precisely nothing.
>
> This love of which I speak is slow to lose patience—it looks for a way of being constructive. It is not possessive: it is neither anxious to impress nor

does it cherish inflated ideas of its own importance.

Love has good manners and does not pursue selfish advantage. It is not touchy. It does not keep account of evil or gloat over the wickedness of other people. On the contrary, it is glad with all good men when truth prevails.

Love knows no limit to its endurance, no end to its trust, no fading of its hope; it can outlast anything. It is, in fact, the one thing that still stands when all else has fallen.

For if there are prophecies they will be fulfilled and done with, if there are "tongues" the need for them will disappear, if there is knowledge it will be swallowed up in truth. For our knowledge is always incomplete and our prophecy is always incomplete, and when the complete comes, that is the end of the incomplete.

When I was a little child I talked and felt and thought like a little child. Now that I am a man my childish speech and feeling and thought have no further significance to me.

At present we are men looking at puzzling reflections in a mirror. The time will come when we shall see reality whole and face to face! At present all I know is a little fraction of the truth, but the time will come when I shall know it fully as God now knows me!

In this life we have three great lasting qualities—faith, hope and love. But the greatest of them is love.

With that, I would like to introduce Dr. Mose Durst who is director of the Unification Church in Northern California. One reason why I really like Dr. Durst and am so much impressed by him is that he is so controversial. If there is something that I don't like in religion it is boredom. And I can tell you that the Unification Church in Northern California is not a boring place at all, nor are the people boring, whatever else you may wish to say about them.

Mose Durst: After hearing the passage from Corinthians, I almost feel that there is nothing more to say...

Essentially, the church in Northern California has sought to embody the Principle in spirit as well as in word. My wife was the pioneer founder of the Oakland Church. She came as a missionary fifteen years ago and was my original inspiration for joining. I suppose they say that when the Jews start converting, it is surely the last days; and when a Jewish Marxist starts converting, it must be not only the last day but the last hour.

Meeting and coming to know the woman who later became my wife had a very powerful effect on me. Her purity, dedication and idealism were very great. She was living things that I had talked about all my life as a professor of literature. It is easy to talk about great ideals, but it is far more moving to actually see a woman struggling to maintain several jobs, working herself to the point of exhaustion, and even contracting tuberculosis as a result, who is still smiling and singing songs of praise to God. That was very moving for me.

Our life in the Northern California church is essentially trying to live as children of God, experiencing a personal relationship with Him in everything we think, feel—in everything we do. So we try to make the experience of God substantial in our lives. In our relationships with people, we endeavor to see every person as a creation of God and to respond to the image of God in each person.

Prayer is virtually the core of our life. Rev. Moon has taught us the idea of prayer as the beginning and end of our life. Flying here I prayed that every place we flew over could be blessed. I prayed for Florida when we touched ground; I prayed for New York when we hit New York. I prayed several times—New York needed several prayers. (laughter) When I sit in a bus or a car or a train, I pray for people who look like they need help. If they don't look like they need it, I pray for them anyway. There is a constant thought of prayer that is a core and guiding basis of our lives. We are constantly aware of establishing a relationship with God while we are focusing on another person. It is like you extend your heart to God and your hands to the world in a very special sense. It is tangible; I taste it when I speak of prayer.

The most inspiring thing for me personally is when I get up and have 5:00 AM prayer with my wife, and we both get on our knees and pray to God. Before we go to bed, we ask God, "Please accept this day; for anything we have done which has been wrong, please forgive us. We pray that we have offered something to you that can comfort you." It is a great and nourishing experience to kneel down with the person I love in the morning and at night to offer that day to God. The Principle or any ideal for us is not reality. Reality is process, change and movement, and the ideals are guides.

Growing up as a Hebrew man, I loved a commentary in the Talmud that teaches that a man of virtue gets up early and prays before the world has a chance to sin. I feel that we claim the world for God by offering to Him the first moment before the day has begun.

We also emphasize study. We study the Bible, we study *Divine Principle* and, whenever we can, we read scholarly works. We draw many of the best students in the country to our movement. I emphasize to people that if they want to understand certain problems they should read the Penguin edition of Matthew, read the *Gnostic Gospels*, or read this or that. I counsel our staff members on how to give people information so that their life of faith can be based on knowledge as well as experience. A life of faith has to come on a foundation of intellectual understanding as well as prayer, emotional experience and acting out the Principle.

Acting out or "actionizing" the Principle is another core of our life. It involves giving in whatever we are doing. We have a motto: "One—actionize, two—actionize, three—actionize, one hundred percent." For me, it is the fulfillment of an existential ideal—to be engaged each moment. If you listen to somebody, listen to them a hundred percent. If you talk, talk a hundred percent. If you are pouring a cup of coffee for somebody, pour it a hundred percent. Whatever you do, do it authentically, with your full being.

I started groups like Project Volunteer and the Creative Community Project in an attempt to apply the wisdom of the world and humanistic psychology (I studied a little with Abraham Maslow) to the depth of *Divine Principle*. I have had experience leading therapy groups at Lewisburg Penitentiary, in pastoral counseling and in the everyday give and take of caring for church members in which I tried to make people feel validated. I purposely chose to teach in an inner-city college because I am concerned about helping students who were beaten by the culture feel valuable. Although I keep to the discipline of literature (somebody asked me what I teach), I try to make people feel valuable. This is also what I teach our members to do. I encourage them to read Maslow and Carl Rogers—to read people who can teach us how to apply the Principle in a practical way. *Divine Principle*, from my point of view, is a framework for value. The Principled person from my point of view, is a value-making person.

Each person can fulfill his own potential, be valuable, become joyful, and draw out value and joy in others. Morality and ethics then come together in an existential convergence in which we are both acting out our personal needs and fulfilling the needs of the other.

We take responsibility directly for our spiritual children. One of the ways in which we seek most to embody the meaning of *Divine Principle* and the meaning of religious life is by trying to take the role of God in relationship to other people. The role of God as we see it is primarily one of heart: caring, serving, giving, loving and healing are the emphases. The purpose of life is to love, and therefore we experience the desire to make good connections with the world. So very much of what Dr. Quebedeaux read is basically what we try to emphasize in "growing" another person. If we meet a person and feel that we have something to offer him and we want to speak to him as God's representative, we have to take on the role of God and serve him or her, care for him, commit our lives to that person. Another motto of ours is "Live or die for our spiritual children." We feel in Northern California that the best way for us to grow individually is to live for someone else.

Rev. Moon spoke at his birthday address yesterday. "Love your enemy," he said. Your enemy may be the person sitting next to you, the person you don't like in the church, the person who treats you badly. If we are truly living a life dedicated to God, then we have to learn to love even our enemies.

I try myself, as the person who is most responsible, to set an example. I witness and visit my home church area several hours a day and have had several spiritual children move into the family. I love being out in the streets, covering Pier 39 to Fisherman's Wharf and around Market and Powell Streets. I claim everything for God in that area. I go to the tops of buildings and look down and I claim the area for God. We get up early on Sundays and go to the Oakland Holy Ground, then to the San Francisco Holy Ground. We claim everything in the Bay Area for God and we pray for the state, we pray for the nation, and we pray for the world.

Whenever I talk to anybody, I feel I have to represent God's heart and God's love. If somebody attends a lecture or seminar or moves into the family, the person who is the spiritual parent tries to live for that person. We seek to learn God's heart by exhibiting God's heart in word and deed for that person. We believe that words themselves have weight and substance and texture and meaning and color and that when you speak a word, you speak your spirit and you speak your heart. When you speak to your spiritual child, a person to whom you give God's love, you have to give it with that spirit. Sometimes your spiritual child has greater wisdom and greater love than you do, and you can receive even more than you gave.

We do not collect members. We seek to find our long lost brothers and sisters. Man has been lost to God. Never think about collecting members. Think about finding brothers and sisters. We seek genuinely to offer God's heart and God's spirit to the person by embracing him and allowing him to embrace us. We allow ourselves to be as vulnerable as we know that he will be if he comes into a deep relationship with God. Vulnerability works in two ways; it makes someone vulnerable when you give love, and it makes you vulnerable when he gives you love. You have to be able to experience both kinds of vulnerability.

We set prayer and fasting conditions for our spiritual children. If someone has a spiritual child, we may set a condition to pray for that person every day at five o'clock in the morning and at midnight. Family members often fast three days or seven days depending upon what they feel they want to do for someone.

The most difficult thing in the world is to build a trusting and loving human being with God's love and trust. The easiest thing is to corrupt multitudes. So it takes a great deal of effort with spiritual conditions to feel that we can take upon ourselves bringing a person to God. The conditions help us to purify ourselves, purify our motivation and our actions, so that the relationship we have with this other person has the deepest base we can create with God and within ourselves. From a psychological point of view, prayer is the ultimate extension of ourselves toward another person. When we set prayer and fasting conditions, we extend the deepest part of our psyche, our soul and our being toward the other. In body and in spirit, we seek to recreate ourselves as we recreate the other. It is a mutual process of recreation to bring someone to God. And when it doesn't work, we feel the pain as much as the other person does.

Also, as God-centered people, we need to establish relationships with other God-centered people. In our relationships with each other, we speak among other things about the need for unity centered on purpose. If our purpose is to love someone, then God can more easily work through unity of love. For example, if I have a spiritual child, everyone will know that I have someone whom I am seeking to bring to God and will pray for him. Someone else has a spiritual child and everyone knows about it and prays for him. We are all seeking in unity to make a base for God to work in the world.

The Oakland family was built first by my wife walking around Lake Merrit all by herself, hardly able to speak English. After a year and a half of faithful effort one sister came. My wife gave everything to her—emotionally, spiritually and even physically (the one room that she was living in). Then she grew with that person so that both together bound in heart and service and love could be God's representatives. Upon that foundation, they could then seek to draw others, and they drew many people eventually.

We are all seeking in unity to make a base for God to work in the world. As I perceive it, Rev. Moon has given us his experience, feeling, and wisdom, so that we can be better than he is. After his sixtieth birthday celebration, he had a meeting in Belvedere that lasted until 3:30 in the morning. He went on and on, giving, pouring out, teaching, loving, serving. He can set a tradition of great value.

I am always inspired by my brothers and sisters who are my heroes and heroines, because I know how much better they are than I am. I see in them great qualities that I have never read about, and I constantly get on my knees and thank God for the purity and the goodness of the human beings with whom I am associated.

We are, in our belief and in my experience, a family based on merit. The people who have the greatest responsibility are the ones who take it. We have got more things to do and more positions of responsibility than you can imagine. We want every person to grow and reach his highest fulfillment and highest ability. We don't motivate people through guilt, but by stimulating their God-nature. We assume that each person has infinite love, infinite creativity, infinite value. This is not just an airy ideal but is meant to be lived, so we encourage every person to take on even the most tremendous responsibility.

Onni and I try to teach our members to see the divine within the other person. If the other person is acting badly, don't dwell on the negativity. Find what is God-like in that person and draw it out. Validate it and emphasize it.

We also emphasize being practical. We are disciplined people in terms of our schedule and what we do. Everything in our life has to be done with accountability in mind.

All California nonprofit corporations like the Creative Community Project, Inc., and Project Volunteer, Inc., have to file financial statements with the IRS and the State Board of Equalization. These are all public records and they are very easy to find. Nobody receives any salary.

The older family members get up at 4:45 and pray together at 5:00. At 5:30 we wake the junior staff, and at 5:45 we wake the other family members, and then we all pray briefly together before morning cleanup. We have a Bible reading at 6:45. People then eat breakfast together and plan their day. Many members in Northern California work at regular jobs, as professors, doctors, engineers and lawyers. We can offer in the morning and the evening all the conditions of a spiritual community, and residents can pursue their careers in a normal way. They come to our community and are able to live spiritually nourishing lives.

We sponsor evening programs three hundred and sixty-five days of the year. A buffet dinner is served at 6:00, at 6:45 there is entertainment, and at 7:15 I give a forty-five minute lecture followed by slides of our projects. We sit down and chat until 9:00, when somebody plays "Happy Trails to You." A bus or van is ready at nine, three hundred and sixty-five days of the year, at every one of our centers, to transport guests to the seminar facility. Seminars are conducted every day of the week, and on weekends: two-day, seven-day, and twenty-one-day seminars.

It is a very organized church. I, personally, am an organized person. Of course, there is a dimension of joyful spontaneity and humor, but to get things done, we have to have a clear purpose and use practical management principles. We take seriously Drucker's idea of management by objectives. We use practical wisdom to solve our problems.

We also take seriously Paul's idea, "Rejoice always, pray constantly..." Naturally, as human beings we experience the whole range of emotions. If hostile critics say stupid things about us, I see red. All I can do is sit down and say, "Glory to heaven, peace on earth. Heavenly Father, please forgive me for my anger."

If you want to be different from the world, you have got to be loving, you have got to be serving, even if you feel miserable. Maybe it is the Jewish mother in me, but I bring people chicken soup myself when they are sick. I try with each person to know their spiritual birthday, to know their needs, to know what clothes they have. If anyone is missing anything, we try to truly serve them in a very real sense.

We emphasize sacrificing for brothers and sisters. The people in the faith do work very hard. Sometimes I worked twenty hours a day in graduate school, and I am sure that many of you as professionals work many hours a day. We can't be arrogant in the Unification Church because we work a lot of hours a day, but we have to serve the people in the faith because they are so actively serving God.

Each day we do some self-evaluation: to what extent have we lived the ideals that we are speaking about? Every night I give a lecture and every weekend attend a seminar. To me, the word is like a prayer when I speak. I could never give the same lecture twice before I came to the Unification Church because I felt, "Well, you have to be unique." Hopefully, I still try to be unique, but the lectures to me have become prayers. When I am listening to the words come out of my mouth, it is just like I am praying. I ask, "To what degree am I the embodiment of these words?" I pray before the lecture, I pray during the lecture, I pray after the lecture. I am listening to the prayer to find out if, in fact, I am living the ideals.

One unique thing that Rev. Moon has offered us and that we use in Northern California is the "trinity" system. A trinity may be anywhere from three people to a hundred people (as it is now in some of our trinities). The trinities provide practical organizational structure. God has blessed us in the last few months, and several hundred people have moved into our Northern California family as core members. We emphasize that the older family members have to be responsible for creating little families within a large family. There are twelve trinity heads, and my wife and I are the directors of those trinity heads. They tell me if anyone is having difficulties, if anybody needs anything, I try to respond immediately. I meet with these trinity heads four or five times a week. We may meet from 11:00 PM to 2:00 AM three or four times a week, just so that we know that everyone is OK and everything is taken care of.

Every trinity head is an advocate for people in the trinity. You talk about consumer advocates. You should hear these "God advocates." They feel allegiance to the people in their trinity. If Ricky wants thirty new cattle for the farm he communicates this to his trinity head. The trinity head says, "Ricky is in my trinity and wants thirty more cattle." Somebody else may say, "Well, wait a second. Virgil wants to regreen the golf course at camp and that is costing ten thousand dollars." "Well, cows are more profitable." We discuss it openly. Everything comes out. There is as much conflict as in any democratic arena, but we try to come to a consensus. We reevaluate each project the week after or two weeks after or three weeks after to see whether it is going well or not. We respect every person's opinion. If members feel that their trinity heads are not representing them well, they can come to other trinity heads or to me directly, and I always have those lines of communication open. I think I am the most approachable person in the Unification Church of California, if not in the world. Everybody can get me. I give out my phone number to anybody, including the hostile people. They can call me any time day or night.

The evening program is important for all of us, whether we have a guest or not. Everybody comes home at 6:00 PM. Our assumption is that the ideal world is already here, at least it is at Bush Street and Hearst Street and Dana Street and Camp K and Boonville. That doesn't mean we are any better than the world, but our assumption is that we should be. I know it is difficult talking to people, talking to strangers; even being nice to somebody can be difficult. People come home, sometimes they are tired, hopefully they are inspired; and when they come home, we embrace them. People are validated, sharing a beautiful meal and the best music available. We make everyone feel that every day. That is the existentialist ideal: we have to recreate our reality every day; we have to greet each other for the first time every time—that is another motto that we live by. We try each day to take that seriously. So when it comes to evening it is a new day. No matter what your day has been like, it is a new day come 6:00 PM.

The weekend seminar has exactly the same purpose as the lifelong dimension of our family. We emphasize three points in the seminar: 1) that God exists, 2) that each person is a child of God, and 3) that by using the Principle we can build a good world, a God-centered world, a heavenly kingdom. A heavenly kingdom for us is a place where people care the most, respect the most and love the most. You may make mistakes. If you have a hard time studying Aquinas and Maimonides, you are still going to have a hard time, but at least your professor will be loving and maybe you can switch courses. Each thing is done with a great deal of care and respect. In a warm and loving family, there is a great deal of love and therefore a great deal of flexibility. In the weekend seminars spiritual parents stay with their guests to represent God for a day and a half so that hopefully the guest will experience a quality of love that he has never experienced before.

The cynical newspaper accounts say, "Why did he go to the bathroom with me?" But at least it is one way of showing that we are really willing to put up with the smelliness and the dirt and the garbage because we have no concepts about this person's value other than that this person is God's child.

The weekend seminar schedule includes three lectures a day, with a discussion after each lecture. We draw out questions. There is also a time for sports. People sleep from 11:00 PM to 7:30 AM—eight and a half hours. The schedule is even more flexible during the week, with meditation time and study hours and hiking and always at least eight hours sleep. If you get a spiritual child, it is wonderful. You go up to the land. It doesn't look too good if you are fasting when your guest is eating, so everybody eats and sleeps. The whole myth of the seminars as heavy indoctrination centers is completely opposite of the truth. The seminar is like ours here in the Bahamas; you are eating and sleeping lots—granted there are hills instead of beaches. It is a vacation for most family members.

The Actionizer program is for graduates of the Camp K twenty-one-day seminar, for those who wish to come into our life. They hear lectures on our theory of education and theory of art, Unification thought, current events, comparative religion (we study Dr. Kim's books), and are exposed to publications put out by the seminary. Our new Actionizers come from different backgrounds and are anxious to go into every area of life. They push the Principle, testing it, pulling it, tugging it, to see how it holds up in real life. People learn to witness, very quickly becoming spiritual parents themselves who are learning how to reflect God's heart and take responsibility.

In capsule form, then, that is both the internal and a little bit of the external of what we do. We try to do what we do well. We have pride in a standard of excellence. Everything that we do we pour ourselves into.

About eight good articles were published on us in the last two weeks, including one carried on page four of the *San Francisco Chronicle*, six columns long. I was on a major T.V. station for a half hour last Friday night. Finally, the media are saying good things. Soon people will be saying good things about us in Northern California. But we do shake people up. We are on every street, on every corner in the Bay Area. People meet us and they are going to see a Moonie smile from now until the end of restoration. Maybe we will have to smile in different ways, but they are going to see us. We are going to be out there. We are going to be singing "You Are My Sunshine" until there is sunshine all over the place. That may cause a certain reaction, and we try to bend over backwards not to offend people or hurt people. People come, they are moved, they confront themselves, they must make a choice for their lives, and that brings about reaction. We hope that it has good effects, but ultimately, each person must choose his own spiritual life. Things fall in many different directions.

Discussion

William Shive: Probably the biggest criticism that comes again and again about the Northern California church particularly is the concept of heavenly deception. We would like to hear anything you might want to say on that.

Mose Durst: "Heavenly deception," as people accuse us of it, means to say or do anything to get a member into the church or to get his money. It is completely contrary to our teaching and practice. The area of difficulty is that several years ago I started the Creative Community Project and Project Volunteer.

I have also done what I think of as a disciplined study on who are the most successful people at religious conversion and why they are successful. One of the groups that is successful is the Mormons, and they don't come up to somebody and say, "Hi, I'm a Mormon. Would you like to move into my church?" What they do according to the Mormon witnessing manual is: Step one, prayerfully select a family with which to get acquainted. Step two, make your own family one that they would want to know. Step three, invite the family to your home. Focus on their interests. Step four, go out together. Do something that they want to do. Step five, tell them that you are a Mormon. There are many religious denominations which emphasize indirect initial witnessing.

We do some of that and we also set up tables each day with signs which say, "Hi! We are the Moonies. You have heard about us, but how much do you know about us?" There are many ways in which we witness.

In indirect witnessing, the point is to listen to somebody, to make a relationship, invite them for coffee, get to know them. Later, invite them to a center. If they eventually come to a one-day seminar, everything clearly says "Unification Church," thanks to Dr. Sontag, God bless his soul. Three years ago Dr. Sontag came up to Boonville. I asked him, "Please help us to make things better. Is there anything we should correct?" He suggested that on the seminar sign-up forms we make it very clear that a person signs up for something involved with the Unification Church.

Here is my experience. A guy is standing at a bus stop. You look at him and he looks like a good guy who doesn't know God. You have four minutes until the bus is going to get there. He has a poetry book in his hand. How can I get to know this person and sincerely seek to give him God's love? I don't want to lay a trip on him. Most people are negative about God. I want to establish a relationship with this guy, so I talk about poetry. If we are both interested in it, I say, "Look, why don't we get together sometime?" I'll meet him for coffee. A week later I'll meet him again. Maybe we'll have lunch together. Then maybe I'll invite him over to our center to meet other people. It is a process. I don't see it as deceptive. The image is, "Well, you didn't say when you first looked at me on the street that you were with Rev. Moon, and that you have an ammunitions factory and make sabre jets that fly around the world." (People have all these strange concepts.) If we talked about God initially, what purpose would it serve? I think it would kill people spiritually.

Over the years, I have set up several groups that I thought would be valuable. I founded the Center for Ethical Management and Planning about five years ago because a number of people in my community are engineers and management consultants. It had nothing to do with the church. Rev. Moon has given us *Divine Principle* and said, "Now go to it." He doesn't call in the morning and say, "How are you doing?" So I created this group and we sponsored a conference on energy, the ethics of energy utilization. The *Daily Cal* called me the day of the conference and said, "Aren't you the director of the Unification Church?" My wife was at that time, so I said, "No, my wife is the director of the church." "Is this conference evangelical?" I said, "No it is not evangelical; it has nothing to do with evangelism. Of course it has to do with ethics, which to me is an essential part of religion." Front page of the next day of the *Daily Cal*, "Is conference evangelical?" It knocked out five of the participants from University of California, Berkeley. Out of the best intentions I would create something because I was inspired to create it, and then, boom, get shot down. People have written letters to my college saying that I am using my position to proselytize. Now, I do go into my office before each class and I close the door and I pray for my students, and if anybody hears me, great, but I certainly don't talk about the Unification Church in my class. All these things build up.

Andy Smith: I was going to ask about heavenly deception because that is the first thing that I usually hear also from people when they find out that I have been to conferences or something like that. The second thing I hear about the recruitment process is the fact that once people are invited to the center they are never left alone. They are never left to be able to be by themselves. Now the way you explain that, is that it is because you are showing love to these people, and you want to be with them all the time, but as it is perceived by some of those people and by outsiders it is because you don't want to give them the chance to think for themselves. In many other religious groups, people are allowed very long periods of time to meditate by themselves, to be alone, to think over what they are doing. Now it was not clear in your presentation whether or not a person really is with somebody all the time, even when they go to the bathroom, as you expressed it, or if in fact they do have some time to meditate. I would just like some information on this.

Mose Durst: In everything other than the initial two days, people have meditation times and study times. That initial two-day experience is an intense and structured experience in which many people have a significant transformation of their minds and their hearts—which, for me, is the conversion experience. If, during that time, anyone wants to be alone, our policy is leave them alone, because the worst thing in the world for our conversion process is to have a negative person. In our seminars right now, we may have two or three hundred people. If one person gets negative and rambunctious, he is going to affect a lot of people. It's easy to leave a person alone; a lot of times that happens. "Don't sit down with me, I just want to go to the hillside for a while." All we do is defer. If somebody really wants to go smoke dope, we will see that they are smoking dope and will say, "Please, the bus is leaving in fifteen minutes, we hope you will be on it." We encourage people not to do anything illegal, immoral and so forth, but the most difficult thing for us is to have a negative person who is causing a disruption. Although there are only three lectures, it is an intense experience. People sit and they talk. They ask questions. They have sports. It is a full day and a half, even with eight hours sleep each day. If a person wants to be alone, we leave them alone. But the seminar is not designed for that. We feel that to give somebody an experience of God is very difficult. It takes much effort to design a seminar where you can create an experience for a person that is truly different from the experiences he has had all his life. If it were easy to bring people into a relationship with God and to transform them, then the whole world would have been transformed a long time ago; it takes a tremendous effort.

Phyllis Lovett: I take it that once they are in Boonville, they have already gone through a certain number of steps. You have already invited them to some of your evening talks. So you have gone through a certain process before you get them there, because people are not going to say, "Yes, I'll go to Boonville for seven or twenty-one days" just at the first meeting. You then take full opportunity of that time in Boonville, because you consider that that might be your only chance.

Mose Durst: Absolutely. But, also, during the middle of the week, everybody works on the farm. If someone hears a lecture then, it is probably only one lecture; and actually people are alone working on the farm and come together for lunch and for dinner, for group meetings and evening entertainment.

Most of the people we get are intellectually probing. They experience a great deal of love and a great deal of care and their eyes may get a little glazed. But as brother Eldridge Cleaver said, "You wonder why the Moonies have glazed eyes? Because they are praying for the fools of the world, and they are crying all the time." We try to give a person a deep experience in a short period of time. Conversion involves being easy, and yet giving a hundred percent. It is like the Zen moment; you pick up a piece of lumber, you know what you are doing. You arrange a flower, you are in there, you are relaxed but you are there. You are playing baseball, but as Ted Williams said, "One of the hardest things in the world is to hit a baseball." So it is both the discipline and the casualness that has to be combined. That is the art of conversion, as far as I understand it.

Thomas McGowan: I have a lot of practical questions. I am not sure if I have time to get to them, but I want to ask one theoretical question which is also theological. You said that you are unity-centered. You don't motivate people out of guilt; rather you draw their attention to their God-centered personality. These are very interesting ideas. But in Unification theology, as I understand it, the Cain/Abel model is important.

The fact that we are fallen people is essential to the theology. I guess my question is this: Are you a Moonie heretic? Or, put another way, do you consider theology important in the conversion experience? I ask this because you seem to be outside the center of Unification theology.

Mose Durst: I think Unification theology is something that we embrace as much as anybody. We teach the Principle, and we don't have any unique principles. It is what is taught anywhere else in the world. In practice, though, it is effective to make people aware that their relationships are based on purpose and value.

It is very easy to confuse people, to say I have something to give you and so you should follow me. Actually I say, "Look, every situation is a value-laden situation and has a great potential for value, and our purpose is to draw this out. Whoever has insight into the value, let it come out. Since I am in a position where I have to initiate, I will tell you what I think about the value in this situation. If you see other things here, please let me know."

It is very similar to when I go into a classroom. When I teach a novel, for example, I have certain things I want to communicate to the students. I don't go in there and say, "Well, what do you want to do today?" I know what I want to communicate; but I am open to the questions, the insights, the information that will come from those students. If they have greater insight than I do, if they have greater perception, which they often do, I'm open to that and then I will change my interpretation and respond differently according to their interpetation. I don't know if that answers your question.

Thomas McGowan: Well, not exactly. Could I take the second part of the puzzle, the God-centered personality? If indeed we are God-centered personalities, why do we need the Unification Church? This is fine humanism, and it is excellent Maslow and so on. But where does the Unification Church come into this? If people are God-centered already, why do they need it?

Mose Durst: Well, Rev. Moon has said that the purpose of the Unification Church is to wither away ultimately, and that this is a process that we are going through to reach a state of maturity. In the process, there are various ways that you can seek to draw out divine nature. We can agree about theology. But the question then is how do you make it real? How do you make people aware that they are loved by God?

Jane Flinn: Early in your talk you mentioned "growing" a spiritual child. I am a little uncomfortable with that phrase. I can hear love. I can hear concern for passing on something that you find valuable. But what happens to the other person's autonomy if you are somehow, as a spiritual parent, perhaps growing something that, like a plant, doesn't have its own volition?

Mose Durst: Remember that I also said that it is a mutual process in which we make ourselves vulnerable? In any relationship you seek to meet in the great dance of life. In the dance, presumably, you have a form that can be pleasing, that can make you more joyful, more creative, more aware and so forth. The growth process is the growth of intellect, of emotion, of will, the growth of heart, all from our point of view centered on love and purpose. It is not just touchy-feely. You know when you close your eyes how you feel when I rub your shoulders and you rub mine. It may feel good, but it may not bring us to a good value place. So growth is a sensitizing of intellect and emotion and will for valuable purposes. But in the process of helping someone else, we have to be as open in our own sensitivity, in our own cognition and in our own volition as the other person. It has got to be a mutual process.

George Exoo: Shortly before I came here, a person who very much loves me and my church in Charleston, when discussing my coming to this conference, said, "You know, George, you are a disarming charmer." Dr. Durst, I find *you* a disarming charmer. I think I have learned some things about effective pastoring from you, because it seems to me that you are a good pastor to a number of people, but in that there may be some problems. I must tell you that I went up to Hearst Street last summer after going to the Virgin Islands, and I was not pleased with what happened up there. One of the things that I observed that bothers me ethically, despite the fact that I think it is very important to minister to people, is that everybody that I questioned on Hearst Street had come into the Unification Church at a point of great vulnerability. Namely, they all seemed to have come in at the point when they arrived in San Francisco without friends, without a job, short of money, etc. They really needed the community which you were offering them. I sense somewhere under your disarming charm there must be a great deal of exploitativeness, pushiness and coerciveness. I sensed pressure up on Hearst Street where I had the hardest time getting out of the door even after I had made my position clear.

Also, in my experience, I almost felt your church was guilty of the classic fallacy, "Everybody is free to choose his faith, but either you choose to go the true way or..." I am not quoting you, but I got the feeling in Oakland that the rest of us who might be Episcopalian or Catholic or whatever have chosen the wrong way even though we are free to choose our faith. That kind of attitude puts a tremendous amount of pressure upon people. If you are at all vulnerable, it is very easy to feel guilt under that kind of circumstance. I don't even know if I have a question. Maybe you can react to my statement. (laughter)

Mose Durst: Well, sorry we didn't get to you at Hearst Street. (laughter)

George Exoo: You have just answered my question. The man understands group dynamics very well and he is a superb manipulator. He is incredible. Part of that can be good and part of it can be dangerous.

Mose Durst: We can look at any situation or look at the quality that a person has and say, "Well, this can be used this way and this can be used that way."

I hope I didn't communicate the idea that we are living truth and other people are not. In fact, I think I emphasized in my talk that often the people that we speak to are better in some ways than we are, and I teach all our members when they go out and speak to people, to listen to them and not to lay a trip on them, because they will probably be better than you are in some ways, know more than you, have more experience than you do.

One of the things we do feel is that responsible people do not abandon their responsibility of offering people a choice. They say "Look, here is something valuable in life. I believe in it, I am living it." Aristotle said that courage is the ability to choose the greater good rather than the lesser. But, you have to exhibit that moral virtue and that courage so that people can make a choice and see what is available to them, can see that there is an alternative to what they have been living. Yes, many people come to San Francisco who have had all kinds of terrible experiences in their lives. We, in one sense, try to set up a situation in which people can choose.

Also, if I could read off the academic honors of our people, the Phi Beta Kappa's and so forth, you would see they are not just dummies that come out there. They see that here is a group of people who are trying to live their ideals, and for many people it is the first time in their lives that they have seen anybody who is trying consistently to live an ideal, and I think it is a good thing. Rev. Moon didn't want to create a new church. He didn't want to start a new sect. He wanted to draw together people based on an ideal. That is our point, trying to draw people together. So all I can say is, yes, we try hard to be successful. If there is something wrong in our purpose, then I stand to be corrected there, and if there is something wrong in the way we act—maybe people put too much pressure on you—then that is something to be corrected. But we want to represent a moral and ethical ideal in a world in which those things are often not taken seriously.

George Exoo: But they may not be in the position to make that free choice if they are extremely vulnerable emotionally.

Mose Durst: Well, my assumption is pretty much that every human being is free to make a choice. Negative parents come to me and they sit down with their child right in front of us and they tell me their child is not free. This is the most disgusting thing that I have ever experienced. Here is their twenty-seven-year-old "child" with a Phi Beta Kappa from the University of Michigan and they are saying, "My boy is not making a free choice by being in this environment." The parents don't believe in God. The parents are not committed to anything. The parents are not trying to bring him to a better place. All they can do is tell this kid that he is somehow moonwashed or something like that. That seems to me the ultimate denigrating remark that one can make to one's own child. I guess I just don't see a problem with freedom.

I do see the problem of choice. People have to make hard choices. We are like a universal Rorschach test: people look at us and they experience where they are. We draw it out, their love, their goodness, their fear, their hate, their bad feeling about peanut butter and jelly, all that stuff comes out—sometimes people open up amazingly quickly. That happens because we stand up clearly for what we believe. This is the irony of people thinking we don't stand up. It is just the opposite.

Don Jones: But surely, even you know the meaning of vulnerability. You have been vulnerable. And you have been less free than you are now.

Mose Durst: Freedom for me is rooted in the concept of value. We are free when we are free to be valuable. For example, when we talk about freedom of the body, presumably that involves a certain health, wholeness and harmony of the body. So you have to know how to nourish yourself properly, to get rest and so forth. If you say, "I'm free to take this poison," well, you can take poison, but then there is no longer any meaning to the concept of a free body.

Don Jones: Yes, but if you are physically sick, you are vulnerable and you are less free to make choices. I mean, you know the meaning of vulnerability. I don't think you are talking seriously.

Steve Post: I would like to say one thing. When I was seventeen, I went to San Francisco for the summer. This was 1969 when many of my friends had gone out to California. You know, the word was out that California was the place to go if you lived in Babylon, Long Island. (laughter) When I got out there I suppose that I was vulnerable because I didn't have more than five dollars in my wallet. I had hitchhiked all the way across the country, and then I lived in the Mission District of San Francisco with my cousin who was a former Green Beret in Vietnam and was living a Bohemian life in that district. When I think about that summer in my life, I realize that if I had met a group like the Unification Church at that time it would have been a positive experience. A lot of my friends' lives were destroyed by contemporary culture. Now I have never been to the Oakland center and I am not going to say too much, but there may be some value you are overlooking in that Unification community.

George Exoo: I grant that there is some value. You know, I recognize the need to minister to the needs of people.

Steve Post: It is a ministry—let us at least begin with that, and then we can discern things, perhaps be critical. But we should understand that it is a ministry. I don't think it is a gimmick.

George Exoo: Let me put it this way: A woman phoned me as a Unitarian to tell me that she didn't want me to come to this conference. When she was giving her arguments, she compared the Unification Church to rapists and to people who beat little old ladies in the street, and I was thinking "Oh, Betty! Here are these nice people, and you have just got it all wrong." She is reacting to a public relations image that has been generated out of Northern California. I hate to see that happen to this woman. Despite the fact that you are heterosexual chauvinists (laughter), I love you and I want to see you succeed. See? And I don't want to see a beautiful open person like this woman in my congregation walking around with the misconception in her head that members of the Unification Church are tantamount to rapists. You have a very serious public-relations problem here, and I hope you take it seriously. Just as I plead for you to deal with the gay community in a sensitive way, I plead with you to deal with this public-relations problem in a sensitive way.

Mose Durst: I hear what you are saying, and it is a problem that we have to work on.

David Simpson: That was exactly the response that we heard in the Virgin Islands. That was after some of us had been involved in a small group discussion where we talked quite frankly about exactly the same issue: the credibility problem that came out of the community in Boonville. Among the articles that I have read and that many other people have read, the most recent thing in the *New York Times Book Review* was written by some people with real credibility. All refer to experiences that people have had in that two-day experience and similar kinds of experiences, and I really do think you are glossing over something very serious.

Frederick Sontag: I wasn't going to say anything; I am a refugee from the theology session. (laughter) As a philosopher who teaches existentialism, I want to offer one little story which adds a note of paradox because I think you are right in what you are saying—there is something different about San Francisco and Oakland and everyone knows it. Instead of making them out as heretics, though, I only want to add one interesting note. I have puzzled through this whole thing myself, as Dr. Durst and Mr. Kim know. All the state and center leaders were sent out to Northern California to go through a training weekend there because Rev. Moon wanted them to see what Northern California was doing. One of the center leaders I know talked to me about this. He looked incredulous and said, "And you know, they are fundamentalist Moonies out there." His comment is very insightful, because, although there is something very different about the Oakland church, at the same time, the zeal for the mission of the restoration and conversion, the whole mission, is there in Oakland. This presents a paradox which is interesting to me.

History of the Unification Church

Neil Albert Salonen

Richard Quebedeaux: This morning we are going to have Mr. Salonen, the President of the Unification Church of America, give a presentation on the history of the church.

Neil Salonen: Good morning. I am happy to join you. I am sorry that I couldn't be with you the entire time. As most of you know, one reason some of us were late is that Thursday was the celebration of Rev. Moon's sixtieth birthday. I guess you have had that explained to you in the last couple of days, but the reason that I bring it up now is because in order to give an adequate history at this point in our movement, a very young movement, we really have to begin with the person of Rev. Moon. I don't think there has ever been a session where we have done this.

I will try to give you significant dates in the development of our movement and our providential understanding of why the movement was expanding like that. From this, I hope to provide a context for you to see current activities in their historical perspective, and therefore have some idea of the way we see the movement in the future.

The first date is 1920, the birth of Rev. Moon, who was born in what is now North Korea. At that time, all Korea was under Japanese occupation, and so he was raised a Christian in an atmosphere where Christianity was persecuted. As such, he had a pretty intense experience.

When he was fifteen or sixteen years old, depending on whether you count the American or the Korean way, on Easter morning, he had the beginning of a series of revelations in which Jesus Christ appeared to him and told him that he was chosen for a mission. Over the next nine years that mission was revealed to him, and he pursued an understanding of how God had been working since the time of the fall of man to bring about the restoration of man to His original ideal. He pursued his understanding of the dispensational missions and responsibilities of what we call the historical families, the families centering on Noah, Abraham, and so on.

That period of revelation, primary revelation, took place from 1935 to 1944. During this time, Rev. Moon studied engineering at a university in Japan. He also was active working in a variety of capacities to help his family. At the end of this period, which was also the end of the war, Korea was divided into North and South. Rev. Moon was in the part that was given to the communists. We believe that he continues to receive revelation, but that it is an outplaying of the basic framework that was developed in this period. We often consider that the *Divine Principle*, in essence, was revealed in this period and that since that time, there has been an elaboration of it or further exposition.

As Rev. Moon studied biblical history, he found that God had been seeking to restore faith, or basically to restore man's relationship with the Word, and that He had been looking for someone who could set up the foundation of faith and substance that we refer to. The first person to successfully do that was Jacob, and therefore, a great deal that happens in our movement is patterned after what we call Jacob's life course. As you know, Jacob spent a period of twenty-one years in Haran after he had stolen back the birthright. Those twenty-one years were broken into three periods of seven, and so we often refer to the twenty-one year course, or the three seven-year periods, as symbolically connecting with the victorious experience of Jacob. On every level, we imagine the successful person is expanding Jacob's course.

Rev. Moon, with that same intention, would have begun a twenty-one-year course at this time if the initial foundation around him could have been set up. It was his desire. It is our belief, that many other groups within the Korean Christian community received revelation to support this mission. It is a very long history. There isn't time to explain it here, but it is our understanding that there were people who could have taken the position of John the Baptist, to testify to Rev. Moon so he could effectively proclaim the Principle during a twenty-one-year course. Had he done that from 1945, it could have been completed as early as 1966. However that was not what happened. Rather than North and South Korea being reunited through free elections as was the original plan, the country has remained divided. Christianity was heavily suppressed in the North. Pyongyang had been known as the city of churches; it was actually the seat of Korean Christianity. But Christianity was heavily suppressed there and Rev. Moon was imprisoned because of his religious teaching. He was imprisoned in a communist prison camp from 1948 until 1950, a period of almost three years. During this time, he was unable to begin his ministry in any significant way. He could neither proclaim the *Divine Principle* nor organize a movement centering on it.

With the beginning of the Korean War in 1950 there was an initial period when the United Nations forces landed, went north and then were swept back. In that initial sweep forward, the prison camp at Hung Nam where Rev. Moon was imprisoned, was liberated. The communist captains were trying to dispose of all the prisoners. He was just about to be executed when the actual liberation came and his life was spared. At that point he and a few followers fled to the southern tip of the peninsula, to Pusan, and there began the Unification Church. Perhaps those of you who have seen our literature have seen the first little cardboard-box house that they built in a refugee camp in Pusan. That was really the first church structure that was erected and the first place where Rev. Moon began to teach the Principle.

Thus, during the period from 1950 to 1954, he was seeking to organize some kind of group, some kind of foundation centering on the mission of Jacob. Jacob had twelve sons who represented the twelve different gates to the new Jerusalem. The twelve sons of Jacob expanded to the twelve tribes centering on Moses, and they would have become the foundation of Israel, the Messianic nation. When Jesus came, he was to unite the twelve tribes, send them out to twelve nations and, in that way, expand the foundation of restoration centering on God's word. However, the tribes of Israel didn't accept Jesus, and therefore, he chose his twelve disciples. Those disciples were spiritual sons, spiritually representing the family of Jacob. Jesus was building his own tribal structure in order to compensate for the lack of support in the tribes of Israel, the nation of Israel, at that time. In the same way, Rev. Moon was seeking to establish a following which would represent the tribe. He needed to make a foundation to restore Adam's family, work through Noah's family and accomplish on the level of Jacob.

He officially began the Unification Church in 1954 in Seoul, Korea, and that is considered the mother church around the world. In this period, he was still seeking to set up the foundation to follow Jacob's course and, most centrally, to restore the position of Adam. When Adam fell, and Cain did not unite with his brother Abel but rejected and killed him, not only Adam himself, but Adam's family, was lost. In restoring the position of Adam, it is necessary first to restore the position of sons. For that reason, Jesus had three chief disciples whose mission was to stand in the same position to him as the sons should have stood in relation to Adam. That would have been the foundation for their restoration.

Between 1954 and 1960, Rev. Moon was seeking to accomplish restoration on the level of Adam's family. In 1960, he was prepared to do that with the establishment of his family. Most of you are a little familiar with his background. His marriage in 1960 came on the foundation of three spiritual sons, the three elders of our church who took that position to him. They and their wives made the foundation for Rev. Moon and his wife to conditionally restore Adam's family. With the establishment in the spiritual, conditional sense of this family, which we call the restoration of the holy marriage Blessing, began a twenty-one-year course which runs from 1960 to 1981.

Everything that has happened from that time until now is within this twenty-one-year period. Therefore, it has what we call providential significance. The entire history of the Unification Church in America falls within this period, and it is seen as part of the outplaying of Rev. Moon's twenty-one-year worldwide ministry.

In preparation for this, Rev. Moon sent the first missionary to Japan in 1958. Actually, Korea did not have a treaty of normalization with Japan at that time, so it was necessary for the missionary to smuggle himself into the country. There were many Koreans living in Japan. During the period of occupation, the Japanese had required all Koreans living in Japan to take Japanese names; that was also done with many Koreans in Korea as well during the Japanese occupation. So, many Koreans of the older generation have two names, a Japanese name and a Korean name. The Japanese were actually seeking to eradicate Korean culture. They were teaching Japanese in the schools, forcing the Koreans to take on new names, etc. The missionary to Japan at that time was Mr. Sang Ik Choi; his Japanese name was Mr. Nishikawa. Mr. Nishikawa smuggled himself into the country and began setting up a foundation on the national level.

We believe that while Rev. Moon was setting up his personal foundation, he was also anticipating the time when that would be expanded to the worldwide level which would be that level that Jesus had not quite reached during his ministry. In 1959, he sent the first missionaries to the United States. Dr. Young Oon Kim came on a fellowship to the University of Oregon at Eugene and, although she came to study and to do some work, she came with the purpose of teaching the Principle. She had lived and studied with Rev. Moon from 1954 until 1959. She had written one English version called *Divine Principle* (she chose the title), which was produced in Korea before she came. Although the quality of printing and even the quality of English was at a minimal level, she brought those things with her. She did a further revision of *Divine Principle*. She typed it herself and ran off copies on a mimeograph machine. She began teaching those who would listen to her.

Perhaps a word or two about her is significant. She had not been raised in a Christian household, but had a conversion to Christianity as a teenager. She went on to become very active in the Methodist Church and in the worldwide ecumenical work of the Methodist Church, attending conferences all over the world. She went to seminary in Japan, and she was teaching at Ewha University, a Methodist-affiliated university in Seoul, at the time that she first heard the teaching of the Principle. She was then in her thirties. She, along with two other professors and a number of students, studied the Principle and decided to join in 1954-55. The reaction from the Christian community there was so intense that she was confronted with the choice of either leaving the university or disaffiliating from the church. She chose to stay with the church and to disaffiliate from the university and give up her position. That particular incident at Ewha University was the source of a lot of the early criticism and of vicious rumors about the church because it was a very ugly incident. The reaction was so intolerant, really following the lines of classic religious intolerance. There was a real effort on the part of the Methodist hierarchy to discredit the early Unification Church movement in any way possible.

Thomas McGowan: What year was that?

Neil Salonen: It was 1955. That was the year that Rev. Moon was in prison for the second time, actually on the trumped-up charge of draft evasion. He was held for three months, but he was released without trial and declared innocent. Christianity is still a minority religion in South Korea, but the Christians have a great deal of influence with the government because of their superior educational system. It was cooperation between the Christians in the government and the Methodist hierarchy that sought to suppress the Unification Church movement at that time and, if possible, eliminate Rev. Moon—"eliminate," meaning imprison him. He was released after three months.

In 1959 then, Miss Kim, as we affectionately call Dr. Young Oon Kim, began her missionary work in Oregon. About the same time, Mr. David Sang Chul Kim also came to the Northwest. He is the same Mr. Kim who is attending this conference and who is currently serving as the president of the Unification Theological Seminary.

Not exactly at the same time, but a few years later, Col. Bo Hi Pak, one of the early members of our church in Korea, who was also a member of the army of the Republic of Korea, came to serve at the embassy in Washington as the assistant military attaché. He was serving not in any way in connection with his church activities but simply because the Washington embassy was his assignment. South Korea and America were at that time closer allies than they are at the present time. Col. Pak felt that it would be possible to make a bridge between various nations and groups through cultural activities. He retired from the military, remained in Washington and formed the Korean Cultural and Freedom Foundation which organized the Little Angels and a dancing troupe called the National Folk Ballet of Korea. They toured around the world under the sponsorship at various times of the United Nations, the Korean government, and others. They have performed throughout the United States. Col. Pak also sought to do evangelical work in the Washington, D.C. area, although often his time was consumed with his other activities.

In 1965 Mr. Sang Ik Choi, who had been the first missionary to Japan, also came to the United States with some of the early members that were converted in Japan. One of those early members is Mrs. Durst, Dr. Durst's wife, who then worked with Mr. Choi in the San Francisco Bay area. She later set up separate activities. So that at one point we had four different independent groups, fraternal but in a sense quite autonomous, like a feudal period before the real national movement was formed. Thus, we had at this time four missionary efforts in the United States, three of them in the Northwest and one in Washington, D.C.

By 1963, Rev. Moon had made several efforts to come to the United States in order to expand the work that was being done in Korea and to connect it to what was happening in America and the rest of the world. We consider it significant that among the first members who joined in the United States in the period between 1959 and 1963 were immigrants to the United States who were still nationals of their European home countries. In 1963 missionaries went to Europe. These included members of the Unification Church who had converted in America and went back to their own countries, pretty much by their own inspiration. We didn't have a major program through which they were officially commissioned and sent. Peter Koch went to Germany and Paul Werner went to Austria. Also one of the first five American members, Doris Walder, went to Italy, even though she didn't speak Italian at that time. From 1963 to 1964 the work was expanding, and finally in 1965, Rev. Moon made his first tour, his first trip outside Korea to the rest of the world.

In 1960, he had set up the foundation to conditionally restore Adam's family, and so in 1960, in addition to his own wedding there was the wedding of three significant couples and they were included in the thirty-six couples. These thirty-six couples represented three sets of twelve couples representing Adam's age, Noah's age and Jacob's age. Strictly speaking, we were trying to restore the innocence of the world before the fall of man. So, twelve of these couples were people who had never had any marital or sexual experience; they were absolutely pure. We refer to them as virgins and bachelors. The second twelve represented the fallen condition of the world, people who had a sexual relationship or a previous marriage, but who were not married at that time. The final twelve represented the moral foundation of the world in the sense of those who were married and who entered the church as a married couple. They had their marriage Blessed by the church. Thus, all possible categories of people were included. So really, the significance of the thirty-six families is twelve, representing the twelve disciples of Jesus, but expanded to thirty-six because of the moral state of the world.

This Blessing took place in 1960. In 1961, there was a Blessing of seventy-two couples. Then in 1963 there was a Blessing of one hundred and twenty-four couples. The significance of these expanded foundations would take a long time to explain, but generally speaking, this thirty-six family group is considered the personal foundation for the mission of Rev.

Moon. Among other things, they were all supposed to be prepared to continue his mission in the event he himself died or could not continue his activities. Thus, they are also considered his personal representatives. Mr. Kim and his family are here; they are included in the thirty-six families. Later today, Col. Pak will arrive; he is also a member of the thirty-six families. The seventy-two families surrounding the thirty-six families roughly correspond to the seventy elders referred to in the Bible. The one hundred and twenty-four families represent the number one hundred and twenty, the expansion of the twelve different gates to enter Jerusalem, really going out into the world. It was Rev. Moon's desire then to expand the foundation of Blessed couples and to restore the Blessing conditionally to the other nations around the world. But, before God created man, He created the environment where man could live, and, therefore, in order symbolically to recreate the environment, the significant work of the first tour was the blessing of holy grounds, one hundred and twenty holy grounds around the world. This is ground which is symbolically dedicated back to God, ground which is conditionally separated from its relationship with the fallen world and is thought of like a seed. Our members attend the holy ground, pray there and seek to become the purified individuals who are entitled to live in a world that is free of sin.

George Exoo: Where are those places in the United States?

Neil Salonen: There is one in every state and since that time, it is also our teaching that members of the Unification Church can expand the holy ground, so if the nearest one is far away from where they are, they can establish a holy ground near them. For example, are you from the San Francisco Bay area?

George Exoo: No. I'm from South Carolina, but I'm very curious where mine is. (laughter)

Neil Salonen: We'll send you a map. We could give a very long talk just on the meaning of the restoration of the holy grounds and even the procedure that was followed, but the significance is that ground was dedicated to God. It is symbolic; it is a condition in advance of the dedication of all the land back to God.

Thomas McGowan: Do you own the real estate?

Neil Salonen: No. In most cases it is public ground. In some cases, very unusual things have happened to the ground. (laughter) Every now and then, you may hear a story of Unification Church members trying to get to a certain ground. It is kind of interesting. There is one spot of ground on the Capitol grounds in Washington, D.C. which is a holy ground. We ourselves wonder how Rev. Moon was ever able to get there to bless the holy ground because it is an off limits area. We are constantly held back from praying there, especially as we are sensitive about public demonstrations. We don't do anything there except pray. We simply go individually or as a group. There is no symbolic ritual or anything like that. We simply consider it a significant place to pray, and to remember the condition that was set. This happened in 1965. Rev. Moon visited for a short period of time in the United States. He visited every state, blessed holy grounds, went on to Europe and continued around the world. That was when one hundred and twenty holy grounds were made.

At this time, he asked Dr. Young Oon Kim to go to England and take responsibility for the mission there. She went to England and began the missionary work. Col. Pak was in Washington and he was given additional responsibility for the work there.

I think I left out one point which is that in 1961, Miss Kim moved her original group of five members from the Northwest down to San Francisco where she incorporated the church in the United States. So the Unification Church of America actually began in the San Francisco Bay area in 1961 under Dr. Young Oon Kim.

In 1966, Miss Kim came back from England and joined together with Col. Pak in Washington, D.C. The National Headquarters of the Unification Church was established in Washington, D.C. at that time. That was the first time that we could be said to have a national movement in any real sense. Up until that time, each group was extremely autonomous with no central direction or good communication.

I, myself, joined in 1967, so the rest of the history I know intimately from my own experience. We were expecting Rev. Moon to come back again and to establish the first Blessed couples in the United States. However, he didn't do that until 1969.

In 1969, Rev. Moon made his second world tour, and at that point the primary reason for the world tour was to extend the marriage Blessing to the faithful members of the Unification Church in the other countries throughout the world. In preparation for this, in 1968, he had the Blessing of 430 couples in Korea. The 430 couples represented the national foundation. They symbolized 4300 years of Korean history and also the 430 years of bondage in Egypt by the Israelites. So this symbolized the blessing of the nationhood into the promised land. We consider that we began the journey through the desert from 1968. Significantly, this was at the end of the first seven-year course that Rev. Moon began in 1960. The end of his first seven-year course was in 1967. With the beginning of 1968, he began the second seven-year course which continued until 1974. During the first seven years, he proclaimed several holidays, and at the end of that time, he proclaimed God's Day on January 1, 1968. We consider God's Day, January 1st, the most sacred day of the year. It is dedicated to God, and it is celebrated on the foundation of the completion of the first seven years of Rev. Moon's twenty-one-year course.

In 1968, he blessed 430 couples in Korea and then he traveled throughout the rest of the world in 1969. He Blessed thirteen couples in the United States. This was amazing to us because he did not appear to be specifically selecting thirteen couples, but it also symbolized the thirteen colonies that began the American nation. In Europe he Blessed eight couples. In Japan he Blessed twenty-two couples, making a total of forty-three couples. Forty-three on the worldwide level is tied symbolically to the 430 on the national level in Korea. At the end of his tour, he returned to Korea and continued the work of the national foundation from 1968 to 1974. It was his interpretation that from 1975 he would come out to the world and seek to establish a worldwide movement. That was his plan when I met him in 1969.

In 1970, he called members from ten different nations who were prepared to be married for the Blessing of 777 couples. He had gone out to the world to give the Blessing to the forty-three couples, symbolically scattering seeds. Seven hundred and seventy-seven couples then represented the harvest coming back to Korea. This Blessing was performed in Korea and the three sevens symbolize the three seven year periods of Jacob or the twenty-one-year course, representing a worldwide foundation. Of the 777 couples, the vast majority were Korean and a very substantial second group were Japanese. The rest were more symbolically included because the movement had not expanded that much. At that time there were seven couples from the United States. The Spurgins were included, and my wife and I. I don't know of anyone else who is here. The Jones were included, and the Edwards.

Thus, from 1970, Rev. Moon was preparing to take his ministry to the worldwide level. In preparation for that he visited the United States again at the end of 1971 and stayed for several months until 1972. When he arrived at the end of 1971, and again at the beginning of 1972, he officially began a three-year period of preparation for his worldwide ministry centering on the United States. Then he came again at the end of 1972 and has remained here fairly consistently since that time. Rev. Moon's ministry and the providence centering on the United States began in 1975.

In 1972, on the celebration of God's Day, Rev. Moon called the first national conference of all members and all leaders of the Unification Church. At that time, he unveiled a plan for pioneering or sending missionaries to every state in the United States which had not been done before that time. Secondly, he selected seventy pioneers who travelled with him and went on a seven-city speaking tour. He hardly spoke English at all at that time, but using two different translators, he traveled to seven cities beginning in New York and sought to proclaim the message of the Principle to the public. At this time, the Religion Editor of the *New York Times* did an interview with Rev. Moon, but didn't publish it because she said he wasn't really newsworthy. Since that time, she has sought several times to have interviews but he now thinks she is no longer interesting. (laughter) At that time he was very, very available and spent time talking to anybody who cared to talk with him. One reason he has made himself a lot less available is not only that he is very busy, but that it didn't pay off enough—also, he has fulfilled his responsibility in this area, and now it is our responsibility to do the talking.

The seven-city tour was quite exciting. We really didn't see how we could do it. We believed at that time that, since he was either a great messianic or pre-messianic figure, the whole spirit world or something would open and a lot of people would come and fill up the halls. Actually that didn't happen. The first couple of talks that he gave were rather poorly attended, and we began to realize that we would have to become capable of moving people, actually persuading them and inspiring them to want to come to listen to his message. This was in 1972. In 1973, he began the twenty-one-city tour starting in New York at Carnegie Hall. The seven-city tour had begun in New York at the Lincoln Center.

Also in 1973, in order to break down cultural barriers, a number of members came from Japan to work together with members from the United States. It was a time of a lot of confusion—language barriers, misunderstandings, the meshing of different value systems—but it was a very exciting time because we all had the same goal, and we literally *had* to work together because we were working together to fill up the halls for

Rev. Moon's tour. Everybody was very faithful to Rev. Moon, everybody wanted the tour to be successful, but we all had very different ideas about the way in which this should be done. In Japan, when you really want to proclaim something, you stand on the street corner with a loudspeaker and really proclaim it. In the United States you can do that but that is not necessarily the way that you persuade people to come. So there are a lot of things that you may have seen our group do that represent a little squirt of Japanese culture, a little squirt of some other culture, all coming together to find an effective way. And we came to appreciate each other a lot. I don't want to make light of it, it was difficult. But it was also wonderful. In my own life this was one of the most difficult periods for me because I had to work together and establish a bond of trust with people. Rev. Moon has said that it is important that representatives of Korea, Japan and the United States become one, one in heart and one in purpose. To do that was not easy; we had to overcome barriers to unity. Our group is dedicated to unification and unity, but we never assumed that comes about by goodwill alone. We realize that it is something that we have to build. So even though we may have some harmony, we expect to feel strong passions of division and to have to deal with them. That is exactly what happens.

The twenty-one-city tour in 1973 was substantially more successful, and it was in this period that a tremendous amount of publicity started to be generated centering on our movement and Rev. Moon. It was also in this period that the movement really began to grow. Until 1972 we had perhaps four hundred members in the United States. By 1973 that number was expanding rapidly. Rev. Moon not only spoke publicly but was hosted at banquets throughout the United States. We received hundreds of proclamations for Rev. Moon Day or Unification Church Day. When we explained ourselves to people face to face, not being reinterpreted by those who might not be in sympathy with our beliefs or not able to understand what we were doing, we got a very good response. What happened as the movement began to grow was that the churches and other organizations began to feel threatened by the rapid growth of the Unification Church. Thus, the period of public criticism of the Unification Church really began.

In 1974 Rev. Moon decided to go to every state that he hadn't yet visited. So we began what we call the thirty-two-city tour which went to the states that he hadn't spoken in on the twenty-one-city tour. Together with a tour later that fall of eight major cities, the work in 1974 included a forty-city tour. These eight major speeches represented the level on which he really intended to speak. Everything before that time was for the purpose of actually training us in public evangelistic work. The eight-city tour began with Madison Square Garden, and we usually consider that the first successful public event. It was on September 18, 1974. Interestingly enough, the Unification Church in America had been founded on September 18, 1961. The date September 18 becomes increasingly significant in our movement. The tour began at Madison Square Garden and expanded. It was extremely successful, and we felt that we ended the second seven-year course from 1968 to 1974 in a very victorious way. We then began Rev. Moon's third and final seven-year course in 1975. This was the end of the Day of Hope tours and represented the fulfillment of national level evangelism.

David Simpson: What does highly successful mean?

Neil Salonen: The places were jam-packed. Literally everywhere the places were jam-packed. At Madison Square Garden one of the doors broke because there was such a crush outside of people trying to get in. Everywhere we went the places were jam-packed. Sometimes there were demonstrators outside who got pushed aside by people trying to get in. It was highly successful by any standard. That is what I mean.

More than that, though, people listened. I had the privilege of being the emcee and introducing Rev. Moon on all those occasions. It was exciting. People listened. He spoke strongly and clearly, and, even though it was through a translator, the people responded. It is not something that could have been packed by our members, because we didn't have that many members. These were people who didn't belong to the Unification Church and had never studied *Divine Principle*, who were responding to the actual message of Rev. Moon, not responding to the image or things that they had heard second or third hand, but responding to what he was actually saying when he spoke for himself.

In 1975, it was his long-stated intention to begin the worldwide ministry centering on the United States. Therefore, he did two things. First he took many of those members who had participated in the Day of Hope tours and formed an International One World Crusade team which conducted activities in Korea and Japan. This year was also the first year that Rev. Moon spoke publicly in his home country of Korea. He spoke in eight cities. Again, there was just phenomenal response. To us this symbolically restored the rejection that Jesus met speaking publicly to his own people.

In 1975 three events took place: one was the IOWC tour and the Day of Hope in Korea, the second was the Blessing of 1800 couples in Korea, and the third was the Yoido rally against communism which was attended by 1.2 million people in Korea. It was the largest rally of its kind that had ever been held and was an opportunity for Rev. Moon to demonstrate his commitment to expose the meaning of the atheistic base of communism and to lead a worldwide religious revitalization in order to confront the challenge of communism.

At the same time, he also sent missionaries to a total of one hundred and twenty countries. Up until that time we had been active in approximately forty countries. But following the Blessing in February, missionaries were trained and three went to every country to which they could possibly be admitted either as missionaries or as individuals in any capacity. One missionary went from the United States, one from Japan, and one from Germany to each country. Those three worked together. No leader was appointed; it was their challenge to somehow find a way to unite and work together. Sometimes they did and sometimes they didn't, but it was their challenge as representatives of those three nations to work together. The missions have been supported by those three nations since that time.

This year, 1980, for the first time, all those missionaries gathered back in New York. Virtually all of them came to the celebration of Rev. Moon's birthday and for a conference to evaluate the success of the last five years' work.

The first worldwide evangelical effort in 1975, which was America's responsibility, was the beginning of the third seven-year course. After the Yoido Rally, Rev. Moon returned to the United States and in 1976 sought to fulfill his reponsibility to proclaim America's responsibility to lead the world in challenging communism and revitalizing its Christian fiber. To do that, we had two God Bless America rallies, one was on June 1st in Yankee Stadium and the second on September 18th at the Washington Monument grounds. Over 300,000 people gathered at the Washington Monument. We consider that rally to be the conclusion of Rev. Moon's public ministry. It was his responsibility to proclaim his message personally to the people of America. Thus beginning in Lincoln Center in 1972 until 1976, he sought to speak personally, even though through a translator, even through periods of criticism, to the people of America. He concluded this responsibility at the Washington Monument rally. Since that time, many people have even thought that Rev. Moon was no longer in the country. We had a prayer meeting in Greenwich Village the other day and one of the news reporters asked me if he would be coming back to the United States, very unaware that he was currently in the United States. Since 1976, the church in America has addressed itself to two things, deepening its roots in the community and attending to the support of the world missions. Those are really the only two things. Of course, that involves a lot, but we no longer have any conditional or providential responsibility like this to fulfill.

Thomas McGowan: Excuse me, Neil, would you consider the Yankee Stadium rally successful?

Neil Salonen: No. I have been to baseball games where they have about a third of the turnout that we had. But for us, the standard of success was overflowing with a turn-away crowd outside.

Thomas McGowan: I was at that one and many people there were neighborhood ruffians.

Neil Salonen: I didn't consider it successful, although my parents went, a lot of my family members went, and they had a wonderful experience. But what we were trying to accomplish was not accomplished. Yankee Stadium represented the second stage, or growth stage. Madison Square Garden was the first significant rally, Yankee Stadium was the second and Washington Monument was the third. The second in the course of three always represents going past the period of crucifixion. So when we have three things to do, we believe that the second thing may be difficult, and it often is. We always believe the third thing will be successful, and so far it always has been. This is not predestination—there is just a tendency.

Since 1977, the church has grown and expanded. I think you have heard a lot about the activities. I have pictures of some of them. After 1981, when Rev. Moon concludes his twenty-one-year course, we believe that each of us personally will begin a twenty-one-year course, and, as such, our movement will grow in even more diverse directions because then it will become the responsibility of the individual members to decide how their lives should be an offering to God and how they can make a twenty-one-year offering centering on faithfulness and on willingness to sacrifice to accomplish substantial achievements. Jacob didn't just go and endure twenty-one years in Haran. He earned his wife, he earned a great deal of goods and he used those things as an offering when he went back to the promised land in order to be accepted. We believe that we must prepare an offering. We teach that everyone must have an offering. So I expect a great deal of diversity in the movement following 1981, not instantaneously, but beginning from that point. I think that those of you who have followed the movement for several years have already begun to see that. We have great tasks in front of us. Some of them are going on in the other conference that is here in the Bahamas where we have a lot to do in terms of hammering out what the movement actually teaches, what it actually stands for. Rev. Moon himself has indicated that following the conclusion of his twenty-one-year course he will devote himself personally to clarification of a lot of points in *Divine Principle*. We treat this year and next year as marking a very sharp turning point in the church, a turning point many members have been expecting since they joined. We don't believe that suddenly things will change, but we think that a lot more responsibility will be put on the shoulders of the individual members. I expect a rush of vitality. A lot of creative talents haven't been used yet.

Discussion

Mary Carman Rose: I am deeply concerned about the assessment of the success of a Unification rally in terms of the numbers of people who attend. The fact that thousands have attended such a rally in no sense guarantees that they derived genuine spiritual benefit from attending. Certainly you'll agree, Neil, that the success of a rally is to be judged primarily in terms of its effects on the individual's commitment to doing the works of love.

Neil Salonen: Yes, indeed Rev. Moon used to say, "If I talk and talk and wave my arms around and the room is full of people then you think it is OK. But if there's only one person sitting there, you would think I am a crazy person. But in reality, what difference does it make?" Also Rev. Moon is like the preacher who says, "I don't preach to the people who do not come to hear me, I preach to those who do."

Andy Smith: In our session on spirituality the other day, Pat explained to us a little about the importance in the movement of the pledge and the pledge service. I wonder if you could maybe recite the pledge for us, and give us a little of the history of the place of the pledge within the movement.

Neil Salonen: Since I don't know what Pat said, you have the advantage of cross-referencing her answer. The pledge is the spiritual responsibility of the Blessed families and it represents their joining together with Rev. Moon in sharing his mission. So they rise every Sunday morning at 5:00 and recite the pledge. That symbolizes their being willing to rise and to go in advance to the world, to sacrifice in sleep, to sacrifice in time. I can give you a copy if you'd like that, but basically it's a pledge of those who have become spiritually united with Rev. Moon in mission. Now the members of the church optionally join to say that. Some may not realize that it is optional. Supposedly some do, because they don't all come. But the fact is that the saying of the pledge is fundamentally centered around the Blessed couples. It really represents the same pledge that Rev. Moon makes to heaven. They are joining him in making that pledge to God.

Andy Smith: When did that start?

Neil Salonen: In this country it started after Rev. Moon's second world tour in 1969. It couldn't have started before because we didn't have Blessed couples before that time. I'm not quite sure, but I think it started in Korea in the middle sixties.

William Shive: What's the present organizational structure in America?

Neil Salonen: Well, we have one big family in America, including the Oakland family. Someone catches the mission and does it according to his or her own creative capability. When I visit the Durst's out in California, it's the same family, the same brothers and sisters. We have a great diversity of members, but we have one organization. We're not as tightly organized as we may appear to be from the outside. Since most of you are not really "outside," I am sure you are beginning to understand that. Rev. Moon has the attitude that if people are sincerely trying to fulfill their responsibility, they need room to do that.

William Shive: I guess accountability is what I'm trying to figure out. What is the line of accountability from any one particular section of the group to the whole?

Neil Salonen: Can you give me an example, say, of an issue? Or would you like me to pick an example?

Thomas McGowan: How about training techniques?

Neil Salonen: In 1975, Rev. Moon set up a training program in Barrytown. He gave a Japanese leader, Mr. Sudo, responsibility for it. The whole movement sent members there, including the family in Northern California and the family in New York. The family in Northern California and the family in New York, for different reasons, both felt, I'm sure, that if they had been running that training program, it wouldn't have been done exactly the same way. But they honored the person who was given the responsibility. So Mr. Sudo trained members in a certain way. There were leaders in New York, there were leaders in California, and leaders of small groups elsewhere that all felt that if they were doing it, they might do it a little differently. But I think they all appreciated the benefits of the way it was done. So we can't all run everything.

William Shive: Well, as president of the church, how are you related to all the parts around the country? Maybe that's the only way to approach the answer.

Neil Salonen: I try to harmonize them.

William Shive: You're not an authority? They don't have to report to you, or be accountable to you?

Neil Salonen: They do report, and legally we do hold the authority. But when Rev. Moon is here, then I feel like I'm operating more as a mediator, or maybe as a channel of communication, between him and the members. So Rev. Moon gives broad direction, kind of philosophical direction. But how we're actually going to do something practically becomes the responsibility of the state organizations for which I'm responsible.

Don Jones: For instance, do you read Jaime's financial report, which she doesn't particularly like to fill out?

Neil Salonen: I don't myself, but my staff does, and Rev. Moon doesn't, for example.

Renée Bakke: You said that those persons who were recently matched will have to wait for the Blessing ceremony until Rev. Moon decides it is the right time for the Blessing. And according to you, this waiting period is based on a revelation concerning the numerical structure of the course of the Unification Church in America and in the world. I don't call that *revelation*; I call it *manipulation*.

Neil Salonen: Are you asking a question?

Renée Bakke: No, I'm giving you what I have to say on the subject.

Neil Salonen: You don't approve of our marriage customs. Is that what you are saying?

Renée Bakke: You can have your marriage customs. I don't believe your basis for planning the time for the Blessing is a revelation. I believe it is a maneuver to bring about a situation in which there will appear to be a numerical structure. Did you get that?

Neil Salonen: Well, I heard it.

Renée Bakke: All right. And I want to comment on something else you said. You also said that Jesus Christ was rejected by his people. Now he was not rejected by all of his people and neither was Rev. Moon. You said that Rev. Moon was later received by his people, but Rev. Moon was not received by all of them, because I know personally the minister of the biggest Christian church in the world which is in Korea. Now I think you'll have to make better statements.

Neil Salonen: I didn't mean to say, and I don't think I did say, that Jesus was completely rejected by his people. He was rejected by the bulk of his people. He was rejected by the leaders of his people. He had to set up his own spiritual foundation. So really, the twelve disciples represented the twelve sons of Jacob, and they were to become like the twelve tribes.

I know very well that Rev. Moon hasn't been completely accepted by his people, in any sense. In fact, the reason that his original twenty-one-year course didn't start in 1945 is largely because of the intolerance of the Christian community in Korea toward any new revelation or message. I would compare that to the leaders of the temple at the time of Jesus. I couldn't think of a more exact parallel. But in 1975, if you count the sum of all the events, over two million people came to hear Rev. Moon speak. And to us that's extremely significant because it represents a level of acceptance of Rev. Moon by his people. That's all I meant to say.

Paul Sharkey: I think that a part of what Mrs. Bakke is reacting to is the way you use what in philosophy we sometimes call "descriptive language." For example, you talk about the timetable of restoration. You need, however, to make it clear in what sense this is a revelation and in what sense by cooperating with that timetable you help to bring about the actualization of the timetable.

Also, is it wise to talk about the "failure" of Jesus' mission? Yes, Jesus was crucified and was widely rejected. But he had and has had since he lived numerous followers. I think, too, that just as a matter of public relations, you need to reflect on how talk of Jesus' failure is going to affect Christians. I don't think you will be successful in the movement, in the

Holy Spirit Association for the Unification of World Christianity, if Christians continue to hear this message that Jesus was not successful.

Neil Salonen: We believe that Jesus' mission was not fully completed and that it has to be completed. We also believe Rev. Moon is either preparing for the completion of his mission or is in the act of doing it himself. That is what we see his position as being. And I know that is not acceptable to those who do not share our faith. But that is the way to understand us.

Paul Sharkey: That is the point. It's a matter of faith. It's not a matter of accepting a conclusion based on evidence. So, when you answer Mrs. Bakke with empirical data concerning how many people accepted or rejected Jesus and how many accept or reject Rev. Moon, that approach is irrelevant. It's ultimately a matter of faith.

Richard Quebedeaux: I don't know how many of you are aware of Bill Bright's "I found it!" campaign that blitzed this country. Bill Bright never has stopped thinking that it was one hundred percent successful, that there were so many converts and so many people who joined the churches as a result. On the other hand, empirical studies have not found that to be the case. But it is the faith of certain people that concluded that it was successful. Maybe you know about Robert Schuller who works on the principle of possibility thinking—i.e., that in fact if you visualize it, if you think and believe in it, it is happening already. And I see this in the Unification Church.

Diana Muxworthy: I'd appreciate it if you could talk a little about the symbolic and theological position of Mrs. Moon and then her personal life—her past and present and what you perceive as her future.

Neil Salonen: Actually, Rev. Moon first married in the mid-1940s, and it would have been his desire that this woman help him achieve God's work of restoration. His first wife could have done it if she could have accepted his life of dedication to the church and his doing the work of the church. And this answers, in part at least, the charge of male chauvinism which some people make against us. The point is that Rev. Moon could not fulfill his mission without his wife's consent and help. And in general, in no sense can one partner decide the commitment of the other. Both of them must make the commitment for the work entrusted to either of them to be fulfilled.

In 1960, Rev. Moon married Hak Ja Han, who was at that time eighteen years old and didn't know the Principle. She was the daughter of a member. Therefore, over the next seven years he educated her. So the first of his three-fold seven-year courses was centered upon solidifying his family. In that time, she became able to take responsibility for her position in that family. We teach that this twenty-one-year course of his is also her twenty-one-year course. In the beginning there was something like a father-daughter relationship between them. But now there is equality. It's very much their position as a couple through which God works.

Richard Quebedeaux: OK thank you very much, Neil. We have to break. Of course, many of you have other questions. Neil, you'll be here through tomorrow?

Neil Salonen: Yes.

Richard Quebedeaux: So you can talk to him privately, and also to Mrs. Salonen if you would like to talk about women's issues or other things.

Belief and Behavior Amid Cultural Change
Some Thoughts on the Dynamics of New Religious Movements Like the Unification Church and Others

Stillson Judah

Stillson Judah: As a liberal Christian, my faith in God depends partly on my belief that He must have revealed Himself historically in the world religions as well as in new religions, whose very existence may indicate some failure of the well-established ones to meet needs under certain conditions at a particular time. As an historian and phenomenologist of religion, I must bracket the question of the truth of any religion investigated, in order to study its phenomena objectively.

This paper then represents some preliminary thoughts about the relationship between belief and behavior in the origin and development of religions, using the Unification Church, the Hare Krishna movement and some of the metaphysical sects of the nineteenth century as examples. In the beginning, I should like to view the Unification Church and other new religions in America in the context of the historical origins of other religions; next, to observe briefly some of the dynamics of beliefs as a basis for particular behavior; finally, to give a brief constructive critique, raising some questions.

All religions are part of some particular culture or subculture, owing their origins to ways in which they have psychologically met human needs during times of crisis. Such crises produce social and individual alienation or lack of identity. Such needs may be due to confrontation with conflicting ideas and values for reasons such as immigration, invasion and oppression, or simply rapid changes in culture.

At such times, religions may originate or change: (1) by forming new syntheses of ideas that ease the conflict, allowing new and firm identifications and commitments to be formed; or (2) by rejecting changes accepted by the established religions, and returning to what is believed to be the original teachings and values; or (3) by discovering a new rationale for the faith that meets personal and group needs. These may not be mutually exclusive categories and any new religion may represent a mixture. Conversions are only the personal aspects of the dynamics creating new religions or religious change. Now for some examples.

Christianity originated during Roman oppression amid a period of Greek acculturation when not only Greek philosophy, but also popular Zoroastrian ideas, introduced during the Babylonian captivity, were influencing the Jewish religion. The resulting confusion had earlier produced the politico-religious parties of the Sadducees and Pharisees, whose differing compromises eventually led to civil war. The success of Christianity, however, with its messianic hope owed much to the final synthesis of these opposing views and others in the Christianity of the New Testament.

It is well known that the Roman oppression led many Jews and Christians to flee into Arabia where their mingling added to cultural confusion there. At the time of Muhammad, even the traditional Arab religion and existing tribal system were experiencing severe difficulties. The final success of Muhammad again owed much to the new revelation which provided a basis for a higher social unity than that of the warring tribes. It also incorporated in modified form the indigenous Arab religion with Jewish, Christian and Zoroastrian concepts to form a new synthesis that was Islam.

As Islam spread into countries of differing cultures, it also added to cultural confusion. Many in India were converted; both Hinduism and Buddhism suffered corruption and the Hindu social system was weakened, because the Muslims did not accept the caste system. The sixteenth century saint, Chaitanya, purified the Vaishnava religion of the sexual corruption caused by these changes, by reinterpreting philosophically the sexual allusions in popular literature as well as the very basis for the caste system. This made it easier to reconvert many former Hindus from Islam, to win over many Buddhists and Muslims, and to preserve and reenforce the Hindu social system. The same religion in modified form has given meaning to thousands of youth in the United States and elsewhere as the Hare Krishna movement during this period of change.

In nineteenth-century America, the combination of new scientific discoveries relating to geology, paleontology, and the doctrine of evolution, together with the beginning of the scientific study of the Bible, challenged scriptural authority. This led again to religious confusion. Liberal churches found meaning in the Social Gospel, which became particularly meaningful to the rising middle class. Others met their needs by denying the validity of the doctrine of evolution and new scientific theories, and reaffirmed the literal truth of the Bible in the new fundamentalist and Pentecostal sects that arose toward the close of the century and thereafter. Still others were not content to go either of these ways. They joined new religious movements which arose in response to the crisis after the middle of the nineteenth century and in the twentieth. These accepted all the new scientific discoveries and theories, but also a belief in a God of science, of principle, or a higher spiritual law for which the physical laws were but a lower correspondent, a shadow of the higher reality, as Swedenborg had proclaimed. Based on a combination of Christian morality, and often a new interpretation of Christianity, together with influences from Hindu philosophy, American transcendentalism, Swedenborgianism, and imported French occultism, etc., they formed new syntheses, the so-called "scientific" religions, e.g., Christian Science, Divine Science, Religious Science, *et al.* As forerunners of psychosomatic medicine and stress-relieving psychotherapies, as optimists, pragmatists, and exponents of the American way of life, they believed God revealed Himself to them through their good health, prosperity and happiness. Like the fundamentalists, with some exceptions, they turned from social activism toward a highly personal religion. One example, the New Thought Movement, is related most closely to Christian Science, Religious Science, Divine Science, and other metaphysical healing movements. Its practices, involving the power of thought, have influenced greatly its general religious behavior. In these related movements, the material world is regarded as a shadow of the spiritual world, and the denial of the existence of matter as in Christian Science, or its acceptance as in New Thought, is largely a semantic problem. Such a belief, not unlike much related Hindu philosophy, has emphasized the spiritual or mental side, so that physical forms of social action to ameliorate conditions have tended to be neglected in the past except for certain well-known exceptions.

While advocating the Golden Rule, these metaphysical groups do not emphasize, as does the Unification Church, the willingness of personal sacrifice for the sake of others, as the sacrifice of Jesus Christ most fully exemplified. This difference, Henry Harrison Brown, one of New Thought's early leaders, pointed out. He said: "It is no longer a struggle for physical existence, but for spiritual expression. This demands not force, not sacrifice, not pain, not suffering, nct labor, but love and love alone." While one must not infer that New Thought adherents were incapable of sacrifice, still *sacrificial* love requiring some personal suffering was unemphasized. Pain was to be denied as a reality. When the Social Gospel movement of liberal Christianity began toward the close of the nineteenth century, Henry Wood, another leader of New Thought, was careful to distinguish the latter's aims. He said: "It does not deal directly with social phenomena, but with their inner springs of causation. I believe the danger that most threatens New Thought... is its more or less intimate amalgamation with other reforms... upon lower planes... Without uttering a word pro or con concerning political socialism... etc., I believe the New Thought should be kept above and distinct."

The Arcane School, a metaphysical and schismatic Theosophical sect founded by Alice Bailey in 1923, while not demanding sacrificial action, is an exception to the above due to its social concern. It also has certain similarities to Unification thought and practices but with significant differences. Alice Bailey's teaching came purportedly from a Theosophical master residing on a high spiritual plane. Her philosophy orients her followers toward a life of not only spiritual self-development toward perfection but also toward a life of service to others. They are to form the nucleus of a new civilization in the New Age now dawning. She revealed that the masters have been working with "the Christ" to eliminate barriers so that the New Age would begin with the return of "the Christ." Like the Unification Church and Theosophy, she distinguished between the person of Jesus and "the Christ." The latter is similar in this respect to the Unification distinction between the person of Jesus and the Lord of the Second Advent. While the Arcane School awaits the imminent return of "the Christ," many Theosophists at one time believed that he was to occupy the body of Jiddu Krishnamurti, who later disavowed such beliefs entirely.

Alice Bailey, like the Unification Church with its belief in indemnity, taught that humanity must play a part to change conditions. This would permit the Messiah to return to bring in the Kingdom of God on earth and to unite Christianity with Buddhism. Instead of the power of indemnity to make these conditions right through prayer, fasting, and sacrificial physical acts as the Unification Church teaches, the Arcane School solves its problems solely through the mind like the followers of New Thought. Alice Bailey's followers serve others by using the Great Invocation. It is ostensibly a translation of an ancient prayer "The Christ," re-introduced to the world in 1945, when because of the terrible world conditions, he decided that he should return. The more it is recited, they believe, the more right human relations will be established, enabling "the Christ" to return.

Thus, the metaphysical movements have solved for themselves the disturbing dichotomy between religion and science by means of their type of mental science. This has satisfied them intellectually, emotionally, and given meaning and direction to their lives through what they experience as the working of God's law.

In this century the religious movements that have been so influential on American young adults have had their major growth, if not all their origins, as a result of the catalytic effects of the protests of the sixties (when most were organized in the early seventies). But the sixties perhaps only increased the momentum of change which Alvin Toffler has called "future shock," a change which he now envisions as marking the end of the industrial age that has succeeded the agricultural one. He calls it the beginning of "the third wave," an entirely new age, socially, industrially, and economically. Besides all the various changes occasioned by the many liberation movements from civil rights to the sexual revolution, there are those produced by the rapid advance in computer technology. Moreover, there are changes brought about by the atomic age itself, when two dominant opposing powers, amid growing critical energy and economic crises threaten the destruction of our civilized world. Such changes, confusion and crises create anxieties and fear. We tend to look for an authority and a leader to give us new solutions and meaning. Many need a definite direction in which to move, and a vision of hope for the future to which they can be emotionally and intellectually committed. Adding further to this confusion, the media are bringing us face to face in our living rooms with all the incongruities of different cultures, ethical and religious views, threatening further our personal and group identities.

As one examines the Principle of the Unification Church, even a critic must regard it as a new synthesis for providing identity in meeting contemporary needs. It combines ideas of Taoism, Confucianism,

Christianity, shamanism, and the principles of science by analogy or correspondence, into one philosophy. Thereby it hopes to unify all religions and cultures, among other things. In furthering this purpose, the Unification Theological Seminary offers an unparalleled opportunity for open dialogue with well-qualified faculty composed of scholars of many faiths. Roman Catholic, liberal and conservative Protestant, Orthodox and Jewish are all represented, while additional lecturers add the dimension of faiths other than those of the Judeo-Christian tradition. Through contributions of still other scholars participating in such conferences as this, in which the theology and behavior patterns have been examined in dialogue, these students will be well equipped to help formulate the future theology of the Unification Church.

In a day when the liberal Christian churches, because of their identification with a changing establishment, fail to provide fixed points of identity and needed experience to internalize them, many are practicing forms of meditation from other religions. The declining membership in liberal churches since the sixties is mute testimony to this at least temporary situation. Others, however, are returning to a new conservatism, rediscovering an identity that is internalized through their experience of the various gifts of the Spirit. These are the growing churches.

The Unification Church offers a new form of conservatism with a black and white moral code giving fixed points of identity and direction. It offers hope for the future, and is working toward restoring a God-centered nuclear family which has been in decline. This is belief in action.

Amid currently divisive cultural patterns, and believing in the necessity for the unification of cultures, it strives to overcome both racial and cultural differences by its practice of combining in marriage, partners of different races and cultures. While trying to contribute to the harmonious unity, it also gives attention to the preservation of what is valuable in each, such as sponsoring its New York Symphony Orchestra, various kinds of rock and jazz bands, as well as its Korean dance troupe, Korean music, and dances and music of other cultures.

As a further attempt to dispel the old historical opposition between science and religion, it not only offers a philosophical type of unity between the two by analogy or by correspondence, but also sponsors annual conferences on the unity of the sciences, in which some of the world's foremost scientists participate and whose results are published in very handsome volumes for the benefit of the whole world.

In a day when even the president of the United States has been accused of not appreciating the real dangers of communism, the Unification Church's Freedom Leadership Foundation has been working not only to inform the world concerning the faults of communism, but also to offer an alternative, which voices some of the protests of the sixties.

In order to work at the grass-roots level in alleviating suffering, and to aid in the transition to the restored kingdom, the Unification Church is developing social programs. I was impressed by the work of the members in Washington, D.C. There, during a party in a racially mixed area, a Black had invited the entire neighborhood in appreciation of what a group of Unification Church workers had done there in bringing understanding and harmony between races.

The work of Project Volunteer started by Dr. Mose Durst in the San Francisco Bay Area and now expanding to Los Angeles and the East is also most impressive. It is not only distributing many tons of food each month to needy people in its area, but it has been sending needed food and medicine to countries overseas. Particularly worthy also are its programs for helping people help themselves, such as the food fair it organized for merchants along Telegraph Avenue in Berkeley; or the kick-off drive it arranged to help SCARE, the Sickle Cell Anemia Research and Education organization; or its seminar in a racially depressed, high-crime area of East Oakland. There it arranged for legal authorities and police representatives to meet with the community in order to instruct the people concerning their rights. They told them how to help themselves legally and how they might be able to alleviate many of their problems.

All of these behavior patterns are manifestations of Unification beliefs in action to help change and to make this a better world, a part of the work they believe is necessary for a material kingdom of God to be realized on earth. They are overt expressions of their faith that the new age is dawning and the Lord of the Second Advent is here.

Such crises throughout history have also engendered belief in a new age and a Messiah in the great world religions: a Kalki avatar for Hindus; a Lord Maitreya, the coming Buddha for Buddhists; a Mahdi for Muslims. Indeed for many occultists in our troubled times there arises an abiding hope in the dawning age of Aquarius; the expectancy of the imminent return of Jesus Christ according to the Mormons, Jehovah's Witnesses, and many fundamentalist sects and movements; and the belief that the Messiah is already here, according to the Unification Church. Unlike a more orthodox Christian view which waits for God's pleasure to bring in the kingdom on earth, the Unification Church believes that the restoration which failed at various points in history again waits for humanity to do its part at this time. This faith gives hope to socially activistic members. They feel that they themselves can do something about our conditions, just as many thought they could in the sixties, even though the greater part depends upon God's grace. For only through such behavior as prayer, fasting, and self-sacrificial action for the sake of others can they indemnify the conditions of the original sin of Adam and Eve. Through such action they believe they make conditions right for converting others toward this goal of creating God-centered families and for furthering the restoration of God's kingdom on earth. Thus through the Principle they have sacralized the secular goals to which many had aspired without success in the earlier protests, when the expected revolution did not occur. Such socially activistic behavior and concern for the problems of the world had most of their roots in the protests of the sixties. In spite of the fact that the statistics were taken in 1976, seven years beyond the height of the protests, and were from those living in areas noted for their conservatism as much as others were for their radical activism, still 40 percent of the Unificationists indicated they had been involved in student protests of the late sixties. This extent of activism compares favorably with 55 percent of 1000 senior males who earlier in 1971 at the highly radicalized University of California Berkeley campus had been involved in the demonstrations. That 62 percent of Unification Church members surveyed indicated they had abandoned their parents' faith because of visible hypocrisy of its adherents and 66 percent cited its incapacity to give a larger meaning to life indicates their depth of ethical and psychic deprivation.* These figures among others point clearly to the existence of alienation and need for a faith that would give them direction and meaning. Further case studies also confirm this.

Although the survey of the Hare Krishna devotees reveals an almost identical percentage of those whose parents' religions lacked meaning for them and also a high percentage of former protestors, at the time of their conversion most had become hippies interested only in their

---

*These two terms may be briefly defined as conflicts in ethical values, and lack of meaning to life, respectively. They were formulated, among others by two sociologists, Charles Y. Glock and Rodney Stark, as explanations for the origin of religions.

spiritual search through drugs. Thus after their conversion, their behavior was not at all directed toward social action which had brought little results, but only toward trying to change people's hearts. One of the devotees expressed their view in the late sixties: "We understand that there is a root cause of all this distress, and so we're going to the root cause of all the problems: pollution, overpopulation, starvation, and wars. All these things are caused by forgetfulness of our real position to render sacrifice to the Supreme Lord... If you see a tree and there's a wilted leaf here and there, the materialistic man says, 'Let's pour some water on the leaf.' But we understand that to help a tree, you have to water the roots, then automatically all the leaves will benefit... Therefore, we are going to that root by reviving everyone's God-Consciousness, so that they benefit from this society." They would say that the material world is the creation of *maya*, God's illusory and inferior energy. Consequently, their principal acts of chanting, preaching, and selling their literature are to help the world return to the Godhead.

When asked to list in order of importance, the reasons for their conversion 58½ percent cited the sound of the *mantra*, which they chanted to give them the religious experience that guided them to Krishna Consciousness. This corresponds to the earlier search of the majority to find salvation through a drug mysticism, since 61 percent had formerly been practicing a spiritual discipline while taking drugs. By contrast only 18½ percent of the Unification Church members cited the devotional service as attracting them to the movement. Correlating again with their social activism, 75½ percent of them gave as their chief inducement toward conversion, the Principle, the philosophy for bringing into being the material kingdom of God on earth. To the same question, only 41 percent of the Krishna's devotees mentioned its philosophy as their chief attraction to the movement, even though their spiritual master had voiced many of their protests in his commentaries on the sacred texts. One should not infer from these factors that the Hare Krishna movement has developed no social concern. Recent developments in the movement already indicate that it is changing, even though its primary goal is still the same.

The Unification Church too, in spite of its involvement in social and cultural programs that follow naturally from its particular beliefs, still puts its foremost efforts into proselytism and fundraising. One survey has reported that these two tasks were the principal work for 52 percent of members responding to a questionnaire. Unfortunately, the media, while unwilling to recognize the Unification Church's contributions to society, have been critical because of the manner in which these tasks are sometimes performed. "Heavenly Deception," a term used for the failure to make clear the relationship of some association or program to the Unification Church, has been practiced according to both former members and some current members, even though there is a stated policy against it. One can understand that deep commitment intensifies the feeling of urgency to fulfill goals one believes to be vital. It has been explained also that the "bad press" has made such practices at times necessary because public feeling has become so strong against the movement. Still, some have given "Heavenly Deception" as a reason for dropping out of the church. Even though the Unification Church is not alone in such practices, as a new movement, it must be doubly careful about its public image. The First Amendment protects beliefs but not practices, if the public feels they are either illegal or too offensive. My fears are not only for the Unification Church. If laws should be made regulating how money is raised or how people are converted, their application could affect the liberty of all religions.

There are also problems concerning the Unification Church's behavior toward its own members. The first is in respect to their physical health. There are those who have dropped out of the movement because the lack of medical attention when they were ill forced them to return home for treatment. Perhaps these have been isolated cases, because certainly care of members depending wholly upon the church as part of an extended family should be a primary concern.

The second problem is concerned with the mental health of some of the members. The Unification Church may be characterized as a communal religious movement with an ascetic discipline. Such is normally designed to increase faith and commitment. Studies have shown that the number of hours members worked are more than the average, had the members been holding positions outside the movement. Psychiatric studies have shown, however, that there is a positive correlation between the number of hours so employed and the scores for well-being. Since discipline itself may not be a negative behavior factor, then my concern is whether such tasks as fundraising are assigned to members over long periods of time without regard to their particular talents, training and ambitions. While I am aware that the Unification Church has attended to this problem very well in many cases, there are examples of dissatisfaction and even dropouts from it because of a lack of personal fulfillment.

There is one final problem which has affected stability of membership. Whereas cultural change may produce needs which new religions may meet at these particular times, such change is a double-edged sword. It may strike with one side at the established religions for not taking a firm stand on changing issues; it may strike with its other edge the new religions which do not make some compromises in the face of dominant changes which its members have supported. A case in point is the changing conditions of women in our society which have affected female members in many of our more disciplined religions. Nuns have left the Roman Catholic Church because of its rigidity. Female devotees of the Hare Krishna movement have dropped out because of the great contrast between the traditional place of women in Hinduism and one espoused by the Women's Liberation Movement. There are also women in the Unification Church, who as members of a new religion aiming to unify all cultures, feel that a Korean pattern of male dominance is being inculcated.

In conclusion, even though there are problems the Unification Church may have in making practical adjustments to change, I believe that it and other new religious movements are playing an important part in meeting the needs of many in these times. Such periods as this throughout history have been characterized by violence of the discontented and alienated. Not enough attention has been given to the role such new religious movements may have played in eliminating crime and violence. The new movements, like the Unification Church, may have played a significant role often unnoticed in changing people's hearts from hatred of society to love, from violent protest and destruction in the face of evil to constructive measures for changing this world into a better place for us all to live.

REFERENCES

Galanter, Marc and Richard Rabkin, et al. "The 'Moonies': a Psychological Study of Conversion and Membership in a Contemporary Religious Sect." American Psychiatric Association, Annual Meeting, 1979, pp. 166-67.

Glock, Charles Y. and Rodney Stark. Religion and Society in Tension. Chicago: Rand McNally & Co., 1965, pp. 247-48.

Judah, J. Stillson. Hare Krishna and the Counterculture. New York: John Wiley & Sons, 1974.

—————. *The History and Philosophy of the Metaphysical Movements.* Philadelphia: The Westminster Press, 1967.

—————. National Survey of Members of the Unification Church, (Date for monograph in progress) 1976.

Discussion

Richard Quebedeaux: I'd like to ask the first question with respect to your comments about the First Amendment, saying that it protects the right to believe but not the right to practice. What about making conversions which could be interpreted as practice? If in fact it doesn't protect, then we're sunk.

Stillson Judah: That's right. I know it and I am greatly worried about it. Once you make a law it's not going to affect only one religion or two religions. It is going to affect the religious liberty of all religions and this is one of the reasons why I joined APRL (Association for the Protection of Religious Liberties) and for some years was its vice chairman. I worked very hard because I felt that our religious freedom was really being greatly jeopardized by some of the protests that were being made by the media. So if they begin making laws concerning fundraising, laws for how people are to be converted, this is going to affect the freedom of all religions. I have an example here, as a case in point. My son was greatly influenced at one time in his life when he was in his teens by the Young Life Movement of which Billy Graham has had sponsorship. After he was married, he and his wife were invited by one of his former acquaintances in the movement to be a chaperone for a lot of young people who were going out for a weekend to have a lot of fun. They were going to have dancing, games and music—they had a rock band and they had gathered a number of these youngsters together and they all went out for this one weekend. I said, "Well look, was it only dancing and singing?" He said, "No, as a matter of fact, there were lectures and discussions. At the end, when each was asked how much this had meant to him or her, some broke down and cried. It was most amazing how at the end of two days the Lord had gotten to so many of them." I said, "Well, if the Unification Church did this in one weekend, they would call this mind-control." So you can't oversimplify this problem. It's not just in the Unification Church. You find this problem in the conversions in many of our Christian churches.

Rod Sawatsky: I want to make an observation. Adversaries of the Unification Church usually apply psychiatric categories to why people join—it is an aberration, it is some kind of deviant response to problems, etc. On the other side, when people leave movements, then people within the movement tend to use psychiatric categories to explain why they didn't stay. And you, in your presentation, tended to give the negative interpretation of that. Now, I think it would be very valuable if someone like you with your academic tools could perhaps typologize, why people leave.*

Stillson Judah: I'm trying to do that. I've been asking everybody. I ask, "Why do you feel that people leave the movement?"

Rod Sawatsky: You mentioned inability to take the discipline and then psychiatric disorders. Is there a type who might, as a healthy-minded person, leave for rational reasons such as a disagreement with management policies?

Stillson Judah: Oh yes, absolutely.

Rod Sawatsky: There is some feeling among some very smart and healthy people in the movement, as I understand it, that there are some changes going on that are actually bad for the movement, such as increasing Korean-ification of management and decisions. Would you call that a rational reason for leaving? Kurt the other day said that when someone leaves, it is usually wrong vision or having lost the vision.

Stillson Judah: Yes, some apparently lose the vision; and this is what I've been working on. But this is a puzzle which has many parts that are hard to discover, and then to put together. I don't think any conversion happens by mind control. Rather, the person has been looking for something, and he finds it. But when a person leaves the movement, it is usually not just for one reason, but for many reasons. These reasons build up and then, suddenly, one particular thing happens, and bang! The person leaves. So I have been trying to discover the intellectual and emotional satisfactions and the guidance which make conversion possible. And I have also been trying to find out what makes a person lose his vision.

*Under the auspices of New ERA, a conference on the "Dynamics of Joining and Leaving the Unification Church" was convened in Berkeley, California, in February, 1981.

Don Jones: Can you imagine that new insight, enlightenment or rationality is the reason for moving out? It was my reason for leaving Youth for Christ. I felt that it was not a loss to me because when Emil Brunner through his books moved me to a new grasp of the gospel, I felt that when I left, what I was leaving was a rather narrow evangelical faith. I thought I was making an advance. Yet people within the group thought that I had back-slidden. They used that category. I think it is the task of responsible scholars, like you, to develop some positive categories to do justice to our experience of having left a movement.

Stillson Judah: Right. That's a big problem. This is why I have been so long trying to write this book.* You can't give any simplistic answer to it. There are many different factors that are involved.

Kurt Johnson: In the long run, I think there is a surety that the initial reasons why people leave are psychological. Even in the order of the Holy Cross, there was a rule: never leave the order in a bad mood. If you are going to leave the order, leave it in a good mood, so that you can deal with rational reasons for doing so. When I was talking to Stillson yesterday, I analyzed my experience of people leaving this movement. You come into the movement looking for an ideal. But there are two psychological types. One is the type who wants to take the responsibility and just build that ideal. He has focused on what he has to offer to help realize that ideal. That person will probably not leave. But the other type is looking for the ideal to be given them by the system itself. And they reach a point very often, where they start to point the finger of accusation: you did not give me the ideal you said, therefore, I will look elsewhere. Do you see that difference in type? My responsibility for the ideal or your responsibility to give it to me? This I see very frequently. That can make the final difference.

Ernest Stewart: I agree with Kurt on the idea of many people leaving because they get a little disillusioned. Too many think the kingdom of heaven is like an escalator that you ride to the top. Suddenly they discover that it is hard work. Fundraising is difficult; witnessing is difficult; the kingdom of heaven is just not floating down out of heaven on the clouds. They have to face themselves and admit that it is more than they are ready for, or more than they want to do.

Paul Sharkey: I need to react against both of those. I think they

---

*Dr. Judah is working on a book which he has tentatively entitled "The Moonies: Conversion or Coercion."

are much too simplistic. I know people who have left for doctrinal reasons. I know people who had the original ideal of social action and vision, but who left because they didn't think the church was going in the right direction. I don't think it is just that lazy people get out because they can't take it.

Kurt Johnson: No, that is a misinterpretation.

Therese Stewart: I agree with Paul. And I base that partly on my experience of having left the community that I was a part of for twenty years. There were so many factors involved in my leaving, so many different motivations that came together in an existential way, that I resist any easy explanation of why people leave. Some people leave and return at another time with a different attitude, a different feeling, having had time to sort things out. It's something that requires a great deal of caution.

Myrtle Langley: In building up the profiles of individuals who join the movement, have you been able to come up with any picture of the social context? This is the intriguing side to me.

Stillson Judah: Yes, it is interesting. Of course, it is hard for me to compare the Hare Krishna social profile with that of the Unification Church. I gathered the statistics on the Hare Krishna movement in the sixties and those on the Unification movement in 1976, and much change has occurred in these years. At that time, the profile of the Hare Krishna movement was that of upper middle-class young adults. Most of them had had some university training. The end of the first year was when the largest percentage of them dropped out of school. They had moved from their own homes and their families to radical places like the University of California campus, and in one year's time they became strongly influenced by the protests. Next, they dropped out of college and moved into the hippie ghettos.

Myrtle Langley: They became marginalized, would you say?

Stillson Judah: Yes, absolutely. Now in the case of the Unification Church members, there is economically a greater sociological spread. And, of course the statistics of the Unification Church show that the ethnic content is different from that of the Hare Krishna movement. In the latter there are almost no Blacks, and I've never seen a Japanese Hare Krishna devotee in the United States. Nor does one find but a few third-world youth in the American movement. They're from white, upper middle-class people of the establishment. Quite often, as far as the positions were concerned, they are people, however, whose fathers were not in the professional class, but maybe were making twenty-five thousand dollars a year driving a truck. They had access to a lot of money, and this is one of the things that comes out very strongly in the Hare Krishna profile. These were young people who had everything given to them. They suddenly decided that money hadn't given happiness to their parents, and that there must be something beyond this materialism. So they went into their hippie jungles and finally, when the drugs no longer satisfied them, they found higher spiritual values in the Hare Krishna movement. They concluded that this materialism was an illusion, *maya*.

Myrtle Langley: Are you suggesting that there is a mobility in the parents' lives which leads to a lack of self-identify in the children? This to me would be a deeper reason.

Stillson Judah: Yes. Many were moving up in status but with probably mixed results. One interesting thing came out unexpectedly. I wanted to make a little survey of the parents of Unification Church members. So, in the Bay Area, I asked the members to make up questions which might be asked concerning their parents. I was trying to see what type of training the different parents had given, to see if I could find differences between those parents who were against their children belonging to the Unification Church, and those who did not object. So we had these various questions. One of the questions which everyone was required to ask was, what type of training did you have which prepared you for going into the Unification Church? Now one of the strange things that emerged was that, instead of most saying there was a lack of love in the family and the need for a new family, a new relationship, it divided fifty-fifty down the line almost exactly. In other words, fifty percent said there was a lack of love in their family; or they were not appreciated; or even though their parents loved them, they didn't show it. But another fifty percent said it was because of the great love of their family, and the strong feeling of love, which they felt, then, should be a part of any family, that explained why the Unification Church was of such great importance to them.

Myrtle Langley: But there was a lack of personal identity?

Stillson Judah: Yes there was. I feel this is so important, this lack of personal identity, the lack of direction occasioned mostly in this period, by changing culture. In our society with its sexual revolution some of the big problems particularly for our liberal churches are: Is homosexuality

OK? Can a homosexual become a minister in that particular church? Is premarital sex OK? Is it all right to live with another person and not get married? These are things which many of the liberal churches are talking about, but there are no decisions. How are most young persons making the transition to adulthood in the establishment going to make this passage without some kind of guidance? Here the Unification Church has a role. The movement has said, this is wrong, this is right. It gives one a basis for meaning.

David Simpson: Does your research throw any light on how people join and leave the established churches? I have this stereotype about a lot of people who never really reflect about the religion in which they are brought up. There are some of us who go through a process of being born into a religious tradition which we initially took for granted or accepted unreflectively. I myself was brought up in a liberal Christian tradition. But there came a time when I had to ask myself whether I would discard it or really join and begin to take my faith seriously. So I'm wondering, Stillson, whether you've looked into the relation between the reasons Moonies join and then stay with the movement or leave it and the reasons people join or leave the established churches. In both cases, as Paul Sharkey said, there are some doctrinal problems—e.g., the Roman Catholic who cannot accept the church's position on birth control.

Stillson Judah: ... or abortion or some things like that; so they leave.

David Simpson: There is another aspect of this question. I am very interested in the experience of the born-again Christian. You go away for two days to a Youth for Christ or a Young Life meeting, and you come back a changed, committed person. Is this like the experience of being at Boonville for a few days?

Stillson Judah: Well, I don't think there can be any doubt about it. I feel that most of our liberal churches do not really offer enough meaning in these times of crisis.

Esteban Galvan: I want to share something that I felt was slighted over yesterday and which has come up again here. While attending a major Catholic seminary in a clinical pastoral education program, I wore a priest's collar, offered chaplain services in a local hospital, preached at a college campus, gave last rites, and heard confessions. Now, I dropped out of that professional commitment to God because I searched and was dissatisfied with my distance from Jesus Christ as a personal reality nor did

I see Jesus reflected in the behavior of the Catholic hierarchy. I believed that when I stood in front of people and I preached of Jesus, I really had to be accountable for those people's lives, at least for the Jesus I represented and preached. I couldn't do it and be honest with myself.

I didn't say it yesterday, but a change has happened with me and so now when I'm fundraising, and I receive money from someone, I feel I can be responsible to that person's work with the sweat and tears that the money represents. Also in the witnessing of our movement, there have been times when I have been challenged in my witnessing because I've had to ask myself whether I really believed in what I was doing. I go through the whole, same thing, asking, is this really true? So there have been times when I've sat down on the sidelines and I've not witnessed because I had to sort these things out, before going on any further.

Stillson Judah: I think that's a healthy condition. The honest facing of doubt is very important. It is one thing that makes the difference between what I would call a healthy religion and fanaticism.

Esteban Galvan: Dr. Judah, through your research have you been able to evaluate the job that the Unification Church is doing in counseling people to stay in the church or to leave, and also in giving those who stay work to do which is spiritually and intellectually fulfilling for them?

Stillson Judah: I haven't really made a complete study of those areas. I know, though, that this is a big risk you are taking and a big responsibility that you take on yourselves. There is one fellow who came to me from the Berkeley group who was dissatisfied and said he was leaving the movement. He went back to his leader and gave his reasons for wanting to leave and the leader advised him to go. I thought this was commendable of the leader. Also, I think there is something very important to say here: If you have somebody in one of the Unification families who is really completely dissatisfied with the church, that person is going to be a troubled and troubling member. He is not going to help the harmony of that group. The best thing is to let him go.

George Exoo: It is clear to me, Stillson, that in these meetings, when we're sitting here with Kurt Johnson, Diana Muxworthy or Arthur Eves, we are talking to people who are a part of an educated elite within this organization. It's also clear to me that there are a lot of workers out there who aren't going to Harvard and who aren't going to Barrytown. For the most part, it seems to me, they are fundraising on the streets, although I may be wrong about that. But whatever it is, they are people who don't have the charisma or brain that is going to enable them to function in Cambridge, Massachusetts, and compete. Did you do any research on the criteria which segregated the elite from the workers?

Stillson Judah: Well, I have asked the question whether the church was taking care of all the particular ambitions of the person. In the New Yorker Hotel, I met a fellow who seemed to be a very bright person, but who was dissatisfied. He had been on the West Virginia basketball team, but because of his size, he was just a guard in the New Yorker. He felt that somehow the church wasn't using him for the abilities that he felt he had, and so for that particular reason, after being a guard for several years...

George Exoo: ...he went from a center to a guard. (laughter)

Stillson Judah: ...I think that he hadn't left at that time, but I wouldn't be a bit surprised if he has left. This is one of the problems that the church has, taking in as many new people as it does. Can it satisfy the personal ambitions of each one? Can it give each individual a sense of fulfillment? A person who never does anything but fundraise might suddenly think, "Gee, is this really what I want to do?" So maybe at a particularly low point when he is particularly tired, he may decide he has had enough, and leave the movement.

George Exoo: Do you feel that the Unification policy of worker bees has integrity to it? Or is it to some extent exploitative? It may be a mixture of both, of course. I don't know whether there is a rational policy. Somebody decided that Diana was going to go to Harvard. Is there a group of people that decide that somebody is going to stay down and wash dishes and clean the toilets all of their lives?

Hugh Spurgin: You're seeing a rather recent phenomenon within the Unification movement. You're discussing what has happened since the Washington Monument Campaign in 1976 (i.e., after the completion of all the various speaking engagements of Rev. Moon). Since 1975-76, people have floated into all kinds of nonevangelical "missions" of special interest to them—into business, education, the arts, and newspapers. Prior to 1975, egalitarianism dominated. Everybody did the same evangelical tasks: witnessing, lecturing the *Divine Principle*, and fundraising. (The same jobs that new members still do their first few months or years in the church.)

In my case, I worked from 1968 through 1975 doing nothing but evangelical work; then in 1975, I was admitted to the Unification Seminary. Every person in this room has gone through that same basic process. But having completed that initial training program, which should help a person develop in his life of faith, they are now doing something else of general interest to them, jobs differing, but nonetheless satisfying. For example, there are certain people who are studying at the seminary, presumably because they are intellectually oriented, while there are other members who are working as security guards.

I know many of the guards in New York and I know that most of them enjoy their work and have little interest in studying. In life, there are always some dissatisfied people, but I tend to believe that in the Unification movement, they are a minority. There are all kinds of people in the Unification Church with diverse backgrounds, interests, ambitions and talents. Some are working in church-sponsored businesses, others in theatrical performances, still others in maintenance and construction. In this conference you, however, are seeing only a certain type of Unification person—the more intellectual type. That is true, but to a considerable degree, people are fulfilling their needs, interests and desires.

George Exoo: Well, if I have an IQ of 70, are you going to make a place for me that's satisfying to me? What if I want to go to Harvard and I've got an IQ of 70?

Stillson Judah: Well, I know they do. Let me speak to this. (laughter) There was one particular member I have known who was not suited for a position of great leadership. He left the movement for a time but now he's back after a number of years. The church has given him a very good job doing the type of work he likes and can do best. It is mechanical work, using his hands, and he's very satisfied.

Therese Stewart: I think again, there are many factors involved and you pointed out one part of it, Hugh. A lot of it has to do with a person's own identity and self-knowledge, too, even knowing what they want to do and how determined and how confident they are to try to make it happen. Also it depends on who the central figure is in a given situation. I've seen Mr. David Kim send many people, young people from the seminary staff, back to school at some point, because he knows that they need to develop a career or trade or something. But then, there are other central figures who may not have that kind of wisdom and that kind of foresight. So I think there are different things that are happening. I think there is a period that everybody goes through, fundraising and different things, but I think that's only part of it. And there are students who are qualified to be at Harvard who aren't there. I mean seminary graduates who aren't there. There are some who went out after graduation to gain more practical experience, and then after a couple of years they went either to Harvard or some other graduate school. So there are all kinds of things that are operating.

Richard Quebedeaux: I have heard that with respect to graduates of UTS who are selected by Rev. Moon to go to graduate school, that there are spiritual qualifications that had to be fulfilled. Is that true, Therese?

Therese Stewart: That's true. But it is also true that the people who Rev. Moon considers have been recommended on the basis of professors' observations, the observation of the people on the staff, like myself, and other criteria.

Richard Quebedeaux: I've heard that some people are turned down on the basis of spiritual criteria.

Mose Durst: There is also a principle of realism involved. Realistically, we offer a whole range of things that a person can do. But some say that they know already what they want to do, and that the church does not offer them the chance to do that. Thus, they may want to work at a particular job or go to school. Now, we are delighted to have any constructive person associated with the movement, so I often tell people to come to the center in the morning and the evening, to try to live a good life, and to uphold the moral principles. And I assure them that I will support them in whatever they want to do. That is, we try to figure out a way to accommodate individual needs into the larger needs of the church. For example, we have a forty-year-old woman in our family who has a need to paint several times a week. She does this. And we send new people who also like to paint, but who do not like the intensities of our spiritual life, out with her. We tell them that if they meet any new people, they should invite them to the center in the evening. So, indeed, we try to accommodate the needs and wishes of the individual who is willing to lead a moral and ethical life.

George Exoo: Mao Tse Tung sent intellectuals to work on the farm because he thought that was where the real life was. Is that why you send some people out fundraising? Or is fundraising the bottom line in unskilled labor?

Mose Durst: My experience of carrying two bunches of flowers into Denny's at two o'clock in the morning is the most existential experience I have ever had. All the lights were glaring and all the people were looking at me and asking why I was walking into Denny's at that time of the morning with two bunches of flowers. From my point of view, to do that, to be that kind of fundraiser, takes the greatest amount of physical and psychological health. I had to re-evaluate what I was doing and why, with all my experience and education, I was at Denny's with two bunches of flowers at two in the morning. You have to have real intellectual, spiritual, and psychological underpinnings to do fundraising for a prolonged period.

Ernest Stewart: I can look back at my own career in the army as a personnel man for many years. I often had to tell a person that he may be a good truck driver but that I needed a cook. (laughter) So we have problems in the church when certain things have to be done. Also I think some young people have never experienced the joy of working. Also, we have some members who have had no work experience. They came into the movement right out of school, and their parents have taken care of them. So there are many things they haven't experienced. On the whole, however, we have many projects and kinds of work that are opportunities for developing creativity.

Thomas McGowan: This is shifting ground just a little bit; I asked some members why they remain in the Unification Church. And there was a small but significant number, ten out of seventy-four, that gave a disturbing response. They said they stayed in because they are engaged to a wonderful person. Now I realize that this was just after the engagement ceremony. Nonetheless, I found this disturbing because it sounds a little bit like behavior modification techniques. If you don't stay, you won't get this spouse. Did you pick up from your research that there is this kind of positive reinforcement? If you are very good within the church, here are rewards along the line, and specifically marriage in this case?

Stillson Judah: No, I didn't.

Richard Quebedeaux: There's another factor. I have a feeling there were some people who have left the church because they didn't get the right fiancé. (laughter) They had a very close attachment to somebody and were expecting to be matched to that person and were not.

Stillson Judah: That is true. I have evidence.

Mary Carman Rose: I have long been interested in the various dimensions of the current study of religions. I dropped out of the Society for the Scientific Study of Religion because of its great emphasis on behavioristic interpretation of religious commitment. The behavioristic approach to the study of religion is important, even necessary at times.

But it is hardly adequate for the study of all aspects of religion. Today there is less use of behaviorism. Instead, we have phenomenology with its bracketing and historicism. Stillson, you yourself started out by saying that you have to bracket the religious phenomena you are studying. I am sure that you will agree with the point that I wish to make. I want to point out that the student of religion is studying the religious beliefs, practices, and commitment of persons who have not bracketed their metaphysical and ontological beliefs. Methodologically this means that you have to go back to the community you have studied and ask the members whether your research does justice to what they really stand for. I know that many academicians who study religion do not do this. They are willing to substitute their historical, sociological, and historicist interpretations of religion for the metaphysical and ontological beliefs which are really of central importance in any religious life.

Diana Muxworthy: The issue of elitism is critical, and because I was mentioned in connection with it, I'd like to respond to it. I know my own situation is unusual, and I have thought a lot about it. If I were to decide to leave the movement now, that would be a critical, critical problem for me. I am grateful for having fundraised as much as I did prior to coming to Harvard. I wouldn't want to be at Harvard (let's put it this way) if I hadn't gone through the experience of fundraising. I regret that I haven't been able to fundraise more in order to get to Harvard, because we are trying to create a new age kind of person who is able to be intellectual, and yet in no way think of himself as separated from those who are not intellectual or educated. This is the kind of person I am trying to make myself into. It's my image of a new kind of person I'm trying to make myself into.

Don Jones: Something that you said, Stillson, triggered off an agenda that I think might be helpful for the academics, whether within the circle of Unification faith or outside. You used the term "healthy" and I take it that humility for you would be a sign of a healthy religious commitment. That is a normative judgment. OK, my response to that, as a professional ethicist who looks at institutions and behaviors from an ethical point of view, is that your report needs a way of making normative judgments about the religions you study. We all make such judgments, but we need precise criteria. We think that the Hare Krishnas are either less or more than holiness Pentecostalism or Unitarianism or vice versa. We can make those normative judgments from different religious normative points of view. However, I am more comfortable with moral categories than I am with psychotherapeutic categories. The term, "healthy," is a psychotherapeutic term. I want to suggest that there are at least ten ways of determining whether a religion is a good religion by using ethical criteria. I'm going to read them off. I think a good religion engenders and maintains the following:

(1) Humility. This is a sign that you have a transcendent perspective and that you do not identify your own articulation of it with the transcendent.

(2) Generosity. This is a sense of other-regardingness, sacrifice, altruism and attention to the interests of others.

(3) Individual freedom. This includes consent or dissent regarding one's destiny. It is the opposite of manipulation.

(4) A sense of justice. This is an interest in equal opportunity in the context of some other variables, such as merit, ability, need, and attention to justice for the disadvantaged.

(5) Honesty. Just as we apply honesty and truthfulness to the marketplace, doctor/patient relationships, and the academic community, we should also apply it to religion.

(6) Respect for human life. This means belief in the sanctity of human life, from an ethical point of view. I would judge Abraham as involved in wrongdoing by taking his son Isaac up the hill with a knife, with intent to kill. Now it is a problem whether the religious-action guide or the moral-action guide is superior. As an outsider, I see the moral-action guide as superior. The person within the faith has a different view.

(7) A sense of proper loyalties to nation, biological parents, spiritual parents, etc.

(8) Prudence. This includes knowing what's going on, rather than hiding from what's going on.

(9) Temperance. If you believe in providence, or whatever the language of the religion is, you don't take shortcuts, you don't hurt people to achieve a short term goal. You wait.

(10) Courage. If a religion engenders personal courage, which I think is the cornerstone of all virtues, then I think it is a good religion.

Now none of these are absolute and some take precedence over others.

Stillson Judah: They sound very good to me. Of course, I see my task differently. You as an ethicist are interested in the ethical and moral dimensions of religion. I am interested in the dynamics of religions—e.g., why people go into any one religion.

Don Jones: Why wouldn't you want to make a judgment about which is a better religion—the Hare Krishna movement or the Unification Church?

Richard Quebedeaux: You know, I asked him to do that.

Stillson Judah: I couldn't.

Don Jones: See, I could do that. (laughter) And I'll tell you. I think the Unification Church, according to these criteria, is superior to the Divine Light Mission, for instance; and I'll say that flat out. I think the Divine Light Mission is an inferior religion, morally speaking. Now the moral point of view is not the only point of view. I'll admit there are other points of view. I would see the snake handling cults in West Virginia as inferior to some other religions, morally speaking.

David Simpson: Did you ever put that in writing?

Don Jones: I haven't.

Stillson Judah: Do it. Those are good criteria.

David Simpson: One of Don's ethical categories was personal freedom. Stillson, what do you make of the member of the Unification Church who thinks he has to ask permission to leave the movement? Have you ever heard of a wayward Catholic asking the priest's permission to not go to church anymore? Or did you ask the Board of Elders' permission not to go to church anymore? Did I ask my minister when I decided for three years I didn't want to have anything to do with the church? Somehow there is a dramatic difference between these cases and the Unification movement.

Stillson Judah: Because they are a family, you see, I think this makes the difference—whereas in most of our Protestant churches, we go to church on Sunday, but we live at home. It's quite different. When you are a part of a group and a family, as it were, and want to leave the family, you ordinarily talk with people about why you're leaving. In the Unification Church you have this feeling of family; you are part of a unity, a social unit; and I think this makes a big difference.

Richard Quebedeaux: It's like getting a divorce.

Stillson Judah: Yes, I think that's a good analogy.

David Simpson: So if you decided to leave the movement, you'd have to move out. I mean, you'd really have to move out.

Stillson Judah: Yes, absolutely.

Hugh Spurgin: It has not, however, always been true that all Unification people have lived communally. In Korea, most members never did. It is true that those who are presently living communally, even though they may have outside jobs, are very involved with their housemates. Moreover, the movement seems to be changing in this respect, due to the newly created home church program and the emphasis upon home church membership.

To live communally is not easy; it is a struggle. Hence, it is also an indication of the greatness of the Unification way that many do live communally.

I have great respect for traditional churches, but it is different when you belong to a Sunday-only style church and don't live with others in your congregation. It is not the same as actually living with those people, and with their various idiosyncracies. Struggle is avoided, but so is an opportunity for growth. Families living together is even more complex. Nora and I have experienced that.

Problems exist but what overcomes them is the presence of God and love for one another. There's incredible diversity within the Unification Church, but what minimizes misunderstanding is a belief that there is something or Someone who transcends all, and a willingness to give unselfishly.

Esteban Galvan: Also, I think that a lot of the persecution that we receive has caused us to grow together, to pull together. This is the same process that Caesar Chavez says about the United Farm Workers' Movement. He said the more persecution they have received, the more religious that community has become. I think it's really true in our situation. I think that persecution has stimulated our community experience in becoming closer to one another and expressing mutual love. I am discovering that not only God, but another brother or sister, another human being, really loves me.

Kurt Johnson: I want to ask David a question. We've been talking about sociology and about coming and going in the Unification Church. I want to ask what's going to be the sociological position of people who are so threatening to you, who don't even want you to be here. What's going to be the sociology of their discovering that we may authentically not only be religious, but actually have something to contribute? Can they move away from the emotional attachment they have to their negativity toward the Unification Church?

David Simpson: Well, I guess just a very quick response would be that I think that those individuals have to go through some kind of a truth finding process in the same way that I may be doing, either with this or with respect to other things that I pursue that I want to get some answers about. And I don't think that I, or any other person, can do that for them. That's what I meant about the whole individual, the need to maintain that private space and that freedom, and I think that their emotional negativism may in some way be an interesting counterpart to the emotional attachment that members within the church find to each other, to the movement and to Rev. Moon. So I don't know how to answer that, other than to say that I think there is a similar amount of psychic energy that is going on on both sides and they ought to get together and talk to each other.

Richard Quebedeaux: The anticult movement has a lot of cohesiveness and a support system, too.

George Exoo: One of the things that keeps people from leaving jobs frequently is investment in pension plans. I have not gathered that there is any kind of pension plan or provision for old age within the Unification Church and I'm wondering if a person leaves, does he leave with absolutely nothing, no investment whatsoever and does that create a problem for people? Do you have any feeling on that or anybody else?

Stillson Judah: That is a good question, I would like to hear some comments.

Hugh Spurgin: Yes, I'd like to answer that question by using the example of my wife's parents' community. Nora comes from a conservative Mennonite community in Lancaster County, Pennsylvania, which opposes insurance. Their idea is that people, rather than insurance companies, should be depended upon when someone is in trouble. As to the Unification movement, currently there are no extensive plans for members. In the future, they are expected to be supported by their congregations, as well as their children and grandchildren.

George Exoo: Are you going to take care of the people who have left along the way?

Hugh Spurgin: No, I'm talking about people who have remained in the church.

Thomas McGowan: Do you think that it would be unsafe to have insurance plans because of something in your eschatology?

Hugh Spurgin: We have had some insurance plans; I'm not saying that we have not. In the past, individuals have had life or health insurance policies. But the stress is placed upon faith that people not legal commitments will take care of you when you are old.

There is also a Blessed couples' fund. It is a fund to which couples tithe and which any family that has a special need, such as a complication during childbirth, could dip into. Unfortunately, that system is not yet as developed in the U.S.A. as it is in Japan, Korea and elsewhere.

Ernest Stewart: I've seen many people off for various reasons—to go to school, go home or quit, or whatever. We don't give them a year's salary or something like that, but we don't send them away with nothing in their pockets. They get a couple of hundred dollars if they are going somewhere close. If they are going farther, they may get a thousand dollars.

Richard Quebedeaux: I think it is true that all this is in its developmental stages. I know a person who has not formally made an exit from the movement. His wife and kids are still in and active. He's trying to get a job and says that fourteen years in the Unification Church have not helped his dossier any, even though he's probably gotten much experience during that time that could be used in any secular organization. Yet who's going to believe it?

Diana Muxworthy: That's the risk that people take when they join.

Jane Flinn: After twelve years with the Franciscans, my husband left with fifty dollars in his pocket and ate off my meal ticket at Harvard his first year, (laughter) . . .

Richard Quebedeaux: Right, it's not just the Unification Church.

Paul Sharkey: I agree with Don that the ethical dimensions of any religion are important and that, judged by Don's ten criteria of the value of the ethical aspects of any religion, some religions are better than others. But there is also the necessary question: What is the purpose of religion? One purpose is the individual's gaining a sense of being accepted. But there are two kinds of acceptance. One is acceptance by the individuals in one's religious community. But there is also one's acceptance by God. This latter is more fundamental than the former. A person might leave the movement because he is looking for this and doesn't believe that he has found it.

Mary Carman Rose: That is an extremely important point, and I am glad Paul brought it up. Many of the Moonies present have talked about the support they find within the Unification family. No one has mentioned the way the Unification Church fosters the individual's relation to God, the Father, but I see this as a remarkable contribution to twentieth-century understanding of the individual's living relation to God.

Rod Sawatsky: In terms of figures of people leaving, what are we talking about? We have been talking about that so much, but I'd like the percentage.

Richard Quebedeaux: Can anybody make a wise comment in terms of the last three or four years, numbers of new members and numbers of exits.

Stillson Judah: I'd like to have those statistics.

Hugh Spurgin: I cannot give you precise statistics, but I would assert that since 1975, there has been an increase in the *percentage* of people leaving, as well as an increase in the number joining. Prior to 1975 in America, ours was a small movement in which most medium-sized cities had between five and ten Unificationists and only the bigger cities had more. But in 1975, there was a change. As I said earlier, many of the leaders were asked to go overseas as missionaries; others joined the various national projects, including the seminary, fundraising teams, the newspaper, etc. That is to say, though still under the Unification umbrella, many of those who didn't go overseas became involved in the nonevangelical activities of the movement. This meant that the American church was left without experienced leaders and had to rely on newly converted nineteen and twenty-year-old kids to take over key local and state positions.

Herein lies one indication of the greatness of Rev. Moon. He is always providing inexperienced people with opportunities to grow, risking the possibility they cannot handle heavy responsibilities, may succumb to temptations, or may leave the church. For instance, in New York City, members confront drugs, alcohol, money, fame, pornography, and all the ills of urban life, not to mention persecution and controversy. Some, no doubt, have been tempted by such worldly inducements and have left the movement—probably more since 1975 than before. But Rev. Moon stresses it is important to face challenges, not avoid them. Even though it is easier to be a saint on a mountain top than in the midst of the hustle and bustle of New York, confronting reality is essential to growth. Parenthetically I might mention also that since 1975, the focus of the Unification Church has been in the cities. Consequently, the diversity as well as the number of members has increased, another factor that increases turnover.

Jaime Sheeran: I was on a fundraising team right before coming to the Bahamas, and the people on that team knew that I was to come here. I want to share something about their hearts and their faith. They are people who are aware of all kinds of options and possibilities available to them and yet they have chosen to continue on with their work of fundraising. I know what keeps them fundraising is the fact that they are experiencing the living God every day while they are out there working hard. For example, I myself, had the option of going out to the field, and one of the reasons I have decided it is good for me to do this kind of work is because it is challenging to me. I think if you want to experience God, you have to challenge yourself to your limits, do something that you've never done before, and then your faith in God can become so real and you'll experience something very deep and valuable. What will we be left with after we die? Will our insurance plans help us then? What kind of insurance will help us with our spiritual lives? The more experiences we have with God, the more we have that is of eternal value. I think this truth actually keeps these people going on the MFT, even though they know that they could have an education and go on to school too. They are experiencing God every day. What school teaches that? So it's just a question of what kind of value system we have.

Richard Quebedeaux: Thank you. Thank you for an amazing lifestyle seminar.

Participants*

Renée Bakke Christchurch, New Zealand

Francis Botchway Professor, Dept. of Afro-American Studies, University of Cincinnati, Cincinnati, Ohio

M. Darrol Bryant Professor of Religion and Culture, Renison College, Waterloo, Ontario, Canada

Mose Durst Director, Unification Church of Northern California, Oakland, California (President, Unification Church of America, New York City)

Arthur Eves Student, Unification Theological Seminary, Barrytown, New York (Will be joining the staff of *The Washington Times*, Washington, D.C.)

George Exoo Minister of Unitarian Church, Charleston, South Carolina

Frank K. Flinn Professor, St. Louis University, St. Louis, Missouri

Jane Zeni Flinn Instructor of English Education and wife of Frank K. Flinn, University of Missouri-St. Louis, St. Louis, Missouri

Durwood Foster Dean, Pacific School of Religion, Graduate Theological Union, Berkeley, California

Esteban Galvan Student, Unification Theological Seminary, Barrytown, New York (Regional Director, Collegiate Association for the Research of Principle)

Lorine Getz Professor in Religious Studies, Cleveland State University, Cleveland, Ohio

Kurt Johnson Director of Interfaith Affairs, Unification Church of America and, Director of International Relief Friendship Foundation, New York City

*The positions held by the participants at the time the Bahamas' conference occurred are listed here. If the present position of a participant is different, that position is also noted in parenthesis.

Donald Jones Professor and Chairman, Dept. of Religion, Drew University, Madison, New Jersey

J. Stillson Judah Professor Emeritus and Librarian, Graduate Theological Union, Berkeley, California

Myrtle Langley Professor, Trinity College, Bristol, England

Leonard Lovett Professor, Fuller Theological Seminary, Pasadena, California

Phyllis Lovett Social Worker, M.S.W., M.R.E., and wife of Leonard Lovett, Pasadena, California

Thomas McGowan Professor, Manhattan College, Bronx, New York

Marianne McGowan Reading Specialist and wife of Thomas McGowan, Tarrytown, New York

Diana Muxworthy Graduate of Unification Theological Seminary, Graduate Student, Harvard Divinity School, Cambridge, Mass. (Graduate Student, Columbia University, New York City)

Wellington Nyangoni Head of African Studies Dept., Brandeis University, Waltham, Massachusetts

Stephen Post Graduate of Unification Theological Seminary, Graduate Student, University of Chicago Divinity School, Chicago, Illinois

Richard Quebedeaux Author, Berkeley, California

Herbert Richardson Professor, St. Michael's College, University of Toronto, Toronto, Ontario, Canada

Mary Carman Rose Professor, Goucher College, Towson, Maryland

Neil Salonen President, Unification Church of America (Graduate Student, George Washington University and President, International Cultural Foundation, Washington, D.C.)

Rodney Sawatsky Director of Academic Affairs, Conrad Grebel College, University of Waterloo, Waterloo, Ontario, Canada

Paul Sharkey Professor of Philosophy and Religion, University of Southern Mississippi, Hattiesburg, Mississippi

Jaime Sheeran Director, Unification Church of West Virginia, Huntington, West Virginia (Staff, New Ecumenical Research Association, Barrytown, New York)

William Shive Director, Berkeley Interfaith Council, Berkeley, California

David Simpson Executive Director, Association of Religious Communities, Danbury, Connecticut

Judith Simpson Wife of David Simpson, Danbury, Connecticut

Andy Smith Campus chaplain, Capitol Area Ministry, Albany, New York

Frederick Sontag Professor of Philosophy, Pomona College, Claremont, California

Hugh Spurgin Graduate of Unification Theological Seminary, Graduate Student, Union Theological Seminary, New York (Graduate Student, Columbia University, New York City)

Nora Spurgin Member of Unification Church, counselor (M.S.W.), and wife of Hugh Spurgin, Unification Theological Seminary, Barrytown, New York

Ernest Stewart Director of General Affairs, Unification Church, Barrytown, New York

Therese Stewart Academic Dean, Unification Theological Seminary and wife of Ernest Stewart, Barrytown, New York

Jonathan Wells Graduate of Unification Theological Seminary, Graduate Student, Yale University, New Haven, Connecticut

Patricia Zulkosky Graduate of Unification Theological Seminary, Graduate Student, School of Theology at Claremont, Claremont, California

Other Books on the Unification Movement

Evangelical—Unification Dialogue $7.95
    Richard Quebedeaux & Rodney Sawatsky, eds.

Exploring Unification Theology $7.95
    M. Darrol Bryant & Susan Hodges, eds.

God: The Contemporary Discussion $12.95
    Frederick Sontag & M. Darrol Bryant, eds.

Hermeneutics & Horizons: The Shape of the Future $11.95
    Frank K. Flinn

Hermeneutics and Unification Theology $7.95
    Darroll Bryant & Durwood Foster, eds.

Orthodox—Unification Dialogue $7.95
    Constantine Tsirpanlis, ed.

Proceedings of the Virgin Islands' Seminar $9.95
    on Unification Theology
    Darroll Bryant, ed.

The Social Impact of New Religious Movements $10.95
    Bryan Wilson, ed.

Ten Theologians Respond to the Unification Church $9.95
    Herbert Richardson, ed.

A Time for Consideration: A Scholarly Appraisal $9.95
    of the Unification Church
    M. Darrol Bryant & Herbert W. Richardson, eds.

Unification Theology $8.95
    Young Oon Kim

Unification Theology and Christian Thought $6.95
    Young Oon Kim

Distributed by
The Rose of Sharon Press, Inc.
G.P.O. Box 2432
New York, N.Y. 10116